W9-BHP-875

CAMUS'S *L'ETRANGER*: FIFTY YEARS ON

Camus's *L'Etranger*: Fifty Years on

Edited by

Adele King
Associate Professor of French
Ball State University, Muncie, Indiana

St. Martin's Press   New York

First published in the United States of America in 1992

Reprinted 1994

ISBN 0–312–06858–1

Library of Congress Cataloging-in-Publication Data
Camus's L'étranger : fifty years on / edited by Adele King.
p. cm.
Includes index.
ISBN 0–312–06858–1
1. Camus, Albert, 1913–1960.   Etranger.   I. King, Adele.
PQ2605.A3734E836   1992
843'.914—dc20   91–24360
                                              CIP
Printed in Great Britain

To the memory of Matthew Ward

Contents

vii

Preface

These essays are dedicated to the memory of Matthew Ward, whose translation of *The Stranger* won the PEN translation prize in 1989. Mr Ward's death in 1990 prevented him from completing an essay on his translation, originally to have been part of this collection. Most quotations from *The Stranger* come from this translation. Some citations from Camus's work are from published translations; some translations are mine. The varying, sometimes contradictory interpretations of *L'Etranger* are, of course, those of the individual essayists.

My debts to scholars in many countries are numerous. I would like to thank John Cruickshank, Brian T. Fitch, Patrick Henry, Elaine Marks, Eric Sellin, Susan Suleiman, and Olivier Todd. Liliane Phan and Monique Guibert, of Gallimard, provided access to their files of reviews and information on sales and translations of *L'Etranger*. Catherine Camus spoke to me about her father's work and its reception. Ball State University supported my work with a summer research grant. Lynne Marozin and Lisa Mercer, my student assistants, deserve special thanks for their help.

ADELE KING

Notes on Contributors

Christiane Achour, born in Algeria in 1946, is presently a Professor in the French Department of the University of Algiers. She specialises in colonial Algerian and Caribbean works. She is the author of *Abécédaires en devenir, Langue française et colonialisme en Algérie* (Alger, ENAP, 1985). *Un Etranger si familier – Lecture du récit d'Albert Camus* (Alger, ENAP, 1985), and *Anthologie de La Littérature algérienne de langue française* (Alger-Paris, ENAP/Bordas, 1990).

David Bradby is Professor of Drama and Theatre Studies in the University of London (Royal Holloway and Bedford New College). He has taught in the Universities of Glasgow, Ibadan, Kent, and Caen. He is the author of *Modern French Drama*, Cambridge University Press, 1984; *Directors' Theatre* (with David Williams), Macmillan, 1988, and has edited *New French Plays*, Methuen, 1989.

Catharine Savage Brosman is the author of *Art as Testimony: The Work of Jules Roy* (1989) and of other studies on Roy. Her most recent collection of poems, *Journeying from Canyon de Chelly*, appeared in 1990, and her *Simone de Beauvoir Revisited* in 1991. She has edited three volumes on twentieth-century French novelists in the *Dictionary of Literary Biography* series and is currently preparing volumes on nineteenth-century French fiction writers.

Gilbert D. Chaitin is Professor of French and Comparative Literature at Indiana University, Bloomington. He is the author of *The Unhappy Few*, a study of Stendhal's novels, and of numerous articles on the French novel and the psychoanalytic theory of narrative.

Deborah Clarke, Assistant Professor of English and Women's Studies at Pennsylvania State University, specialises in twentieth-century American fiction, women writers and feminist criticism. She has published articles on Faulkner and Toni Morrison, and is finishing a book: *Robbing the Mother: Women in Faulkner*.

Jean Daniel, born in Algeria, has been a writer and journalist in France since the 1940s, where he began *Caliban*, a magazine for which Camus wrote. He was editor of *L'Express* from 1955 to 1963. Among his books are *Le Temps qui reste* (1973), *Le Refuge et la source* (1977), and *DeGaulle et l'Algérie* (1986). He has been editor of *Le Nouvel Observateur* since 1964.

K. N. Daruwalla is a well-known Indian poet and short story writer. His sixth and most recent volume of poems was *Landscapes* (Oxford University Press, 1987). An earlier volume, *The Keeper of the Dead*, won the Sahitya Akademi Award in 1984. He edited *Two Decades of Indian Poetry* (1980). A collection of short stories, *Sword and Abyss*, was published in 1979.

Frantz Favre, *professeur agrégé* of classical literature, teaches at the Lycée Corneille in Rouen. He is on the executive committee of the Société des Etudes Camusiennes and has published articles on Camus in the Camus Series of Revue des Lettres Modernes.

John Fletcher is Professor of French at the University of East Anglia in Norwich. He has published widely on contemporary French Literature and is perhaps best known for his books on Samuel Beckett, Claude Simon and Alain Robbe-Grillet. His most recent work was a highly acclaimed translation (with Beryl S. Fletcher) of Claude Simon's novel *The Georgics*.

Michel Grimaud teaches in the Department of French at Wellesley College in Massachusetts (USA). His main research interests are interdisciplinary issues in the human sciences (he is co-publisher of a journal entitled *Empirical Studies of the Arts*), forms of reference and address in French and English, and social and linguistic aspects of street naming. He is editor of a journal on Victor Hugo (Paris, Minard). He has most recently published articles on naming and onomastics in *Le Français moderne, Names, Poetics, Poétique, Pszichologia*.

Alec G. Hargreaves is Senior Lecturer in French at Loughborough University, England. He is the author of *The Colonial Experience in French Fiction* (London: Macmillan/New York: Humanities Press, 1981), *Immigration in Post-War France* (London: Methuen, 1987), and *Immigration and Identity in Beur Fiction* (London /New York: Berg, 1991) and has published articles in the *Journal of European Studies, French Review, Modern and Contemporary France, Contemporary French Civilization*, and *Modern Fiction Studies* among others.

Rosemarie Jones is Lecturer in French in the School of European Studies of the University of Sussex. She has published on the *romans antiques* and on Camus, and she is currently working on *pied-noir* and Algerian Francophone novels.

Adele King, Professor of French at Ball State University, published *Camus* in the Writers and Critics Series in 1964. She has also published books on Proust, Nizan, and Camara Laye, and *French Women Novelists: defining a female style* (Macmillan, 1989). She is co-editor of two series for Macmillan: Modern Dramatists and Women Writers.

Christiane P. Makward, Associate Professor of French and Women's Studies at Pennsylvania State University, specialises in contemporary French literature, Francophone women's studies and translation. She has published numerous articles; her books include *S. Corinna Bille par elle-même* and *Ten Women's Voices in Theatre from the French*.

Patrick McCarthy is Professor of European Studies at the Johns Hopkins University Bologna Centre. His publications include *Camus, a critical biography* and *Camus' "The Stranger"*.

Vicki Mistacco is Professor of French at Wellesley College. She has written articles and papers on twentieth-century French novelists including Gide, Mauriac, Robbe-Grillet, and Duras and is the author of another feminist reading of Camus: 'Nomadic Meanings: The Woman Effect in "La Femme adultère".' Her current research is on the avant-garde, women's writing, and the eighteenth-century novel.

Hélène Poplyansky, born in the Soviet Union, is now a doctoral student at the University of Toronto, where she is writing a thesis on the reception of *L'Etranger* in various countries.

Jan Rigaud was born in Paris and educated in North Africa and the US. He now teaches at Villanova University. He has published interviews on Camus and is now completing a book on Camus.

Emmanuel Roblès, born in Oran, studied in Algiers where he was part of a group of young writers, including Camus. Among his novels are *Cela s'appelle l'aurore, Un printemps d'Italie, Venise en hiver,* and *Le Vésuve*. *Les Hauteurs de la ville* won the Prix Fémina in 1948. As a reporter and lecturer, he has traveled widely. He also writes for television and the cinema, for which he has collaborated with Luis Bunuel and Luchino Visconti. In 1973 he was elected to the Académie Goncourt.

Vilas Sarang is Professor of English at the University of Bombay. His most recent publication is a collection of short stories, *Fair Tree of the Void* (Penguin, 1990), translated by the author from the Marathi. He has also published books of criticism, poetry, and a novel in Marathi. Many of his stories have been published in such journals as *Encounter* and *London Magazine*.

Peter Schofer, Halverson-Bascom Professor of French, has taught at the University of Wisconsin-Madison since 1968. His areas of interest include nineteenth-century French poetry, rhetoric, and film. His publications include *Poèmes, pièces, prose* (1973), *Rhetorical Poetics* (1983), and *Autour de la littérature* (1986). He is now completing research for a book on Baudelaire's prose poetry.

Olivier Todd was educated at the Sorbonne and at Cambridge. He has published in such magazines as *The New Statesman* and *Hudson Review* and has collaborated on British and French television programmes. He has also worked as a journalist for *France-Observateur* and le *Nouvel Observateur*. His last journalistic job was editor-in-chief of *l'Express*. Now a full-time writer, he has published fourteen books (including seven novels). In *Un fils rebel* (1981) he writes of his relationship to Sartre.

Albert Wendt is of the Aiga Sa-Tuapepe and Sa-Tuala and Sa-Patu of Samoa. His novels, short stories, and poems have been published in many countries. Among his works are *Sons for the Return Home*, *Pouliuli*, *Leaves of the Banyan Tree*, and *Flying-Fox in a Freedom Tree*. His latest novel is *Ola* (Penguin Books, 1991). He teaches New Zealand, Pacific, and Commonwealth Literature at the University of Auckland, New Zealand.

Introduction: After Fifty Years, Still a Stranger
Adele King

After fifty years it is obvious that *L'Etranger* has joined the canon of great books and belongs alongside such classics of the humanities as the works of Kafka and Dostoievsky. Its relationship to *The Trial* and to the Grand Inquisitor is more than a matter of possible influences, it is an engagement in the grand debates of western and, apparently, universal humanity concerning such matters as the individual and society, freedom and responsibility, the absurd and meaning. The seeming lack of connection between events and feelings, the ironies and the incongruities of the trial, the sense of alienation and the feeling that despite the lack of meaning life may be worth living offer a counterpoise to the deeper despair and hopelessness of that other great work of the 'existential' period, *Waiting for Godot*. They both speak to us of a world in which community, God, nature and other kinds of transcendence no longer seem credible. Yet with *L'Etranger* we feel that such despair is questioned and that even when accepting his death Meursault is, in his seeming inarticulateness, symbolic of a complex and wide range of human emotions concerning the fundamental issues of life, issues of more importance than the passing political and social problems upon which many writers have established their reputations. The supposed death of God does not mean that life can be reduced to ideology, theory, politics or other obsessions.

The chapters in this book form a collection of essays that is a celebration of one of the masterpieces of twentieth-century literature, not by simple praise but by showing how much Camus's first novel still engages the attention of a wide variety of readers. Contributors discuss the historical context of *L'Etranger*, the text, its reception and influence on various writers, and compare the novel to the work of others. Although several chapters present differing readings of such recurrent questions as *when* Meursault tells his story, and several are critical of Camus in relation to the Arab population of pre-independence Algeria, the contributors are in agreement about the lasting value of the novel and its emotional impact on each new generation of readers during the past fifty years. Vilas Sarang (Chapter 5) whimsically suggests that Meursault is allowed to live in return for telling his story so well, and of course Meursault does continue to live. His story speaks to readers, has been an influence on many writers, and has given rise to a vast body of critical commentary. It contains a liberating spirit for those unhappy with the conventions of society – its religious and cultural restrictions, its insistence on legalism, its hypocritical standards.

L'Etranger has attracted readers throughout the world, including many who have never thought about Camus's humanism, or studied the debates surrounding *L'Homme révolté*. Translations of *L'Etranger* exist, according to the Gallimard files, in the following editions: Afrikaans, Albanian, American, Assamese, Basque, Bengali, Bulgarian, Catalan, Czech, Danish, Dutch, English, Finnish, Franco-Chinese, German, Hebrew, Hindi, Hungarian, Icelandic, Indonesian, Italian, Japanese, Kannada, Macedonian, Malayalam, Malaysian, Maltese, Norwegian, Polish, Portuguese, Punjabi, Rumanian, Russian, Serbo-Croat, Slovene, Spanish, Swedish, Tamil, Telegu, Welsh. Edouard Glissant (p. 343) also mentions a Martinican writer who translates novels into Creole, which he publishes himself in type-written versions, among them *Mun andewo-a*, a Creole version of *L'Etranger*. Camus's work sells the best of any on Gallimard's list and *L'Etranger* is the best-selling of his novels, with over six million copies sold in French (as compared to over five million for *La Peste*, or 1 300 000 for Malraux's *L'Espoir*). At least four million copies in English have been sold in the United States. In Japan, Camus is the most widely read of French authors. In Germany, over 750 000 copies of a paperback edition have been sold.

As Vilas Sarang's, K. N. Daruwalla's and Albert Wendt's essays here show, readers in varying cultures can identify with its hero, find relevance to their own experience. In Lilyan Kesteloot's survey of authors read by black African and Caribbean writers in the 1950s and 1960s (p. 285), Camus is one of the few names cited among twentieth-century French novelists. A critic has found a direct reference to *L'Etranger* in the work of the Ghanaian author, Ayi Kwei Armah (Steele, p. 10). Camus has influenced such Indian novels as Arun Joshi's *The Foreigner* and Anita Desai's *Voices of the City*.

I have been reading Camus, you know. He says, 'In default of inexhaustible happiness, eternal suffering at least would give us a destiny. But we do not have even that consolation, and our worst agonies come to an end one day' . . . Happiness, suffering – I want to be done with them, disregard them, see beyond them to the very end. (Desai, p. 40)

Many readers feel great sympathy for Meursault. He seems 'everyman'; he is not a Malraux hero, nor a Gide aesthete, nor a Sartre intellectual. His life is not 'strange' in the way that those of Dostoievsky's or Kafka's heroes may seem to be outside our usual experience. The seemingly 'natural' tone with which he tells his story creates a bond between narrator and reader. Meursault is a hero with whom we identify because of the very banality of much of his experience. Part of his appeal is the message that everyone can have his rebellion, it is 'a universal right of man' (Barilli, p. 206). *L'Etranger* appeals to all those who, unlike some critics and unlike the rather conventional Marie, are not shocked when he sleeps with her the day after his mother's funeral.

The novel creates a particular complicity between narrator and reader. We as readers are the only witnesses to the murder. We have seen the world through Meursault's eyes: eyes different from those of the typical first-person narrator. Initially we know Meursault less well than we know other narrators, but as we become accustomed to his strangely objective vision, we may in fact feel closer to him. Meursault becomes, as Vilas Sarang says, a brother for the reader.

Part of *L'Etranger's* appeal to many readers is its very unliterary, unnovelistic approach. It is not 'high culture', just as *Waiting for Godot*, perhaps the other major work of western literature to attain such a degree of influence in the post-Second World War world, is not concerned with heroes who express themselves with eloquence. At the same time, however, *L'Etranger* satisfies our need for a classical order. The continuing interest in this novel may reside as much in its art as in its ideas. As Camus himself said in 1947, when Gide received the Nobel Prize: 'If great works sometimes command respect in their own time by the ideas they express, it is by their art that they survive' (interview with Emmanuel Roblès).

Each generation has its own dominating political concerns, its own battle with 'History'. In the early 1940s Meursault seemed to many readers to give voice to those who reject not only social conventions, but also that historical transcendence which was Nazism. By showing the inability of the legal system to understand Meursault, *L'Etranger* attacks the methods of European legalism which 'contributed to Nazi oppression' (Weisberg, p. 114). In the intervening years, Meursault could be a hero of the young who felt alienated by the Cold War or the Vietnam War.

The experience that Conor Cruise O'Brien describes is repeated by new generations of readers:

> To a generation which saw no reason for hope, it offered hope without reason. It offered a category – the Absurd – in which logical, psychological, philosophical, and even social and political difficulties could be encapsulated, and it allowed the joy of being alive, in the presence of death, to emerge. It was neither a revolutionary message nor an especially moral one; but it was a singularly sweet and exhilarating message to a whole generation that was also pleased to think of it as revolutionary and moral. (p. 34)

Edmond Charlot describes Camus's early readers in Algeria:

> *L'Etranger* brought us . . . assurance. A man, a friend that we loved was capable of expressing what we felt. Crying a little before the world our rebellion against its absurdity. It was a declaration of absurdity, an illustration, an example, but no one was taken in: it was also a clear cry, a rebellion against this absurdity . . . Everything was said and perfectly said, with the words of ordinary people . . . All of us felt ourselves to be 'strangers' . . . Those who challenge authority in 1969 are like those of 1936. They feel themselves to be 'strangers' as we did then. (Sellin, pp. 164–5)

On another level, the rich symbolism of the novel, with suggestions of levels beneath the surface of the narrative, speaks to what are perhaps universal psychological tensions in our relations to parents, friends, lovers. Camus's symbolic universe seems a new version of a common experience, 'leading untiringly from life to death, from innocence to guilt, from the kingdom to exile, and also from death to life, from guilt to innocence, from exile to the kingdom' (Gassin, p. 261).

The techniques of narration – the narrator who says 'I' but never analyses his own motivations, the use of the *passé composé* to indicate not only a non-literary mode but also a temporal ambivalence, the neutralising effect of the tone of Meursault's voice – tend initially to make us unaware of what is distasteful in his story and of the fact that he has killed a man. Raymond, for instance, is a thoroughly disagreeable character, but his nastiness is only noted in the novel when Meursault comments in the final chapter that Raymond was less admirable than Céleste. In a dramatisation of *L'Etranger*,[1] just how much a scoundrel Raymond was came through forcefully for the first time to me, because everything is neutralised by the way Meursault tells his story. (An inability inherent in dramatisations to capture this neutralising effect undoubtedly explains the limited success of play or film versions of the novel, even though critics have often commented on how Meursault's method of narration suggests a camera eye, simply registering phenomena.)

Similarly, Meursault neutralises the murder, at least in so far as it has a human victim. The murder is not so much taking the life of another human being as entering himself a path that can only lead towards his death. Readers sympathise with Meursault to such an extent that we almost tend to forget he is a murderer at all. But then, of course, we remember, and are aware of the way in which Camus is being ironic, deliberately subverting any simple moral message. We realise we have felt great sympathy for a man who not only has committed a murder and fired four shots into a dead body, but who does not seem to feel sorry for what he has done. Partly of course our disgust with the trial, with the explanation of the judges, makes us almost forget the murder as a crime. We have become witnesses to Meursault's basic honesty and can accept the murder as a result of chance. Have we, however, as many critics have suggested, read the novel in too optimistic a fashion, a fashion to some extent encouraged by Camus's own preface to the American edition of 1955? It is evident that some readers have not shared this view, finding Meursault to be 'inhuman', 'abnormal', 'odious'. (Fitch, p. 56) René Girard reads in *La Chute* a denial of the premise of the 'innocent murderer' and thus Camus's rejection of his own earlier work. As K. N. Daruwalla comments in Chapter 6 if reason cannot, or at least should not judge Meursault, 'that is easier said than done'.

When we look again at the early articles by well-known writers, it is clear that they read their own preoccupations into the novel. Sartre, while giving a perceptive analysis of many of the techniques Camus uses, argues especially for the philosophical import of the novel. Jean Grenier sees in *L'Etranger* an indication of its author's nostalgia for a lost paradise. Grenier (pp. 37–8) is one of the early critics, however, to find Meursault unsympathetic, scornful, strained.

Nathalie Sarraute (p. 57) describes Meursault's 'fugitive thoughts' in a way that suggests he may be experiencing something similar to the 'tropisms' of her own work. But then she finds that Meursault's refined taste and sensibility lead him back into the psychological. Roland Barthes in *Le Degré zéro de l'écriture* (1953), discussing 'neutral writing', removed from literary language, says such writing is 'innocent ' and commences with *L'Etranger*, where there is almost an 'ideal absence of style'; 'the social and mythological characteristics of a language are abolished for a neutral state'(p. 67). Soon afterwards, however, Barthes himself will speak of the mythological characteristics of *L'Etranger*. In a 1954 essay, he begins by analysing *L'Etranger* as a sociological phenomenon like the electric battery (p. 61), and then finds a 'mythology' of the sun in the novel.

Robbe-Grillet's examination of the neutralising effects of language turns into a search for anthropomorphism and symbolism, the ways in which Camus is *not* writing the *new novel* of Robbe-Grillet himself. John Fletcher, however, points to all that Camus taught the *new novelists* about the unreliability of data, the creation of reality by the text (Chapter 18). Robbe-Grillet's more recent comments expand on his earlier article, while clarifying the influence of Camus on his own work. An interesting sidelight is the importance he attaches to the newspaper clipping Meursault reads in his cell, and its influence on his own *Voyeur*. He sees the reading of the clipping as a sign of the 'humanist temptation' confronting Meursault, the return to the world of texts (p. 225). He also gives another interpretation of the murder scene, not in terms of psychology but in terms of epistemology. Meursault feels a certain balance between the fullness of the world and the essential emptiness of his consciousness (not an emptiness attributable to any peculiarity of the character himself, but rather to the basic emptiness of all consciousness in a Husserlian perspective). Meursault finally, however, cannot 'digest' the world. Thus he must create a scandal, the four shots into the dead body (p. 221).[2]

Other influential earlier criticism includes Robert Champigny's *Sur un héros païen* (1959), a model for seeing in Meursault's vision more than a contemporary existentialist ethic; and Maurice-Georges Barrier's *L'Art du récit dans l'Etranger d'Albert Camus* (1966), which established a line of close textual analysis. Such analysis has shown, for example, that early critics were mistaken to state that there was a lack of conjunctions in the novel, or that Meursault did not use images. Peter Schofer (Chapter 13) points to the power of metaphor in shaping our response to *L'Etranger*. Perhaps the best explanation for the wealth of critical attention is our sense that there are no simple psychological explanations, no analyses of feeling, that the novel is a 'stranger' to our normal ways of reading, and we must find some way to hold on to it. We do not naturally expect to experience the absurd while reading. The work of the best critics, like that of Barrier himself, does not keep the critic or the reader from being struck 'as on the first day, by the inertia of the character and the *absurd* inherent in his life. Simply rereading the book suffices to make us forget that it was an object of study' (Barrier, p. 1).

In spite of the textual puzzles, *L'Etranger* is the story of a man who commits an unpremeditated murder, a story with some problems about verisimilitude, but also in many ways a story about events that could have happened. My own experience teaching the novel has often been a salutary reminder that for first-time readers the novel tells a fairly straightforward story, does not demand any symbolic interpretation.

How to view Meursault is perhaps the central problem. The novel is set in Algeria in the 1930s, among a working-class *pied-noir* community. But, beyond that, what can be said with any certainty. How much do we know about the 'narrator' of the story? *When* does he tell this story? What is his relation to others? Meursault can be seen as a man who becomes aware of his life, or as a man who has always been aware of his life, but distrusts language and therefore does not *want* to attempt any explanation. Meursault can seem Champigny's 'pagan hero', but he also carries the baggage of the centuries separating him from the early Greeks. He often feels 'guilty'. Why does Meursault give such prominence to external reality? Does he want to escape from his internal problems? If so, is he aware of what he is doing? Are his references to being 'judged' proof that he is aware of some fault he does not want to admit?

To what extent does Camus sympathise with his hero? How close is Meursault to Camus himself? What credence should we place on his later comments, such as his evaluation in 1955 of Meursault as 'the only Christ we deserve'? Emmanuel Roblès (Chapter 1) notes the many ways in which Meursault resembles

his creator, and reminds us of the essential Algerian reality of
the novel. The Camus that Roblès's essay evokes here has a
belligerent side and an interest in the odd misfits of society, not
so different from Meursault's traits, and removed from a Camus
we have often too easily considered primarily as a highly prin-
cipled moralist, opposed to violence. The world of Meursault
is violent, but it is also Camus's world.[3] Perhaps Meursault is
less a 'stranger' to Camus himself than we first thought. Barrier
showed that certain tics of language – appropriate to Meursault's
'anti-literary' voice – are also prevalent in Camus's later writing.
These include the frequent use of *un peu*, and phrases that
indicate what Barrier terms 'the obsession with a double point
of view' (p. 76), such as 'd'une certaine manière, sans doute,
d'ailleurs.' Ghani Merad (1975) studies in detail the ways in
which Meursault understands, reasons, displays intelligence,
observes and describes as a poet. Merad even sees Meursault's
way of smoking cigarettes as that of a poet, as if the tobacco
were a drug. Meursault's principles are those of an Arab world
which has influenced the European population, and are often
those of Camus himself.

A number of critics – from Sartre on – have considered that
Camus substitutes his own voice for that of Meursault at critical
moments. The lyrical and rhetorical passages have been seen as
aesthetically unsatisfactory, uncharacteristic of Meursault, the
voice of the author intruding too noticeably, or a regression to
the level of explication. Camus would seem to agree with those
(like Jean Daniel in Chapter 2) who find an authorial intrusion.
This was a carefully considered decision: 'I decided on it
because I wanted my character to reach the only great problem
through the path of what is natural and everyday' (*Carnets II*,
1964, p. 30). If, of course, Meursault's story expresses many of
the psychological tensions of Camus himself, if he owes much to
his creator's personality – including a disillusion with ambition
after he had to abandon his studies, a frequent desire to with-
draw into himself and observe others from a distance – is it
necessarily an aesthetic shortcoming that he also shares some
of Camus's thoughts and his style? Yet Meursault is a mask.
Frantz Favre (Chapter 3) sees Camus projecting his Nietzschean
temptations onto Meursault. Others (such as Jean Gassin, 1985)
have seen Meursault as a way by which Camus can project
outside himself certain psychological tensions. In a perceptive

early analysis of *L'Etranger*, Rachel Bespaloff (1950) noted: 'Gide showed him how to use the *I* to express with the maximum detachment the most intimate experience' (p. 137).

The personality of Meursault has been, since the novel first appeared, the most discussed facet of the novel – both by literary critics and by readers who respond to Meursault as a brother. The form of *L'Etranger* has also frequently been discussed: the balanced two-part structure, the stylistic inventiveness. It has been called a *conte* in the tradition of Voltaire. It can be read as a myth of summons, quest, return to history and transfiguration (Abbou). It can be seen as metaphysical speculation, an illustration of the absurd defined in *Le Mythe de Sisyphe* (as Sartre thought), or a story with limited relevance to Camus's essay.

Another frequent problem has been how and when Meursault tells his story. Why are there so many problems about the time of narration, inconsistencies of which Camus was surely aware? While the occasional use of the *passé simple* was probably a slip of the pen, Camus plays with references to time (as did Gide in *Les Faux-Monnayeurs*).[4] Did he intend the reader to be conscious of these inconsistencies? Barrier suggests that the reader simply accepts them, but my own experience has been that many readers are quickly aware of the problem. Because we see the world through Meursault's eyes, we also become interested in how he tells his story and when, especially since, at least initially, he does not seem to be the type of person to tell a story at all. Gilbert Chaitin (Chapter 12) examines some of the many and varying answers, and the relationship of the process of narration to Meursault's psychological development. The puzzle will perhaps never be resolved to the satisfaction of all readers.

In recent years, two debates have become especially prominent among Camus's critics: the ethnic identity of the victim, and Meursault's (and Camus's) relationship to his mother. Is *L'Etranger* an indirect condemnation of colonialism, or does it show the unconscious colonial or even racist attitudes of the author? Camus's work deals with so many problems that still confront us that we may tend to look for its relevance to other moral dilemmas that at first sight may be peripheral to the novel. *L'Etranger* as a subtle foreshadowing of future violence between the *pied-noir* and the Arab, or as an indirect confrontation with the author's own possible ambivalence is not, I believe, what first strikes most readers. If the Arabs look at the *pieds-noirs* 'ni plus

ni moins que si nous étions des pierres ou des arbres morts'
(p. 1161), Meursault similarly regards the Arabs and also the
many of the *pieds-noirs* he knows in the same fashion. While
Marie, Salamano, Céleste, Raymond accept Meursault, who
wants to be liked and to be accommodating to others, the way in
which Meursault describes people lends some credence to
earlier readings that saw him as basically 'outside' society. But
is he racist? He does not comment at all on either Arab victim –
Raymond's mistress or the man who is killed.

Racist attitudes would be at variance with anything Camus
wrote and with comments by many of those who knew him.
(His daughter, Catherine, while admitting that her father was
'sexist', denied that he could have been in any way 'racist'.
Indeed she remembered that if the children made a remark that
could be interpreted as racist, Camus was strict in rebuking
them.)[5] With our increasing consciousness of ethnic diversity
and the problems of the post-colonial world, however, the fact
that Meursault's victim was an Arab has been read in new ways.
Conor Cruise O'Brien (1970) thinks that the court in the trial
scene is like a European court; this constitutes a denial of
colonial reality. 'Artistic truth was contrasted with, and placed
above, forms of justice in society' (p. 103). Germaine Brée (1974)
replies that O'Brien's interpretation comes from 'his own rather
schematic view of Western guilt' (p. 151). Are we, with our present concern for the problems of colonisation, decolonisation,
ethnicity, reading too much of our post-independence sensibility,
and perhaps guilt, into the novel? Non-Western contributors to
this collection – Albert Wendt,[6] Vilas Sarang – do not dwell on
the fact that Meursault's victim was an Arab. In an age when we
are perhaps overly conscious of 'the other', Meursault's recognition that he is a stranger to the Arabs, and that they are strange
to him, should not strike us as more than simple honesty.
Hélène Poplyansky's survey of Soviet criticism of *L'Etranger*
(Chapter 8) shows that overly political readings of literature
have their evident shortcomings.

Several replies to the question of the Arab in *L'Etranger* can be
advanced. Some have said that, far from being hostile to the
Arabs or denying the reality of their presence, Meursault is
influenced by them. 'The whole work is a denial of free will. Is it
the influence of Islam, which is very close, being incarnated in
French mentality? *Mektoub*. It is written. Useless to fight, to

react' (Malabard, 1946, p. 120) Camus himself seems to lend credence to this idea when he writes in his notebook for 1937–9: 'What does the superman type ('le type du surhomme') mean for the world of Islam?' (*Carnets I*, 1962, p. 101) Perhaps the Arabs – representatives of a world which refuses materialism, 'interpreters of a world in which art and dream exist together' (Abbou, p. 253) – are the 'other' in quite a different sense from the political one we tend to see at present. So the murder might be an unconscious recognition by Meursault that he can *not* enter their world, a world in which he would prefer to live. Another possibility, related to inter-cultural influences is that Meursault, as Vilas Sarang suggests, is close to Indian thought. (Perhaps this is one reason *L'Etranger* has been translated into eight Indian languages.)

Jean Daniel (Chapter 2) raises questions of the larger political import of the novel, a significance which is linked to the moral and metaphysical dilemma we have faced since the mid-nineteenth century. If Meursault is not finally innocent, because innocence is an impossible desire for oneness, his lack of innocence is of larger scope than the fact that the victim was Arab. Similarly, Vicki Mistacco's feminist reading of *L'Etranger* (Chapter 14) goes beyond the fact that Camus, like so many authors of his generation, saw women as 'others', as lesser beings. We should remember Serge Doubrovsky's (1960) comment:

> At a time when history has become for many people the unique dimension of the human drama, Camus restores another, under-lying dimension, without which history would not exist. (p. 162)

Psychological or psychoanalytical criticism, such as that of Alain Costes, Jean Gassin, Jose Barchilon and Donald Lazere, analyses Meursault particularly in relation to his mother. Is he guilty of incestuous/murderous intentions towards her? And then, how does this relationship reflect Camus's own tensions, expressed in some of his early essays? How did his childhood, growing up without a father, influence his imagination, his use of the essential images that recur in his work? Emmanuel Roblès's account in Chapter 1 of meeting Madame Camus gives one side of the coin. Is there another? In terms of Meursault's ambiguous relationship to his mother, were the judges in some way correct to condemn him for his conduct at her funeral? Vicki Mistacco suggests that psychoanalytic readings neglect the working of the 'feminine maternal' in Camus. The deeper level of psychological tensions in the story can explain at least to some extent the strong enduring attraction of L'Etranger, which is not just a literary puzzle, an experience of absurdity for the reader, a classical work of aesthetic genius, but also an appeal to some of our least admitted fears, compulsions and ambivalences.

Recent interpretations also consider the relationship of L'Etranger to Camus's early work: the previously unpublished work in Paul Viallaneix's collection of 1973, and La Mort heureuse. In this day of 'theory', Camus's use of language in L'Etranger, how the novel can be read as a commentary on language and hermeneutics, has also become prominent. Brian Fitch (1982) sees the real concern of the text as the activity of interpretation, 'the reader reads the story of his [sic] own activity' (p. 67). Examining the 'intra-intertextuality' of Camus's work, he sees Tarrou's notebooks in La Peste as reproducing the text of L'Etranger, which is thus resolved as written. Uri Eisenzweig (1983) studies Meursault's distrust of writing (l'écriture), which is always dirty, either insignificant or violent, either a game or a lie. (Might there be a relationship here to the fact that Camus's mother was illiterate – a rare occurrence for a writer, except in parts of the Third World?) Eisenzweig's study of how Meursault uses and how he mistrusts language returns us to a political meaning. Faced with the anti-individualist conception of identity promoted by Nazism, Meursault rejects a 'totalitarian account' of his life (p. 148).

Is it possible to find any incident, sentence, even detail that has not been subjected to some critical analysis? No one, to my knowledge, has discussed Meursault's smoking with reference to Camus's tubercular lungs, or commented on the prison guard's statement concerning masturbation. While Gassin sees 'la petite automate' as a figure for death, and Eisenzweig sees her as playing the game of writing, neither explains why only she and the young journalist (usually considered sympathetic to Meursault, and perhaps a figure for Camus himself) do not fan themselves at the trial. The journalist, incidentally, wears a blue tie, but blue, according to Costes (1985), is for Camus the colour of an 'anguished aggressive move towards an Arab' (p. 70). There is more ambiguity throughout the novel than has frequently been recognised. Despite or perhaps because of its economical understatement, the composition of the novel is so rich that every word seems fraught with meaning. Yet, each time we read 'Aujourd'hui maman est morte ... Cela ne veut rien dire', we are again fascinated by the voice of Meursault.

Notes

1. Alain Illel's adaptation of *L'Etranger* (Paris: Théâtre de la Main d'Or, 1987–9).
2. Robbe-Grillet's use of a term related to eating can be linked to recent psychological interpretations of Meursault.
3. As Maurice Weyembergh has observed, Camus is not so much opposed to violence as to the justification of violence. (p. 372)
4. For this observation I am indebted to a paper by John A. Lambeth, 'Anachronism in *Les Faux-Monnayeurs*', read at the Kentucky Foreign Language Conference, April 1990.
5. My interview with Catherine Camus, 26 July 1989.
6. Albert Wendt's comment, in a letter to me of 8 August 1990: 'Yes, I've always had the killing of an Arab in my head – but no serious reservations about it.'

Works Cited

Abbou, André, 'Le quotidien et le sacré: introduction à une nouvelle lecture de *L'Etranger*', in Gay-Crosier, pp. 231–67.

Barchilon, Jose, 'Profondeur et limite de la psychologie de l'inconscient chez Camus: les jeux du narcissisme', in Gay-Crosier, pp. 17–36.

Barilli, Renato, 'Camus et le Nouveau Roman' in Gay-Crosier, pp. 201–14.

Barrier, Maurice-Georges, *L'Art du récit dans L'Etranger d'Albert Camus* (Paris: Nizet, 1966).

Barthes, Roland, *Le Degré zéro de l'écriture.* (Paris: Gonthier, 1970, 1st edn, Paris: Seuil, 1953).

Barthes, Roland, '*L'Etranger*, roman solaire' in Lévi-Valensi, pp. 60–4. (First published in *Club*, Bulletin du Club du Meilleur Livre, vol. 12 (1954), pp. 6–7.)

Bespaloff, Rachel, 'Le Monde du condamné à Mort', in Lévi-Valensi, pp. 136–40. (First published in *Esprit*, vol. 163 (1950), pp. 1–26.)

Brée, Germaine, *Camus and Sartre* (London: Calder & Boyars, 1974).

Camus, Albert, *Carnets* (Paris: Gallimard, 1962).

Camus, Albert, *Carnets II* (Paris: Gallimard, 1964).

Camus, Albert, *Théâtre, récits, nouvelles.* (Paris: Gallimard, Bibliothèque de la Pléiade, 1962).

Champigny, Robert, *Sur un héros païen* (Paris: Gallimard, 1959).

Costes, Alain, 'Le Double meurtre de Meursault', in Gay-Crosier, pp. 55–76.

Desai, Anita, *Voices in the City* (Delhi: Orient Paperbacks, 1985, first published, 1965).

Doubrovksy, Serge, 'La Morale d'Albert Camus', in Lévi-Valensi, pp. 157–66. (First published in *Preuves*, vol. 116 (1960),pp. 39–49.)

Eisenzweig, Uri, 'Les Jeux de l' écriture dans L'Etranger de Camus, *Albert Camus: 6* (Paris: Minard, Lettres Modernes, 1983).

Fitch, Brian T. *The Narcissistic Text.* (Toronto: University of Toronto Press, 1982).

Gassin, Jean, *L'Univers symbolique d'Albert Camus* (Paris: Minard, 1981).

Gassin, Jean, 'A Propos de la femme "automate" de *L'Etranger*' in Gay-Crosier, pp. 77–90.

Gay-Crosier, Raymond and Jacqueline Lévi-Valensi (eds), *Albert Camus: oeuvre ouverte, oeuvre fermée* (Paris: Gallimard, Cahiers Albert Camus: 5, 1985).

Girard, René, 'Camus's Stranger Retried', PMLA, vol. 79 (1964), pp. 519–33.

Glissant, Edouard, *Discours antillais.* (Paris: Seuil, 1981).

Grenier, Jean, 'Une Oeuvre, un homme', in Lévi-Valensi, pp. 36–40. (First published in *Cahiers du Sud*, February 1943.)

Kesteloot, Lilyan, *Les écrivains noirs de langue française: naissance d'une littérature* (Brussels: University of Brussels, 1963).

Lazere, Donald, *The Unique Creation of Albert Camus* (New Haven: Yale University Press, 1973).

Lévi-Valensi, Jacqueline (ed.), *Les Critiques de notre temps et Camus* (Paris: Garnier, 1970).

Malabard, Jean, 'L'Oeuvre d'Albert Camus', *La Revue de l'Universite Laval*, October, 1946, pp. 118–22.

Merad, Ghani, '*L'Etranger* de Camus vu sous un angle psycho-sociologique', *Revue Romane*, vol. 10 (1975), pp. 51–91.

O'Brien, Conor Cruise, *Albert Camus of Europe and Africa* (New York: Viking, 1970).

Robbe-Grillèt, Alain, 'Nature, humanisme, tragédie', in Lévi-Valensi, pp. 64–6. (First published in *Pour un nouveau roman* (Paris: Editions de Minuit, 1963).)

Robbe-Grillet, Alain, 'Monde trop plein, conscience vide', in Gay-Crosier, pp. 215–29.

Roblès, Emmanuel, Interview d'Albert Camus, Radio Algérie, 1947.

Sarraute, Nathalie. ' "Le Psychologique" dans *L'Etranger*', in Lévi Valensi, pp. 56–60. (First published in *L'Ere du soupçon*. (Paris: Gallimard, 1956). pp. 22–31.)

Sartre, Jean-Paul, 'Explication de *L'Etranger*', in Lévi-Valensi, pp. 41–56. (First published in *Situations I* (Paris: Gallimard, 1947), pp. 99–121.)

Sellin, Eric, 'Interview d'Edmond Charlot', *Albert Camus 3.* (Paris: Revue des Lettres Modernes, 1970), pp. 153–65.

Steele, Shelby, 'Existentialism in the Novels of Ayi Kwei Armah', *Obsidian*, vol. 3 (1977), pp. 5–13.

Viallaneix, Paul, *Le Premier Camus: suivi d'Ecrits de jeunesse d'Albert Camus* (Paris: Gallimard, 1973).

Weisberg, Richard, *The Failure of the Word: The Protagonist as Lawyer in Modern Fiction*. (New Haven: Yale University Press, 1984).

Weyembergh, Maurice, 'L'obsession du clos et le thème des camps', in Gay-Crosier, pp. 361–76.

Part One
Contexts and Influences on *L'Etranger*

1

Camus, Our Youthful Years
Emmanuel Roblès
of the Académie Goncourt

I had arrived in Algiers at the beginning of September 1937 to do my military service while pursuing my studies at the Faculté des Lettres, where I had enrolled the previous year, from Oran, the city where I lived then. I was told that a young theatre company, Le Théâtre de l'Equipe, was going to present *La Célestine*, by Fernando de Rojas, a play from the classical Spanish repertory that was on my university syllabus. Taken by a friend from my battalion, I went to the Maison de la Culture, near the University. Seated at the back of the theatre to follow the rehearsal, I was able to observe as well the director, who also played the part of Calixte.

He was a boy of about my age, but thin and pale, obviously in precarious health but full of an ardour, energy and passion which could be seen every moment when he went from the third row of the auditorium to the stage. He would give his instructions from below, then climb up to play his scene, and go back down, often wiping his brow and his cheeks which were glowing with sweat. That was Albert Camus, my friend told me, who during a break in the rehearsal introduced us to each other. When he saw me in my air force uniform, he immediately asked me if military life wasn't too hard. (He had been invalided out of the service.) I said that the only inconvenience for me was the loss of my freedom. I understand, he replied. We'll see each other in a few minutes, won't we? And we can talk.

We arranged to meet in a café not far from the Maison de la Culture, where he joined me, smiling, and surprisingly without any trace of being tired. Our first conversation was about the theatre and about Spain. I learned that we shared a common background, he as the son of a mechanic, and I the son of a mason. Neither of us had known our fathers, who died in our infancy. (In fact, I am a posthumous child.) And our mothers, both of Spanish descent, did housework to support us. It is possible that these similarities contributed something to establishing between us a fraternal friendship that never faltered.

It seems to me important, now, to note that Albert Camus spent more than half his life in Algeria. Born in November 1913 in a small locality in Constantinois, he lived in Algiers (after the death of his father, killed in 1914 on the French front) until 1939, when he was obliged to leave for France because the colonial administration gave him problems. Thus he lived in Algiers for twenty-six years, to which we should add his time in Oran, from 1941 to the middle of 1942. The influence of this Mediterranean world, of its fleeting lights and its gold and green dusks, the exaltation of the body on beaches near the city, all that happiness of the senses imbues a number of Camus's works and, as we know, penetrates Meursault's story from one end to the other.

I knew that Camus, after an attack of pleurisy caught during a football game on a rainy afternoon, had become tubercular because he neglected his illness. He never spoke about it, but would disappear sometimes for several days, reappear again, always with the same pallor. One evening, at the University Café, he came to meet me, looking unusually sad. When I asked him, rather stupidly I admit, how he felt, he replied: 'Ah, I'm not going to take long to die.' This was said, I should add, with the lightly ironic tone he adopted for a rather serious disclosure.

During the next days, I decided to reread *Noces*, which had been published by Edmond Charlot, and among so many revelations about its author, I remembered this one, from 'Le Vent à Djémila':

On peut être là, couché un jour, s'entendre dire: 'Vous êtes fort et je vous dois d'être sincère: je peux vous dire que vous allez mourir'; êtrè la avec toute sa vie entre les mains, toute sa peur aux entrailles et un regard idiot. Que signifie le reste: des flots de sang viennent battre à mes tempes et il me semble que j'écraserais tout autour de moi.

You can be lying in bed one day and hear someone say: 'You are strong and I owe it to you to be honest: I can tell you that you are going to die'; you're there, with your whole life in your hands, fear in your bowels, looking the fool. What else matters: waves of blood come throbbing to my temples and I feel I could smash everything around me.

But, a little further in the same text Camus adds that faced by the certainty of death he does not want to lie, nor be lied to: 'Je veux porter ma lucidité jusqu'au bout et regarder ma fin avec toute la profusion de ma jalousie et de mon horreur.' *'I want to keep my lucidity to the last, and gaze upon my death with all the fullness of my jealousy and horror.'*[1] And so for Meursault in his prison, as soon as he has lost the innocence in which he lived, the rebellion that comes to burn his conscience when he knows what the sentence of death signifies. We could, obviously, compare many citations from *Noces* and *L'Etranger* that speak of a similar spirit.

Camus and I also met in Edmond Charlot's book store, Les Vraies Richesses. In a little office contrived in the loft, Camus read manuscripts for Charlot or worked on a novel, 'L'Indifférent'. Perhaps it was the first title for *L'Etranger*. As for me, I was writing a story in the breathing space I could get from my military duties or take away from my study of Spanish. I gave him my text and I remember a quotation he retained, and the tone he took to approve it. I had written: 'Les hommes passent comme l'eau d'un fleuve et parce qu'il y a toujours des hommes on oublie que ce ne sont pas toujours les mêmes. On finit par se croire éternel comme ces foules.' *'Men pass by like the water of a river, and because there are always men we forget that they are not always the same. We end up believing ourselves eternal like the crowds.'* And Camus, in a low voice, murmured: 'That's it, that is really it.'

About this obsession with death on Camus's part, I can now reveal a feature unmentioned until now, which I had decided to omit in my account of 4 January 1960, which appeared in a special issue of an Oran magazine.[2] As soon as I learned, through journalist friends, of Camus's accidental death, I immediately went with my wife to his house, Rue Madame, where we arrived before Francine. She knew nothing when she came in. Her sister Christiane took her aside to tell her the terrible news. I drove her in my car to Villeblevin, and went in with her to the room in the town hall, guarded by police to prevent any of the already numerous journalists and photographers from entering. Francine allowed only me and Doctor Camus (striking homonym) near her. The body was lying in its trench coat on a long table. The face bore a scar across the whole forehead and another was scratched across the left hand. Camus seemed to be sleeping. After a moment of quiet, I heard Francine murmur: 'His hands, his beautiful hands . . .' Made nervous by her sorrow, she caressed them slowly, then turned towards the doctor to ask him, in a low voice, 'Are you certain that he is dead?' The question surprised me. 'But Madame', said the doctor, who was also disconcerted, 'his neck and spinal column were broken. Look ... his two wounds haven't bled. His heart stopped with the impact.' 'It's just', Francine said, pitifully, 'that he often told me to be sure.'

But let's go back to the Camus of Algiers. He loved this city and only the demands of his literary career kept him in Paris where, he told me one day, he appreciated neither the physical nor the moral climate. He has Meursault tell Marie, who has questioned him about Paris, 'C'est une ville sale. Il y a des pigeons et des cours noires. Les gens ont la peau blanche.' *'It's dirty. Lots of pigeons and dark courtyards. Everybody's pale.'*[3] He confided to me a little after the war, 'Have you noticed? Here when night falls people go home. Back in Algeria, when evening comes, everyone hurries to go out.' And this difference seemed to him essential for distinguishing two worlds that were in his eyes very far from each other.

The nostalgia for Algiers, the city he loved the most in the world, was so intense that one day when he had come up to see us on our hill in Bouzarea, he stayed for a long time looking below him at the luminous bay in the tender sunlit morning. And told us both how lucky we were. Soon afterwards, he asked my wife and me to find him a similar villa on this crest. A few days later my wife discovered one and I hurriedly wrote to tell Camus, but got no reply because he had just left for Lausanne to see a doctor. As soon as he returned to Paris he sent a telegram to accept the offer. Too late. In the meantime the house had been rented, much to his regret. This location was quite sought after, and offers to rent or sell were rare.

During our time in Algiers, he was always like a brother, generous and very indifferent to money. I speak from experience. Because, as a soldier, I only had my pay, he sent me one day to the barracks a money order for 600 francs (1938 francs!) with a letter that I have kept in which he told me that he was not expecting this money and that I could keep it until I was able to give it back. In the same way, he got me French and Spanish tutoring, as his philosophy lessons, he said, were enough for him. (Meursault, as well, is faithful to his friends, Céleste, Emmanuel ...)

The attention he paid to those he admired was accompanied by an attraction for those who were solitary, marginal, all those who were not reconciled to an order they had not chosen. So we went sometimes, in the evening, to the Rue des Trois-Couleurs, at the foot of the casbah, a section that has now disappeared. There was a little bar, Chez Coco, run by a dwarf with an enormous torso who had to climb on a platform to be at the right height to serve his clients – a mixture of seamen, dockers, prostitutes, legionnaires, as well as, in a corner reserved for them, guitarists, accordionists, or bizarre individuals, one of whom displayed himself naked, with all his body, from the neck to the buttocks, tattooed with a single scene of a fox hunt; one can guess what was the terrier. Almost every evening there was that sort of attraction. We can find in Meursault this interest for those who have come down in the world, such as that doubtful fellow Raymond Sintès, or that half-bum Salamano.

On nice days Camus and I went to swim on the nearby beaches, such as Sidi-Ferruch, and to get there we took the bus, the same, of course, that Meursault, Marie and Raymond will take to reach the Massons' beach cabin on the fatal day of 'quatre coups brefs frappés sur la porte du malheur', '*knocking four quick times on the door of unhappiness*'.[4] Camus swam very well, going out to deep water, full of ease and energy (as when he played football or – as I would see him in 1941 in Oran – going by bicycle towards Aïn el Turck and the beach). We can find the same taste for the sun, the sea and physical exertion in Meursault, for he too knows how to swim well and proves it in his swim with Marie in the port. He runs easily to take the bus to Marengo and to catch a truck on the quays faster than his friend Emmanuel, with whom he works for a shipping company (like Camus for the Algiers firm of Schiaffino).

This as well: in the autumn of 1938 I witnessed an incident, rue Michelet, in which Camus came up against a Communist militant who reproached him for his 'cowardly desertion of the Party'. I remember Camus's cold anger at this provocation; I thought he was ready to make a sharp reply if the other fellow became too menacing. Meursault, as well, is courageous and would know how to fight, as we can see in his attitude during the fight with the Arabs, when Sintès is wounded. Meursault shows no trace of fear.

When *Alger Républicain* was founded, Camus suggested that I collaborate and, of course, it was a matter for him of getting me to earn a little money. As I was in the military, I could not sign my own name, and used such pseudonyms as Pétrone or Emmanuel Chênes. (Camus even had me write a serial novel, that I titled *Place Mahon.*) In the daily newspaper he had several columns, including the court reports. I can verify that he transposed his experience in the trial scenes, which Visconti filmed in the same courtroom of the

Cour d'Assises in Algiers. As a collaborator on the film, I followed all the shooting and I remember that on the evening of one of the sessions, I heard, like Meursault, the cries of newspaper vendors and the cheeping of the sparrows that held court in the trees of the adjoining square.

Finally, in the difficulty of communicating between Meursault and his mother, I can find an echo of what we know (from *L'Envers et l'endroit*) about Camus and his own mother. Sometimes he invited me on Sunday to have lunch at the home of his mother and his uncle the cooper, in the small apartment the brother and sister shared in Belcourt. I remember that this woman with white hair, a delicate smile and a look of kindness, spoke very little and willingly kept herself apart. She hardly cheered up if I tried to talk to her in Spanish. Camus adored her, was always considerate of her, showered her with gifts. One Sunday she told me, in a hushed voice: 'Yes, he is a good son, a very good son.'

These few memories I have gathered seem to me to show how much Camus has given Meursault of his own substance.[5] And the character he created, Meursault, has today entered fully into that family of great literary myths that never cease to move or intrigue the conscience of mankind.

Translated by Adele King

Notes

1. *Essais* (Paris: Gallimard, Bibliothèque de la Pléiade, 1965, p. 65). 'Le Vent a Djemila' from *Noces*. Translation in *Lyrical and Critical Essays*, Philip Thody (ed.), Ellen Conroy Kennedy (trans.) New York: Alfred A. Knopf, 1969), p. 78.
2. 'Visages d'Albert Camus', *Simoun*, no. 31.
3. *L'Etranger*, in *Théâtre, récits, nouvelles*, (Paris: Gallimard, Bibliothèque de la Pléiade, 1962, p. 1156). *The Stranger*, Matthew Ward (trans.) (New York: Alfred Knopf, 1988), p. 42.
4. *L'Etranger*, p. 1168. (Ward translation, p. 59.)
5. Camus himself admitted this in his notebooks for 1942 (*Essais*, Paris: Gallimard, Bibliothèque de la Pléiade, vol. 2, p. 1926): 'Three people were used for the composition of *L'Etranger*: two men (one of them me) and a woman.') The other man had told him the story of the gratuitous crime one of his friends committed against an Arab.

2

Innocence in Camus and Dostoievsky
Jean Daniel

I have written, we have all more or less written, that the amazing
return to Camus that we are witnessing signals a refusal of history.
It is also at least partially an unwillingness to take refuge simply in
transcendence and a sort of active moral consent to rebellion and
to happiness. Everything has indeed been said on this theme, but I
would like to make two preliminary observations which will help
me to give you the latest stage in my own, obviously subjective,
view of Camus.

The first observation is that our return – which is also an appeal –
concerns a body of work that the author considered incomplete. To
Charles Poncet, he said that he had only completed a quarter of the
plan he had elaborated when he was twenty. Claude Vigée reports
more precisely that, in the last months of his life, Camus saw in his
books published until then only the first stages of a future work
that alone would matter and would give him his true place in our
century. From *L'Etranger* to *La Chute* everything was only tentative,
a preparation for the major work, gaining the Kingdom had to be
done through the desert of Exile. How can we, in these conditions,
rely on what is incomplete?

My second observation is that it may seem paradoxical to see a
society return to a way of thinking or appeal to an attitude, when
both advocate the heroism to be found in contradiction rather than
furnish answers and certainties. Undoubtedly we can find justifications to refuse or to resist, but we cannot say that they will leave
us sleeping peacefully. Nor does Camus offer any of those wise
architectural schemes, any of those secure cathedrals which we can
enter to receive the light. He proposes neither a global system nor a
definitive view of the world and, in fact, this 'director of thought' is
more an example than a teacher, more a witness than a judge, more
contagious than persuasive.

In these conditions it would be risky and unfaithful to Camus to return to him pretending, as religious thinkers have often done, to complete his work in his place, or finding, thanks to a reductive interpretation of his thought (and even, I would say, of his impulses) a complacent acceptance of disillusion which would permit us, as he would say, to face our armchairs in the direction of the apocalypse. We must ask ourselves why we have this strange need of Camus, which becomes an acceptance of explosion, a consent to contradiction, a welcome to mystery, not in order to dance once more on volcano tops with the dandies of aestheticism, but in order to continue to play, in the company of those humiliated or offended by history, this accidental, useless and pathetic role which humans have inherited as they accept a history in which we have not been consulted.

Nothing is less comfortable or less reassuring than Camus's witness, and I would like to propose as an illustration of this the basic theme of innocence, with reference to Dostoievsky as a counterpoint. What is striking each time that we look at Camus's itinerary is how quickly he settled into nihilism, and how continually he referred, explicitly or not, to a lost paradise, one in which the individual would have been either happy or justified, both terms signifying innocent. From the beginning nihilism is everywhere. It is the reverse side of everything, and obstructs our perception of the other side. Men are mortal and they are not happy. 'There is no love of living without despair of living', he wrote at the age of twenty-four. Contemplating the world without hope of another life brings forth the notion of the absurd and of individual rebellion, while the spectacle of history and its crimes gives birth to rebellion. The only excuse for God is that he does not exist, while the relationships that individuals have created among themselves by agreeing to use a coded vocabulary organise misunderstandings and reinforce solitude. Meursault is condemned to death because he did not cry at his mother's funeral. And Jan the Czech is killed by the mother and sister whom he came to help. People die for the same reason as Meursault: 'He didn't know how to find the word that was needed. And while he was looking for words, they killed him' (Kafka).

Let me come back to Meursault. Primitive, logical, spare, hardly full of wonder, his existence oscillates between that of a deaf child and that of a stone in the sun. Everything that happens to him before the murder he accepts with a gentle indifference. His humour, which

Camus thought did not sufficiently interest readers, comes from the fact that he will not be turned away from his mineral, stone-like logic. When he is offered friendship or love, he is willing, but says that really it is all the same to him. This is the state that Meursault, when he remembers it, is going to consider happy; he is going to regret it but in such a way that his character is changed, without our being aware of it. And I wonder if we are faced with an un-recognised intervention or a weakness on the part of the author. This indifferent man is undoubtedly innocent in the sense that peasants give to the word; but he does not have the ability to experience consciously a communion with the world, or to express his rapture. So, at the instant when, struck like Oedipus by the fatal command to kill, he becomes cosmically pathetic and concludes:

> J'ai compris que j'avais détruit l'équilibre du jour, le silence exceptionnel d'une plage où j'avais été heureux. Alors, j'ai tiré encore quatre fois sur un corps inerte où les balles s'enfonçaient sans qu'il y parût. Et c'était comme quatre coups brefs que je frappais sur la porte du malheur. (p. 1168)

> *I knew that I had shattered the harmony of the day, the exceptional silence of a beach where I'd been happy. Then I fired four more times at the motionless body where the bullets lodged without leaving a trace. And it was like knocking four quick times on the door of unhappiness.* (p. 59)

There, suddenly, it seems to me, the author of *Noces* intervenes in Meursault's tenderly indifferent universe. The hero lived with the happiness of stones, or, at most, of waves; here he announces the end of exaltation and of joy. It is as if, in spite of himself, Camus the novelist could not keep from lending to Meursault a sort of inner life which was really his own. This is a small uncontrolled insertion of the author's message, of the type we see often in Dostoievsky, where it is sometimes a detriment to the logic of the novel. At the end of *The Idiot* the great anti-occidental tirades have nothing to do with the character. In the earlier life that Camus has given Meursault, there was some surprising emotion. Meursault, indifferent to everything, shivers in his prison when he suddenly hears the swallows tearing through the twilight, and when he feels like kissing a witness at his trial. The need for friendship will be present as well in all the indifferent, cynical, cruel heroes Camus will create.

Is it in this previous life that innocence consisted of not knowing that he would kill, that he would need to take revenge on the person (presumably Arab) who had attacked his mother? (Alain Costes) Before the murder, Meursault is innocent without knowing it; he discovers, at the very instant of the murder, that he has broken with happiness, but in an irresponsible manner, one that could be imputed to the gods. After the murder, having become responsible, Meursault decides to elude all the traps of words, of the judges and even of the priest, in order to go to the limits of a freedom that caused him to lose happiness. This simple being enters the realm of death as a cunning god in his kingdom. He goes so far as to demand that men curse him. He discovers, in fact, that innocence does not exist. And this is the idea that I want to propose to you for Camus. Innocence is a state of ignorance. You can live through something innocently. But innocence does not exist. Innocence is a nostalgic desire for something that is missing, the reflection of another life that does not exist. You can sometimes find this reflection on the face of Franciscan monks in a convent in Fiesole, as Camus describes them. But these monks have retreated from the world, and they are only innocent of what they do not participate in. In solitude but not in solidarity. There remains the face of a child. There in a child is Meursault, but the gods strike him down.

Like everyone else, probably, I change my mind every five or ten years about the symbolism of Meursault, as I do about almost all the great heroes of literature and history. For a long time I thought that Meursault said everything because he had nothing to say; or, more precisely, because he wanted to express nothing, not say nothing but make nothing positive, because words and silence are both false. Now I think that there is more and something else. Meursault understands instinctively that one can only live in this world in the present moment, without hope, without a future. What he says does not admit making plans that contain even a bit of confidence in any kind of next day, any minimum of optimistic certainty that another moment could follow the present one. His words are perpendicular, not linear. There is no resignation to what could be fate, which would be a sort of wisdom. His reflexes imply nothing; they are. Later, when Meursault looks at the destiny that he accepts, and is going to bend and precipitate in order not to submit to it, he suppresses, he empties time, already refusing the illusion that history has a sense. Even more, by refusing the priest, he deprives men of the feeling of innocence executioners want to have when they kill. He goes to the limit of his logic of rebellion. There is a Nietzschean dimension to how this hero leaves the world.

Speaking of Prince Muchkine, of the 'idiot' (which means as well the innocent), Dostoievsky says in his *Notebooks*: 'The idiot is not of this world and his coming among men is extraordinary. He is called a sheep. He mingles with sinners without losing his purity.' This is true. But just like Meursault, he will not be innocent. He will even provoke the worst disorders. The two heroes cannot be brought together without artifice. But the two creators of these heroes have the same conception – tormented, difficult, imprecise and in any case nostalgic – of innocence. Remember the famous dialogue:

> Can the harmony of the world rest on the tears of a child, any child?
> I don't think so, replies Alioscha to Ivan Karamasov.
> Would you consent to be the architect, in these conditions?
> No, says Alioscha softly, even though he believes in God.

And the dialogue continues until it establishes that if God exists he is not innocent, that it is an unbelievable paradox, and that it is perhaps a paradox to believe.

For an understanding not only of Camus but also of our time, the importance of Dostoievsky cannot be overestimated. Muchkine, the idiot, the innocent, includes more than Meursault. His creator says of him that he is morbidly proud to the point that he cannot avoid thinking of himself as a god, but that at the same time he has the clear-sightedness to despise himself and to do so in a way that must be infinite. He is Christian and at the same time he does not believe. I am not sure that Camus–Meursault and especially Camus–Clamence, would reject this description, at least partially accurate, of themselves.

Innocence as much as imposture is at the heart of Camus's key book, which is, in my opinion, *La Chute*. The settling of accounts with intellectuals that it contains used to seem essential to me, but seems secondary today. It is the most audacious and risky self-critical confession that has ever been if not written at least published – except, perhaps, Dostoievsky's, a soon forgotten confession, *Notes from the Underground*. The circumstances in which this confession was written are quite edifying. Immediately after the emancipation of the peasants in the 1850s, Russia went through an intense political crisis and the rise of extremes, which divided public opinion into a revolutionary party and a counter-revolutionary party. Some of the circles to which Dostoievsky had belonged in his youth began to elaborate a terrorist conception of revolution.

Chernychevski's book soon appeared, the famous *What is to be done?*, which was to become the breviary of the Russian revolutionaries, long extracts of which Lenin knew by heart. Dostoievsky discovered with horror the extreme uses of the socialist ideas that had led him astray. He went into seclusion and in a few months wrote *Notes from the Underground* in order to vituperate with boundless irony, like Clamence in *La Chute*, the 'judges with clean hands'. He wrote by looking into his own past; he even constructed characters who merely reflected an earlier self he now disavowed. This is the fall.

In 1867 Dostoievsky went to the Peace Congress, a demonstration in Geneva by the European left. Whom did he meet there? Garibaldi, Louis Blanc, Victor Hugo, Edgar Quinet, Stuart Mill and Bakunin. In short, everyone. And, amazingly, everyone seemed to agree with the ultra-violet speeches of the orators and with the declarations from the floor of revolutionaries who had not been invited. One year earlier, terrorist attacks had multiplied in Russia, most notably the attack against Czar Alexander II. Dostoievsky became convinced that such refined liberals, no matter how seductive and harmless they seemed, were finally accomplices in the crimes committed or preached by the current apostles of the void. It was then that he decided to write *The Possessed*, or *The Demons*, a work which would mean so much to Camus. Again it would be a question of innocence. No longer simply this time to say, as I would argue, that it does not exist, but to denounce the exploitation that could be done of the need for innocence – of the famous nostalgia for innocence.

If I have said that Camus's confession is hazardous, unless it was secretly and willingly a way of mortifying himself, it is because he knew perfectly well that his friends, all those who knew him well or slightly, could recognise the author in the hero, identify him, watch and take note of his mistakes and weaknesses. But the question remains: what can still be saved after the universe of *La Chute*? I have just reread it and I am still shocked. Religious thinkers or analysts may undoubtedly reply that the person who can in any case be saved is the author. But to suppose that the confession of sin washes and makes innocent, addressed to a god who has regulated his indulgences, his small and great pardons; to suppose that the famous catharsis procures virginity and deliverance, is not to realise that we are only in the presence of an inventory of sophisticated remorse, of tricky repentances or of a cynical means of auto-disintoxication. It is really a question, again, of the realisation – how superbly mocking – of lost innocence, of impossible communion, of the loss of paradise and the inescapable descent into hell. Clamence is not pursued by remorse for a crime but by the idea that he was able without remorse to allow a crime to be committed: that young woman who throws herself from a bridge follows him and makes him question himself about innocence. Remember the terrible end:

> 'O jeune fille, jette-toi encore dans l'eau pour que j'aie une seconde fois la chance de nous sauver tous les deux.' Une seconde fois, hein, quelle imprudence! Supposez, cher maître, qu'on nous prenne au mot? Il faudrait s'exécuter. Brr ... ! l'eau est si froide. Mais rassurons-nous! Il est trop tard maintenant, il sera toujours trop tard. Heureusement! (p. 1551)

> *'O young woman, throw yourself into the water again so that I may a second time have the chance of saving both of us!' A second time, eh, what a risky suggestion! Just suppose, cher maître, that we should be taken literally? We'd have to go through with it. Brr ... ! The water's so cold! But let's not worry! It's too late now. It will always be too late.* (p. 147)

Fortunately! It will always be too late, that's the Pontius Pilate Complex and the secret weapon of our era.

It is Clamence who, in spite of or because of his truculent cynicism, speaks best about nostalgia for innocence and about a guilty conscience. Clamence lives within and experiences the world, according to Ruth Reichelberg, as a world of fault, even if in other instances we are taught (as Camus does) that there is no more fault and no one before whom to feel guilty and at fault. Clamence, citizen of a world without god and without saviour, continues to experience things as if God were not completely dead. He is thus doubly guilty. Guilty of not believing and guilty of this very guilt, since there is no one before whom that guilt can be justified.

> 'Que voulez-vous' [says Clamence] 'l'idée la plus naturelle à l'homme, celle qui lui vient naïvement, comme du fond de sa

nature, est l'idée de son innocence. De ce point de vue, nous sommes tous comme ce petit Français qui, à Buchenwald, s'obstinait à vouloir déposer une réclamation ... "C'est que, ... disait le petit Français, mon cas est exceptionnel. Je suis innocent!" Nous sommes tous des cas exceptionnels.'(pp. 1516–17)

'What do you expect? [says Clamence] The idea that comes most naturally to man, as if from his very nature, is the idea of his innocence. From this point of view, we are all like that little Frenchman at Buchenwald who insisted on registering a complaint ... "But you see," ... said the little Frenchman, "My case is exceptional. I am innocent!" We are all exceptional cases.' (p. 81)

But then, and here Camus is speaking, where is innocence?

Les empires s'écroulaient, les nations et les hommes se mordaient à la gorge, nous avions la bouche souillée. D'abord, innocents sans le savoir, nous étions coupables sans le vouloir, le mystère grandissait avec notre science. C'est pourquoi nous nous occupions, ô dérision, de morale. Infirme je rêvais de vertu. Au temps de l'innocence, j'ignorais que la morale existât. (*L'Eté*, pp. 870–1)

Empires were crumbling, men and nations were tearing at one another's throats; our mouths were dirtied. Innocent at first without knowing it, now we were unintentionally guilty: the more we knew, the greater the mystery. This is why we busied ourselves, oh mockery, with morality. Frail in spirit, I dreamed of virtue! In the days of innocence, I did not know morality existed. (p. 164–5)

Here we can see what the feeling, or the illusion, in any case the lived experience, of innocence implies: 'It's all over with innocence and the light of Greece. We have entered the world of sin and of generalised guilt', wrote the philosophy student in his 'diplôme d'études supérieures' on Plotinus and Saint Augustine. Innocence leads to lyricism, to seriousness, and to the illusion of immortality. Where does it come from? When does it visit us? We know that for Camus it is first of all a matter of the body and the light. This light, he said, quickly becomes unbearable to young men when they are only men who feel they are still young. Although the body continues to yearn for the burning light we find that we are suddenly moving away from those shores where the triumph of the senses assured us of glories and justification. Hours lived in innocence are like arrows; they do not have the roundness of days of which Giono spoke, in a book published by Edmond Charlot which Camus read in Algiers. We find ourselves neither thrown into the world, nor abandoned by the gods, but merely cast back upon ourselves. What is to be done as soon as we leave this kingdom if not follow our route into an eternal exile? Tarrou says in *La Peste*:

> Quand j'étais jeune, je vivais avec l'idée de mon innocence, c'est-à-dire avec pas d'idée du tout ... Tout me réussissait, j'étais à l'aise dans l'intelligence, au mieux avec les femmes et si j'avais quelques inquiétudes, elles passaient comme elles étaient venues. Un jour, j'ai commencé à réfléchir. (p. 1420)

> *When I was young I lived with the idea of my innocence; that is to say, with no idea at all ... I brought off everything I set my hand to, I moved at ease in the field of the intellect, I got on excellently with women, and if I had occasional qualms, they passed as lightly as they came. Then one day I started thinking.* (p. 222)

In fact, Tarrou had begun no longer to feel *justified*, that is the key-word, by the triumphant burning rays of the light. 'At its origin innocence is the absence of moral life. Grace touches us lightly when remorse is excluded' (Stendhal's comment on Madame de Renal).

At the age of twenty Camus understood why Rimbaud had decided one day to quit writing – simply because he had said everything. Through Rimbaud we can understand the feeling of lost innocence in Camus. After having seen what man believed he could see – starry archipelagoes, unbelievable flora of the sea – the boat no longer wants to leave the drunken state that led it into all the fantastic adventures and the unlimited debauchery of the world of childhood. He can no longer do anything except be stranded on a far-away, unknown beach: the future Abyssinia. The boat is drunk because it embraced the cyclones of an enclosed world where the lightning itself offers protection, an innocent world, as complete as the absolute world of adolescence. One cannot come back from this absolute world. After the illuminations, there can only be the season in hell. After the Promethean defiance, nothing is left except reaching the cities of wandering. This is the passage from the absolute to the human, from intensity to duration, from passion to tenderness, and this passage cannot be done without a real break, equivalent to a death from which one can only get out through mockery, like Clamence. Through humour as well, Camus would add.

But to stay awhile with Clamence. He has sullied even the memory of happiness. Undoubtedly he lived with this innocence-ignorance, and it is what remains, hardly luminous, a small gleam in the greyness of Amsterdam. His happiness, he knows, was made from others' ignorance, lived at the expense of others. The sun is black in his truth-tale from which nothing can be saved. Not even Christ.

No, not even Christ, accused of suffering on the cross not from a passion to save men but pursued by remorse for having been the only one to escape the Massacre of the Innocents. It is not possible to believe in a reconciliation with the world or with creation. No more can one believe that the sweet Scipion, whose misfortune is to understand everything, is going to save Caligula – who exercises on Camus–Clamence a disconcerting and unbearable fascination. Remember the beginning of *The Brothers Karamasov*, the novel that Freud considered to be, along with *Oedipus Rex* and *Hamlet*, one of the three monuments of universal literature. It is the father, Fiodor Pavlovitch Karamasov, who speaks like a luciferian hero with torrential, devastating and contagious cynicism. This is all the seduction of which evil is capable. This is the happy apocalypse. Against Father Karamasov, Dostoievsky imposes the vigorous and Franciscan softness of Starez. Against Clamence, there is no one. Or rather, there is this mute listener, abused, perhaps even conquered, to whom Clamence is supposedly speaking.

This is where the problem of an unfinished body of work comes up. After Clamence, what? The first man? Autobiography set against autocriticism? The rediscovery of the divine? Camus confirmed after *La Chute* that he did not believe in the immortality of the soul or in the resurrection, without, however, being an atheist. Still retaining a sense of the sacred, he stays in the community of men, and his kingdom, even after all the exiles, is only that of humankind, with, at its heart, a nostalgia for something which is hollow, negative, a reflection: innocence.

It would have been tempting, in fact, to imagine for Camus an evolution, a Dostoyevskian end. The absurd is not the opposite of belief, which can itself be absurd. Saint John did not see the resurrected Christ, but he believed more strongly than Saint Thomas, who touched him. We have invented ways to make God innocent, judging the reasons there were for believing in him, and haughtily avoiding the problem of evil. Nothing will justify, in Camus's written work or in reports of what he said, such a step. Undoubtedly Dostoievsky followed certain Camusian paths and Camus was fascinated by the universe of Dostoievsky. The author of *The Idiot*, in a famous speech he gave at the end of his life to celebrate the anniversary of Pushkin's death, replied that there is only one religion, Christianity, and only one people to serve this religion, the Russian people. This man, at the end of the last century, after having digested all the currents of history and participated in them, after having put on stage and given life to the most representative heroes of his time and ours, foundered on the idea of election, of a chosen people – with, as usual, the same noble considerations that have accompanied this idea. One is chosen to bear witness, to be the best, not to dominate but, on the contrary, to show, etc. The debate, on which the philosopher Levinas has shed considerable light, has for a long time divided the Jewish people. The concept of election conceals potential dangers and virtual explosives. Oddly, we can find the same arguments in Dostoievsky's writing against materialism, socialism, occidentalism and atheism, as in the writing of certain Islamic fundamentalists – if not Christian fundamentalists.

The only reply rests, I believe, in the forty pages of *L'Homme révolté* devoted to Marxism (which Evelyne Pisier has examined with relevance). For beyond the drift of Marxist thought, Camus strives to eradicate the internal philosophy of the Marxian universe. Going further than his master Jean Grenier, he discovers the religious sources of the new revolutionary hope. In order to cheat monstrously the absurd human condition, unable to look either the sun or death in the face, society invented transcendence not only through God but through history. Camus does not cite Ernest Renan who, well before Spengler, had shown how far back the totalitarian and apocalyptical traditions of the prophets of the good society went. From Buddha to Cyrus, from Job to Elias, from Saint Augustine to Hegel and to Bakunin, all the visionaries have extolled a discipline of the heart to prepare the redemptive furnace, unavoidable prelude to every paradise. Everything then was promised to the zealots who followed the road of this religious wisdom, which was termed science when revolutionary hope was born. Marxism will be denounced in this fashion by Camus, not only, as is said now, as an ideology that functions like a religion, but as a true religious ideology. It is a scientific messianism of bourgeois origin, of which the short-term prophecies have been shown to be false, and the long-term prophecies demand the sacrifice of generations. The famous end of history has no sense, no more than the kingdom of heaven. It is at this moment that Camus achieves a coherent thought against totalitarian theocracies. At this moment as well he discovers that innocence and guilt are at the heart of every religion and that Marx reintroduces the fundamental elements of a religious vision, fault and its corollary, punishment: 'Marxism is a doctrine of guilt for man, of innocence for history.' Man is always in a situation where he can be accused of slowing down the journey that leads to a classless society, to the end of history, that is to the kingdom of innocence that we find again here, as in Dostoievsky's *Diary of a Writer*. Nothing in Camus's essential path permits us to imagine a leap from the sense of the sacred to a recognition of the divine.

It is evident that each of us can finish the message or be contented with the unfinished work. As for me, I know exactly what I will take from it: a religion of unbelievers for a generation that has seen Nazism, Stalinism, decolonisation, nuclear danger, crisis.

Translated by Adele King

Works Cited

Camus, Albert, *Théâtre, récits, nouvelles* (Paris: Gallimard, Bibliothèque de la Pleïade, 1962).

Camus, Albert, Essais (Paris: Gallimard, Bibliothèque de la Pléïade, 1965).

Camus, Albert, *The Stranger*, Matthew Ward (trans.) (New York: Alfred A. Knopf, 1988).

Camus, Albert, *The Fall and Exile and the Kingdom*, Justin O'Brien (trans.) (New York: Random House, Modern Library, 1964).

Camus, Albert, *The Plague* (New York: Random House, 1972).

Camus, Albert, 'Retour à Tipasa', from *L'Eté*, in Philip Thody (ed.) *Lyrical and Critical Essays*, Ellen Conroy Kennedy (trans.) (New York: Alfred A. Knopf, 1969).

3

L'Etranger and 'Metaphysical Anxiety'
Frantz Favre

By considering briefly the relationships of both Nietzsche and Camus to metaphysics, we will try to define what *L'Etranger* owes to Nietzsche. The existence of a debt at least cannot be denied, as Camus took care to warn us: 'C'est fini pour aujourd'hui, monsieur l'Antéchrist'.[1] *'That's all for today, Monsieur Antichrist.'* (I, p. 1176; W, p. 71).

Such an assimilation of Nietzsche continues to surprise us. There is not, it would seem, any similarity between the moderation which Meursault habitually shows and the passionate violence of Nietzsche's attack on Christianity: 'I condemn Christianity! I bring against the Christian Church the most terrible accusation that has ever been uttered.'[2] But what is more Nietzschean than Meursault's fidelity to the earth and his obstinate refusal of God. To the chaplain who asks him: 'Aimez-vous donc cette terre à ce point?' *'Do you really love this earth as much as all that?'* (I, p. 1209; W, p. 119), Meursault does not condescend to reply at all, as if he were imbued with Zarathustra's message: 'I implore you, my brothers, be true to the earth and don't believe those who talk to you about superearthly hopes.'[3] Meursault seems to remember Zarathustra's following words – 'they hold life in contempt, they are moribund' – when in his anger he shouts at the chaplain that 'il n'était même pas sûr d'être en vie, puisqu'il vivait comme un mort'. *'He wasn't even sure he was alive, because he was living like a dead man'.* (I, p. 1210; W, p. 120.) There is, however, no trace of antitheism in this character whom we hardly see questioning himself about the strangeness of our condition. We can find in him a feeling neither of frustration nor of rebellion, nothing which usually nourishes the 'passionate disbelief' of the author.[4] His final anger is directed against the chaplain, not against God. If it is true, as Schopenhauer says, that man is 'a metaphysical animal', the prosecutor is right to stress Meursault's inhumanity.

36

There is, on the other hand, a character in whom this 'metaphysical anxiety' is manifest: the examining magistrate. Undoubtedly he abuses the authority of his position to try to influence Meursault, but his nervous tics betray a real concern, and we cannot doubt the sincerity of his indignation and his incredulity when confronted by a disbelief that is so calmly stated:

Il m'a dit que c'était impossible, que tous les hommes croyaient en Dieu, même ceux qui se détournaient de son visage. C'était là sa conviction et, s'il devait jamais en douter, sa vie n'aurait plus de sens.

He said it was impossible; all men believed in God, even those who turn their backs on him. That was his belief, and if he were ever to doubt it, his life would become meaningless. (I, p. 1175; W, p. 69)

Such an admission, let us recognise, seems rather improbable. It proves, however, the existence of a mental attitude sufficiently prevalent to arouse Nietzsche's sarcasm:

Egotism against Egotism: How many there are who still reach the conclusion: 'Life would be intolerable if God did not exist!' Or, as it is said in idealist circles, 'Life would be intolerable if it did not have an ethical foundation.' So, there must be a God (or an ethical foundation for life)! In reality it is completely different. A person who is used to this idea does not want to live without it; the idea is thus necessary for his preservation – but what a presumption to assert that everything necessary for my preservation must really exist! As if my preservation was necessary! What if others believed the opposite! If they refused to live accepting these two articles of faith, and if, these articles were true, life would no longer seem to them worth living! And that is how it is now![5]

Camus also placed himself in the lineage of Nietzsche when he wrote to Pierre Bonnel: 'I only object to believing that the need for a principle in metaphysics means that principle exists' (II, p. 1424). Without wanting to give undue credence to a too narrowly determinist notion of influences, which must be considered deeper the more they are diffuse, we could also be tempted to establish a link between the above citation from Nietzsche's *Dawn of Day* and the affirmation of *Le Mythe de Sisyphe*: 'Il s'agissait précédémment de savoir si la vie devait avoir un sens pour être vécue. Il apparaît ici au contraire qu'elle sera d'autant mieux vécue qu'elle n'aura pas de sens.' *'Before it was a question of knowing if life had to have a meaning in order to be lived. It seems here, on the contrary, that it will be lived so much better if it does not have any meaning.'* (II, p. 138.) 'Lived better' (*mieux vécue*) because lived more freely and more intensely, with only the consciousness of death and the equivalence of all values. Here we rejoin Meursault and his certainty that he has lived as it is fitting to live.

What Meursault, in his anger, replies to the chaplain is less an argument than an affirmation of a certain way to live and to die. This should not surprise us as long as we remember the importance for both Nietzsche and Camus of the idea of a style of living.[6] If, as Camus maintains, 'the only superiority as an example that Christianity has' lies in its 'search for a style of living' (C, p. 31), we can comprehend that the example of 'the only Christ we deserve' (I, p. 1929) might belong, although in the opposite sense, to the same aesthetic order. The stylistic unity of Meursault's fate is based, like Nietzsche's proceeding, on an unfailing demand for truth. Certainly Meursault does not claim, like Nietzsche, to confront the dangerous problem of the meaning of this demand, and of the very value of truth. The goal towards which he climbs, however tragic its conclusion, takes more humble paths. The honesty which would be, according to Nietzsche, the 'ultimate virtue of free spirits'[7] is not an honesty Meursault fulfills on the high summits of philosophical heroism, but rather at first in the routine framework of his daily existence. There he already shows a rare need for economy and accuracy of expression. 'C'est que je n'ai jamais grand chose à dire' (I, p. 1173), as he will explain later to the examining magistrate. We might be astonished at the magistrate's reaction, as he says he is interested in Meursault but does not push this further and is satisfied with such an explanation. He hardly seems to suspect that there could be deeper reasons for Meursault's laconism and his refusal to use hyperbole. Everything takes place, however, as if Meursault, without formulating his position openly, distrusts the mythic function of language operating in what Robert Champigny has called 'theatrical society, antiphysis'.[8] Convinced, like Nietzsche, that 'Every word is a prejudice'[9] Meursault feels repelled by the need to use words. Faced by a court which, because it is caught in the trap of mythical language, fails to realise what is happening and indulges in the formal games of the judicial ritual so far as almost to forget the accused man, Meursault gives up trying to defend himself.

De temps en temps, j'avais envie d'interrompre tout le monde et de dire: 'Mais tout de même, qui est l'accusé? C'est important d'être l'accusé. Et j'ai quelque chose à dire!' Mais réflexion faite, je n'avais rien à dire.'

There were times when I felt like breaking in on all of them and saying, 'Wait a minute! Who's the accused here? Being the accused counts for something. And I have something to say!' But on second thought, I didn't have anything to say. (I, p. 1195; W, p. 98)

Meursault's refusal to consider marriage as 'une chose grave' (I, p. 1156) can be compared to this aphorism of Nietzsche:

'It is obvious, for instance, that a marriage is worth only as much as those who contract it, so in general a marriage has little value. As for "marriage itself", it has no value, nor does any other institution.'[10]

The fictional world created by language cannot, however, be reduced to the single dimension of moral values and social conventions. Language orders our perception of the world, making it intelligible to us by projecting on the indistinguishable reality of what will happen a network of our logical categories. Nietzsche never stops insisting on the perfectly illusory character of our depiction of the world, which presumes the existence of acting substances and of causal links between identical phenomena:

We should not interpret the necessity we feel to create concepts, species, forms, purposes and laws (a world of identical cases) as if it would allow us to establish what the true world is; rather it is our necessity to adjust to ourselves a world which makes our existence possible; in this way we create a world that seems to us determinable, simplified, intelligible, etc.[11]

Meursault's reluctance to explain himself, to oppose to the fictional but logical Meursault composed by the judiciary the real Meursault, would come then from his very Nietzschean conviction that 'nothing happening in reality corresponds strictly to logic'[12]. This conviction is as well shared by the reader, whom the narrator, at the beginning of his story, has taken care to sensitise to the irrationality of the world through the atomised vision of a consciousness 'transparent to things and opaque to meanings'.[13]

To this affirmation of the irrationality of the world is added a denunciation of the 'lie of faith in God'.[14] This is a denunciation which, taking into account its philosophical implications or the gravity of the circumstances, can seem the highest accomplishment of that demand for truth which is common to Nietzsche and to Meursault, and the paradoxical source of which would be, according to Nietzsche, Christianity itself:

> We can see that what really triumphed over the Christian god was Christian morality itself, the idea of truthfulness that was applied with increasing strictness, the Christian conscience sharpened in the confessional and transformed into a scientific conscience, into intellectual cleanliness at all costs.[15]

Although we can find Nietzschean elements in Meursault's rejection of the Christian god, if only in the pride of taking upon himself his own destiny – 'Quant à moi, je ne voulais pas qu'on m'aidât', '*I didn't want anybody's help*' (I, p. 1208; W, p. 117) – Meursault's final violence seems to me to owe more to circumstances than to theory. He revolts less against Christianity than against the chaplain's will to impose his own belief. Without the awkward insistence of the priest, Meursault would probably have been satisfied with only his refusal to waste the little time he had left with God. But such indifference is undoubtedly more provocative than any hostility. Nothing is more significant in this respect than the incomprehension shown by certain Catholic critics, no matter how penetrating they can be in other matters, for whom this indifference can only be a 'numbness of conscience' which destroys 'what is most precious in man: his desire for transcendence'.[16]

'That's all for today, Monsieur Antichrist' can therefore seem an attempt to create humorous distance, allowing the examining magitrate to arm himself against Meursault's disbelief, the provocative nature of which he had felt in such a passionate manner earlier. The naturalness of this attempt to make the situation less dramatic can, however, surprise us. The examining magistrate seems to have adapted himself to his Antichrist, who himself admits that he was taken in by the cordiality. Not that he was flattered by such a term, which hardly suits his nature, but because he has always shown himself to be sensitive to any display of sympathy and because he undoubtedly felt some satisfaction in seeing his disbelief treated with as much naturalness as he himself experienced it.

For it is indeed naturalness that characterises Meursault. By this we mean not only that simplicity and absence of prejudices shown by his conduct, but also – and more deeply – his reduction to *phusis*, to a state of consciousness, more mythic undoubtedly than real, which excludes neither sensitivity nor lucidity, but rather value judgements and 'metaphysical anxiety'. Nietzsche is perhaps again a source for such a character. Knowledge, he writes, does not necessarily lead to despair or to suicide. We can even imagine happy temperaments that accept it with detachment or serenity:

> A person would live finally among men and with himself as in nature, without praise, reproach, enthusiasm, taking delight as at a play in many things which formerly frightened him. He would be free from pomposity and would no longer feel the goad of thinking that he was not simply nature, or that he was more than nature. Of course, as I said, a good temperament would be necessary, a peaceful, mild and basically happy soul.[17]

This airy lightness of spirit, which does not worry about the lack of meaning in existence, takes pleasure in 'soaring freely, without fear, over men, customs, laws and traditional evaluations of things'.[18] This is a state Nietzsche strove to attain, that Nietzsche whose atheism is perhaps less precocious and less spontaneous than he likes to pretend:

> 'God', 'immortality of the soul', 'salvation', 'the after-life' are ideas to which I have not paid attention, with which I have not wasted my time [as Meursault refuses to waste his time with God], even when I was a child – perhaps I was not ingenuous enough for that! Atheism for me is not the result of something and still less an event in my life; it comes naturally, it is instinctive.[19]

Undoubtedly Nietzsche forgot, in this late and somewhat rewritten self-portrait, the atmosphere of Protestant piety which had surrounded his childhood. He was more accurate – and deeper – when he wrote:

> We are no longer Christian, we have gone beyond Christianity because we have lived not too far from it but too close and especially because it is from it that we issued; our piety, more harsh and more delicate at the same time, keeps us today from still being Christians.[20]

It is nevertheless true that all the force of his philosophy tends to free us from the metaphysical-moral vision of being and from even the idea of God, 'the greatest objection to existence'.[21]

It is tempting to oppose to this affirmation of radical atheism[22] Camus's admission to Ponge: 'You got it right in your observation: it is true that I am still a "nervous" man and that I cannot rid myself of metaphysical anxiety' (II, p. 1666). Nietzsche seems indeed to have broken with metaphysics better than Camus. Where Nietzsche's problem is to return man to himself and to reconcile him with life, Camus poses questions on the way in which man, once returned to himself in a world from then on absurd, can confront the injustice of his condition and overcome his nostalgia for a metaphysical meaning: 'Savoir si l'on peut vivre sans appel, c'est tout ce qui m'intéresse', 'Knowing if one can live without calling out, that's all that interests me.' (Le Mythe de Sisyphe, II, p. 143). This confrontation without hope is rebellion. The Camusian atmosphere can thus be defined in its originality, its nostalgic frustrations and its rebellious tension mixed, singularly, with lyrical impulses and a happy sensuality. We are far from the grand Nietzschean 'yes' to Amor fati. In Nietzsche there is no metaphysical rebellion in the sense Camus understands, but rather a rebellion against metaphysics. Camus seems to interpret Nietzsche according to his own problematic when he imagines at the origin of the Nietzschean proceeding a metaphysical rebellion that Nietzsche would have finally betrayed with Amor fati:

> Le oui nietzchéen, oublieux du non originel, renie la révolte elle-même, en même temps qu'il renie la morale qui refuse le monde tel qu'il est.

> The Nietzschean affirmative, forgetful of the original negative, disavows rebellion at the same time that it disavows the ethic that refuses to accept the world as it is. (L'Homme révolté, II, p. 486, R, p. 77)

What Nietzsche questions is less the human condition than man's attitude towards his condition. It is not God who is guilty of injustice towards man, but man who is guilty of injustice towards life. For Nietzsche it is a question of freeing man from God, and not of raising a protest against him.

Meursault could have replied, like Camus, to the chaplain: 'The world is beautiful and outside it, there is no salvation' (II, p. 87; L, p. 103). But in spite of the exclusive love of this earth he shares with his author, he is surely more Nietzschean than is Camus. When, at the threshold of death he feels 'prêt à tout revivre' 'ready to relive everything' and open with happiness to 'la tendre indifférence du monde' (I, p. 1211), he consents, unlike Camus, to the great Nietzschean affirmations of Eternal Return and *Amor fati*.

Such a surrender was not of course foreign to the author of *Noces*, who admitted that 'au coeur de [sa] révolte dormait un consentement', *'at the heart of [his] revolt consent is dormant'* (II, p. 88; L, p. 105). This consent could sometimes go as far as a desire to become part of the mineral indifference of the world: 'Quelle tentation de s'identifier à ces pierres, de se confondre avec cet univers brulant qui défie l'histoire et ses agitations!' *'How tempting to merge oneself with these stones, to mingle with this burning, impassive universe that challenges history and its agitations'* (*L'Eté*, II, p. 830; L, p. 130). Camus's temptation to join the world of stones is not of course without its Nietzschean precedent: 'How we should turn to stone – By becoming hard, very slowly, like a precious stone – and finally by staying there, peacefully, for the joy of eternity.'[23] Camus's humanism, however, remains reticent when faced by these two fundamental concepts of Nietzsche's thought: Eternal Return and *Amor fati*. He can only accept the first by interpreting it in a sense that was surely not Nietzsche's, for whom Eternal Return is inclusive, not selective, and could not be reduced to commemorative echoes of 'des moments culminants de l'humanité', 'the highest moments of humanity' (C2, p. 28). And, for Camus, human nature itself seems incompatible with Nietzsche's second concept: 'C'est par le refus d'une partie de ce monde que ce monde est vivable? Contre l'Amor fati. L'homme est le seul animal qui refuse d'être ce qu'il est.' *'It is by refusing part of this world that we can live in this world? Against Amor fati. Man is the only animal who refuses to be what he is'*. (C2, p. 259).

If it is true that 'the works of a man often retrace the history of his nostalgia or his temptations, almost never of his proper history' (II, p. 864), we can be permitted to see in *L'Etranger*, in spite of the subdued character of its hero, Camus's strongest Nietzschean 'temptation'. From the very fact that he pushes to the limit a refusal of any metaphysical concern, embodying it in the character of Meursault, Camus lets us see his own concern. The deepest paradox of L'Etranger would then be that Camus has entrusted to a 'natural' hero, one exempt from any painful conscience[24] the duty of expressing, through its opposite, his 'metaphysical anxiety'.

Translated by Adele King

Notes

1. For details of the works referred to by symbols (I, II, etc.) see the list of Works Cited following those Notes.
2. *Antichrist*, no. 62. (All references to Nietzsche give the section or chapter numbers only.)
3. *Thus Spake Zarathustra*, Prologue 3.
4. P. Viallaneix, 'L' "Incroyance passionnée" d'Albert Camus', *Albert Camus: 1* (Paris, Minard, Lettres Modernes, 1968), pp. 179–97.
5. *Dawn of Day*, no. 90.
6. Frantz Favre, 'Camus et Nietzsche, philosophie et existence', *Albert Camus: 9* (Paris, Minard, Lettres Modernes, 1979), pp. 65–94.
7. 'Honesty, if that is our virtue, one from which we cannot escape, we free spirits – we want to work at it with all our spitefulness and with all our love, and we will never tire of "perfecting" ourselves in our virtue, the only one remaining to us' (*Beyond Good and Evil*, no. 227). Also see *The Will to Power*, vol. II, bk 4, ch. 2, no. 63.
8. Robert Champigny, *Sur un héros païen* (Paris: Gallimard, 1959), p. 76. English translation, *On a Pagan Hero*, Rowe Portis (trans.) (University of Pennsylvania Press, 1969), p. 41: 'Language which comes to me ready made is not merely logos, it is mythos. For it translates, or better it *is* formal society, theatrical society, antiphysis. It is not merely the language of knowing and comprehending: it is the language of belief. It assumes a sort of autonomous theatrical existence, fascinating and deceptive: it is collective myths.'
9. *The Wanderer and his Shadow*, no. 55. This comparison was noted by C. Gadourek, *Les Innocents et les coupables, essai d'exégèse de l'oeuvre d'Albert Camus* (The Hague: Mouton, 1963), p. 82. Note, however, that this second part of *Human, all too human* was not in Camus's library.
10. *The Will to Power* (French edn, vol. II, bk IV, ch. 4, no. 248).
11. *The Will to Power* (French edn, vol. I, bk I, ch. 2, no. 135).
12. *The Will to Power* (French edn, vol. I, bk I, ch. 2, no. 111).
13. Jean-Paul Sartre, 'Explication de l'Etranger', *Situations I* (Paris: Gallimard, 1947), p. 107.
14. *The Genealogy of Morals*, vol. III, no. 27.
15. *The Gay Science*, no. 357 (repeated in *The Genealogy of Morals*, vol. III, no. 27).

16. J. Onimus, *Camus* (Paris: Desclée de Brouwer, 1965), collection 'Les ecrivains devant Dieu', p. 67.
17. *Human, all too human*, no. 34.
18. *Human, all too human*, no. 34.
19. *Ecce Homo*, 'Why I am so cunning', no. 1.
20. *The Will to Power* (French edn, vol. II, bk IV, ch. 5, no. 404).
21. *The Twilight of the Idols*, 'The four great errors', no. 8.
22. We should, of course, make a distinction. The Nietzsche who proclaimed himself 'the last disciple and the last initiate of the god Dionysus' (*Beyond Good and Evil*, no. 295) was not a satisfied atheist, a withered soul incapable of any religious impetus. Some texts even let us glimpse after the death of God a resurgence of the divine – but a divine freed from moral categories, a refound paganism based on 'the religious affirmation of life in its entirety, of which nothing is denied or taken away' (*The Will to Power*, French edn, vol. II, bk IV, ch. 5, no. 464). 'You say that it is a spontaneous decomposition of God, but it is only a moulting; he sheds his moral skin. And soon you will find him again – beyond good and evil' (*The Will to Power*, French edn, vol. II, bk IV, ch. 5, no. 407).
23. *The Dawn of Day*, no. 541.
24. Meursault only feels and admits a physical fear when faced by the perspective of annihilation: ('J'avais seulement peur, c'était bien naturel', I, p. 1207). But the last sentence of *L'Etranger* does pose a problem. Can we pretend that Meursault is deprived of any painful consciousness when he suffers in his solitude so much as to hope for the presence of cries of hate? Is it necessary, as we stated in a previous study (see note 5), to admit some doubts on the Nietzschean authenticity of Meursault's final serenity? We no longer think so, because this suffering is not metaphysical, and does not exclude in any way the reality of the happiness that Meursault admits. The Nietzschean tonality of this happiness – a minor tonality, the only one that fits a 'man who, without any heroic attitude, accepts dying for truth' (I, p. 1928) – now seems to us evident, even if happiness is not a Nietzschean value, even if it is to his anger and not to a truly acquired philosophical conviction that Meursault owes the state of being 'purgé du mal, vidé d'espoir' (I, p. 1211).

Works Cited

Quotations from Camus:
I : *Théâtre, récits, nouvelles* (Paris: Gallimard, Bibliothèque de la Pléiade, 1967).
II : *Essais* (Paris: Gallimard, Bibliothèque de la Pléiade, 1967).
2 : *Carnets II*, janvier 1942 – mars 1951 (Paris: Gallimard, 1964).

English translations:
L : *Lyrical and Critical Essays*, Philip Thody (ed.), Ellen Conroy Kennedy (trans.) (New York: Alfred Knopf, 1969).

R : *The Rebel*, Anthony Bower (trans.) (New York: Alfred Knopf, 1982).
W : *The Stranger*, Matthew Ward (trans.) (New York: Alfred Knopf, 1988).

Quotations from Nietzsche in this essay were taken from the French translations in Camus's own library (marked *) or from editions which he might have had. (*Translator's note*: Rather than relying on standard English translations of Nietzsche, I have reproduced in English the wording and style of the French that Frantz Favre has cited.)

* *Humain, trop humain*, A.M. Desrousseaux (trans.) (Paris: Mercure de France, 1899). (English title, *Human, all too human.*)
Ainsi parlait Zarathoustra, H. Albert (trans.) (Paris: Mercure de France, 1912). (English title, *Thus Spake Zarathustra.*)
* *Aurore*, H. Albert (trans.) (Paris: Mercure de France, 1930). (English title, *Dawn of Day.*)
* *L'Antéchrist.* H. Albert (trans.) (Paris: Mercure de France, 1920). (English title, *The Antichrist.*)
* *Le Crépuscule des idoles*, H. Albert (trans.) (Paris: Mercure de France, 1920). (English title, *The Twilight of the Idols.*)
* *Ecce Homo*, H. Albert (trans.) (Paris: Mercure de France, 1921). (English title, *Ecce Homo.*)
* *La Généalogie de la morale*, H. Albert (trans.) (Paris: Mercure de France, 1948). (English title, *The Genealogy of Morals.*)
Le gai savoir, H. Albert (trans.) (Paris: Mercure de France, 1901). (English title, English title, *The Gay Science.*)
* *Par de là le bien et le mal*, H. Albert (trans.) (Paris: Mercure de France, 1941). (English title, *Beyond Good and Evil.*)
Le Voyageur et son ombre, H. Albert (trans.) (Mercure de France, 1927). (English title, *The Wanderer and his Shadow.*)
* *La Volonté de puissance*, vols I and II, G. Bianquis (trans.) (Paris: Gallimard, 1935, 1937). (English title, *The Will to Power.*)

Part Two
The Reception of *L'Etranger* and its Influence on Other Writers

4

Discovering *The Outsider*
Albert Wendt

Like Albert Camus, I am of two worlds: Polynesian (Samoan) and Papalagi (European). I grew up in a Samoa which was already colonised.

In 1953 at the age of 13, I left Samoa, the sacred centre, and a large extended family and a communal way of life to study at a boys' boarding school in New Plymouth, Taranaki, New Zealand. From perpetual sun and heat to the winter cold and the puritanical culture of a spartan boarding school modelled on the private schools of England. Like Camus leaving Algiers to live in Europe. I couldn't speak English and I was one of only seven Pacific Islands students in the school. To escape, to survive, I learned English quickly and withdrew, to a large extent, into books and the school library. I became a 'bookworm'. I was fortunate that two of my teachers had a passionate love of literature and they encouraged me to read everything. They introduced me to writers such as Aldous Huxley, George Orwell, James Joyce, W. B. Yeats, Virginia Woolf, T. S. Eliot, W. H. Auden and hundreds of popular writers. With my teachers' encouragement, I also started writing stories and poems.

In my reading I was searching for the voices which said what I wanted to say and understand but didn't yet have the facility to articulate, for the writers who could define me and where I was at. I would later find, described in Camus, that I was living in *exile*, but I didn't know how to define that condition. Much of my reading was also pure escapism, to get away from life in my boarding school. With this background, I was made for Albert Camus, as it were.

I didn't know what career to pursue so after high school I decided to go to Teachers' Training College.

It was during 1958, my first year at Ardmore Teachers' College, that I first read Camus – and it was *The Outsider*. My head exploded, my heart thundered as I gobbled it up in one reading. Here was the book, the testament, I'd been looking for to help understand myself.

It articulated aptly/poetically/lucidly what I'd felt and wanted to say about myself and living in exile in another country. I was bowled over by its poetic lucidity and open vulnerability. The novel invited me into its heart, into the blazing sun which was lodged there, and into its way of life which freed me from being a closet existentialist – and defined and mapped out that way of being, for me. Meursault was the 'hero' I'd been looking for. His way and style of existing made more sense to me than most of the other 'heroes' in modern fiction.

I read and re-read *The Outsider*, gulped down *The Myth of Sisyphus*, and went on a binge of reading everything Camus had written: his other novels/essays/and plays. I was lucky that at Teachers' Training College the librarians reserved for me all the new poetry/fiction which came in. They also ordered Camus's work they didn't have at that time, so I could read them. (Librarians have a soft-spot for bookworms!) Camus is one of the few writers whose whole body of work I have tried to read.

Camus's style of writing was also the way I wanted to write: unadorned, simple on the surface but with complex depths. And it wasn't just writing: it was a way of life, of enduring and finding 'hope' in a world that seemed absurd, of creating my own meanings through my writing to sustain myself in a planet without God. (I'd been raised in a very staunch Christian family. Some of my relatives were missionaries in places like Papua New Guinea!)

At Training College, I started writing 'seriously'. Camus emerged in my work; I didn't mind his obvious influence. As I matured as a writer, I took his style (and the style of other writers I admired) and combined it with mine: a fusion of Sisyphus pushing the rock up the mountain and the Polynesian trickster demi-god Maui who challenged the atua (gods) and stole their secrets, and his eventual death in Hine-nui-te-Po, the Death Goddess. I've woven out of my ancient Polynesian heritage and Camus and all my other literary ancestors a way of writing/seeing/being.

The characters in my first novel, *Sons for the Return Home*, have no names. The only person I name in the novel is Albert Camus, it is my tribute to him. The main character in that novel is a young Samoan university student. He falls in love with a pakeha [white] woman; he buys her, as a present, a book by Albert Camus. Much of the main character reflects the character of Meursault: searching for permanence in exile, refusing to lie, living in the present yet wanting to know more about his Samoanness and his ancestors.

The woman he falls in love with is like Marie. And the intensity of their love and sexual relationship is like Meursault's and Marie's, I think. I didn't deliberately model them on Meursault and Marie. Looking back on it now, I was developing my own brand of existentialism, my own ways of mapping and giving a face to my countries (Samoa and New Zealand) and people, in that novel.

In 'Flying Fox in a Freedom Tree', a novella and the middle book in my large novel, *Leaves of the Banyan Tree*, the trial scene, in which Pepe, the rebel protagonist, confronts the bewigged Judge, reflects Meursault's trial. Pepe is the pagan rebel trying to live honestly/ defiantly in a colonised present. Of course, Meursault's trial is reminiscent of the trials in Kafka and other existentialist writers. Strange, yet 'natural', how trials in fiction are about other trials in other fiction; how writers are about other writers; how novels are about other novels! (Everything has a genealogy.)

'Maman died today. Or yesterday maybe. I don't know. I got a telegram from the home: "Mother deceased. Funeral tomorrow. Faithfully yours." That doesn't mean anything. Maybe it was yesterday' (p. 3).* That's the opening of *The Outsider*, and what an opening! I've tried but haven't succeeded in writing an opening like that in any of my novels, an opening that looks casual and ordinary yet is extraordinary: clean, unfussy, to the heart of Meursault and who he is. The prose, like Meursault, refuses to pretend it is more than what it is, but it *is* more in its complex reverberations, doubt, and refusal to lie.

Though I've gone on to develop my own philosophical world, the existentialism of Camus, and, especially that of *The Outsider*, remains a vital strand of that world.

Over the years as a teacher and lecturer, I have sometimes taught *The Outsider* to my students. (Most of them have been touched and altered by the novel, the same way I'd been affected by it.) Every time I've taught it, memories of my beginnings as a writer and my first real gropings toward a philosophy that has allowed me to live sanely in an insane world, return vividly, lucidly.

The Outsider is one of the few novels I still re-read – and most of it is still fresh to the taste of my sight. It is part of the valued mythology that is my life.

Note
* This translation is from *The Stranger*, Matthew Ward (trans.) (New York: Knopf, 1988).

5

A Brother to the Stranger
Vilas Sarang

We are twins, the Stranger and I. Twins, or almost. The Stranger was born on 15 June, 1942; I was born on 11 June of the same year. Separated at birth by language and geography, we encountered each other many years later.

But, could it not be said that the Stranger died in the year 1942? Was he not executed in that year? It's confusing, this mix-up of birth and death.

Did he really die, though? The book does not say so. The book only gives us the Stranger's story in his own words. It is presumed that he was executed after he had narrated his story. I like to think that this did not happen. I like to imagine that, for telling his story so well, so truthfully, the Stranger was pardoned and allowed to go free. In the chapter on 'Absurd Creation' in *The Myth of Sisyphus*, Camus quotes Nietzsche: 'We have art in order not to die of the truth.'[1] The Stranger 'agrees to die for the truth', as Camus notes elsewhere;[2] the telling of the truth, let us believe, saved him.

I read *The Stranger* (as *The Outsider*, since British editions continue to dominate India) some time around 1961. I had already read some Hemingway, including *The Old Man and the Sea*. I had also read Kafka's *The Trial*. I think this was good preparation for reading *The Stranger*. The description of that book as 'Kafka written by Hemingway' may be wrong on certain counts, as Sartre has pointed out.[3] But there is also a very real sense in which the three authors relate to one another. There is a certain spirit of detachment and acceptance that they share. The serenity of *The Old Man and the Sea* is especially close to the spirit behind *The Stranger*, though the latter book could not possibly have been influenced by the former. (Let us leave it to Hemingway specialists to ponder whether the reverse was true.) So it is not the style that relates Camus to Hemingway. As Philip Thody has pointed out, Camus almost certainly read Hemingway in French translation, limiting the possibilities of stylistic influence; the uniqueness of the use of the *passé composé* is

51

Camus's own[4]. It is the spiritual kinship that is significant. Meursault is called 'taciturn' in the novel itself; the persona of the tight-lipped, no-nonsense but inwardly humane hero is present in Hemingway from the beginning. Then, too, like Kafka's hero, Meursault displays marked passivity and acceptance. Meursault can scarcely be said to rebel against fate, or society, or absurdity. In this Camus's hero is very non-European, non-Western. The novel is a form of protest. Camus recognised this, and said so in *The Rebel*. ('The novel is born simultaneously with the spirit of rebellion and expresses, on the aesthetic plane, the same ambition').[5] *The Trial* and *The Stranger* are not representative of the Western spirit. Kafka the Jew had something 'Eastern' in him; the early Camus, close to Algeria and to Arabic culture, had also something 'Eastern' in him. (In *The Plague* and *The Fall*, both of which are so clearly novels of protest, as also in *The Rebel*, Camus has finally assimilated himself to the Western ethos.)

It seems to me that I, like several other Indian writers and readers, was attracted to certain modern Western writers because I found, largely unconsciously, a spiritual kinship with them. In the 1960s – my formative years – I wrote long essays (in Marathi) on four of the Western authors that appealed to me most: Kafka, Camus, Sartre and Beckett. The essays were collected in 1983 under the title *Sisyphus and Belacqua*. Along with the Camus of *The Stranger* and the whole of Kafka, the whole of Beckett is so close to the Indian spirit. There is the same passivity, acceptance and pessimism. Beckett was deeply influenced by Schopenhauer, and the latter's kinship with Indian philosophy is well known. Beckett even uses the motif of rebirth, which is so peculiarly Indian. Incidentally, Meursault is scarcely Sisyphean; in his passivity, lassitude and indifference, he is closer to Belacqua. Of the four authors I chose, Sartre is the one I feel least close to. Sartre's appeal to me was largely intellectual. There is something in Sartre which ultimately puts me off. In his insistence on action, in his 'hardness', Sartre remains indomitably European. I expressed my feeling at the end of my essay on Camus by adapting Dryden's famous statement: 'I admire Sartre, but I love Camus.'

It is only recently that I have been able to see how close *The Stranger* is to ideas native to the Indian mind. Meursault's famous 'indifference' is a version of the detachment advocated by Indian philosophy. This strikes us right at the beginning of the novel. Meursault's attitude towards death is the ideal Indian one. It is not that he is heartless towards his mother; he has long ago achieved a calm acceptance of death and other realities of life on earth. (In fact, this attitude prefigures his later acceptance of his own fate. In spite of the 'all too human' shivers he experiences from time to time at the imminent prospect of facing the gallows, Meursault's general temper remains equable. Between his mother's death at the beginning and his own death towards the end, there is thus a fine structural tie-up.) Meursault behaves in conformity with Krishna's advice to Arjuna in the *Bhagavad Gita*:

> For to the one that is born death is certain ... Therefore, for what is unavoidable thou shouldst not grieve. Beings are unmanifest in their beginnings, manifest in the middles, and unmanifest again in their ends, O Arjuna. What is there in this for lamentation?[6]

Camus was familiar with Indian philosophy, and may have been deeply, if unconsciously, influenced by it. His mentor Jean Grenier introduced him to and guided his reading in Indian philosophy.[7] There is a reference in Lottman's biography to Camus reading the *Bhagavad Gita* under Grenier's influence around 1931 (p. 51). Camus himself refers to Vedanta philosophy in *The Myth of Sisyphus* in relation to Grenier's *Le Choix*, describing it as 'a book of great importance' which 'establishes ... a veritable "philosophy of indifference" ' (p. 47).

In *The Myth of Sisyphus*, Camus refers to Schopenhauer only once in passing (p. 6), although the subject of his book, suicide, is also the subject of an essay by the German philosopher. This neglect of Schopenhauer may be due to Camus's desire to suppress and obliterate the Idealist in him, an aspect of Camus I shall touch upon later. Camus was certainly quite familiar with Schopenhauer's thought, as evidenced by his essay, 'Schopenhauer and Music', wherein he gives a neat summary of Schopenhauer's philosophy (see *Youthful Writings*). Bergson's attempt to sidetrack reason and intellect had appealed to Camus (see the essay, 'The Philosophy of the Century', in *Youthful Writings*), and the same may have attracted him in Schopenhauer's thought. ('For Schopenhauer the will is something extra-intellectual that cannot be defined with clarity and logic. One can consider it, in short, as the irrational principle of all life', Camus notes in the essay on music; *Youthful Writings*, p. 106). It is interesting to note that, in the 'Essay on Music', Camus prefers the aesthetics of Schopenhauer to that of Nietzsche (p. 120).

Schopenhauer's thought, which is so close to Indian philosophy, may have contributed to Camus's early work, *The Stranger*. The early Camus was strongly attracted towards mysticism and there is much of that in Schopenhauer as well as Indian philosophy. Schopenhauer finds the Buddhist doctrine of Nirvana ('blowing out,' release, or liberation) closest to his own vision. Schopenhauer's discussion of the 'turning of the will' is of interest. To quote a summary of it:

> Thus we can certainly refer to the utterly different attitude towards everyday life and experiences characteristic of the man in whom the will has turned; the change in the viewpoint from which he regards the world, so that things which to most of us present themselves as motives for action or 'interests' appear to him to be matters of no consequence.[8]

A description that fits Meursault surprisingly well. In this context, one might particularly think of his replies to his employer regarding 'change of place', and to Marie regarding love and marriage. To continue with the quotation:

> One can speak, too, of the altered vision that allows him to see in death, not an event to be feared, but rather something to be welcomed ... we have only to compare the serenity and profound air of calm that distinguishes the characters and shows in the faces of saints and mystics with the turbulence, dissatisfaction, and misery that are the dominant themes of most human lives. (Gardiner, p. 298)

Schopenhauer speaks of purely unselfish or disinterested action, inspired solely by another's distress, and approves of quietism and asceticism, of the 'giving up of all willing' (Gardiner, p. 298).

All this may not apply wholly or literally to Meursault, and one certainly does not wish to turn him into a saint. And yet, there are significant points of connection. After all, Camus did speak of Meursault as a kind of Christ (if only as 'the only Christ we deserve', see Afterword in Laredo, p. 119), and not, I think, purely ironically. The serenity and air of calm we observe in Meursault can appear almost saintly, and there is an element of quietism and asceticism, as well as altruism, in his character. Too much has been made of the Greek paganism in Camus's philosophical make-up. There is actually little sensuality, and scarcely any hedonism, in *The Stranger*.

Meursault is, in fact, indifferent to worldly or physical satisfactions. He may enjoy his moments with Marie, but he makes no effort to accumulate such moments in the manner of the Don Juan of *The Myth of Sisyphus*; he prefers to spend a whole Sunday merely lounging about in his apartment in solitude. He displays a saintly indifference towards food and is content to eat eggs out of the pan, without bread because he cannot be bothered to go down and buy some. After sending his mother to the Home, he has not lorded it over the apartment. He has not acquired more possessions, nor thought of marrying now that he has the whole apartment to himself. He has, in fact, ascetically retreated to a small part of the apartment:

> It suited us well enough when Mother was with me, but now I was by myself it was too large and I'd moved the dining-table into my bedroom. That was now the only room I used; it had all the furniture I needed, a brass bedstead, a dressing-table, some cane chairs whose seats had more or less caved in, a wardrobe with a tarnished mirror. The rest of the flat was never used, so I didn't trouble to look after it.[9]

It is a monkish existence, lacking any will towards territorial occupation, or care for worldly goods. Meursault can spend a long time simply watching the sky (p. 31): a good candidate for becoming a Buddhist monk. Later, describing his prison days, he tells us: 'I often thought in those days that even if I'd been made to live in a hollow tree trunk, with nothing to do but look up at the bit of sky overhead, I'd gradually have got used to it' (Laredo, p. 75). This is not far from the Zen Buddhist monk who spent years staring at a blank wall. The Buddhist rejection of the idea of a personal God who created the world and whom, as his creatures, human beings should worship and obey, attracted Schopenhauer; it also fits perfectly well into the world-view of *The Stranger*. Meursault is a potential Lord of Emptiness. One could look upon him as 'the only Buddha we deserve'. (When Camus married Simone Hié at the age of twenty and went to live in a new house on the heights of Algiers, a plaster Buddha adorned a window desk board; see Lottman, p. 74.)

Meursault's adherence to the truths he perceives is uncompromising at times. See his reply to Marie as to whether he loved her; his reply to his employer about going to Paris, and about 'change of life'; his reply to Marie again as to whether he would marry her and whether he considered marriage a serious matter;

and finally his reply to the examining magistrate as to whether he believed in God (pp. 42, 48 and 73). Meursault's uncompromising 'No' is simply plain-speaking, and not intentional brutality. In fact, Meursault is quite considerate, understanding and accommodating in his relations with others. He takes care not to hurt or embarrass people as far as possible. He treats Salamano with sympathy and understanding. In Raymond's case, his behaviour is purely altruistic. Time and again, Meursault goes out of his way to help him out, with no selfish motives attached. Otherwise committed to telling the truth, Meursault tells a lie to the police for Raymond's sake, putting friendship and doing good above truth. Although he would not approve of the word 'love', it is clear that Meursault possesses a deep and genuine feeling for his mother. It comes through in a subtle, oblique manner at rare moments, as when, at end of Chapter 4 in Part I, he says: 'I realized he [Salamano] was crying. For some reason I thought of mother.' (Meursault throughout refers to his mother as *maman*, and not as *mère*.) Meursault embodies sympathy, altruism and selflessness typical of a man in whom 'the will has turned', and not unworthy of a saint.

The asceticism inherent in the character of Meursault is present in Camus's other early work. Of the 1938 book, *Noces*, Paul Viallaneix writes: 'The gifts of life at hand are ... precious to him. But he celebrates them with measure. The poet of *Nuptials* is an ascetic, not a sybarite' (*Youthful Writings*, p. 13) The altruism of Meursault becomes more pronounced and clear-cut, and more saintly, in the character of Dr Rieux in *The Plague*. But the tracing of such continuities is not part of this essay.

That the Existentialist/Absurdist Camus should reveal himself as an Idealist should not come as too much of a surprise to those familiar with the case of Sartre. No doubt it took Sartre's sensational revelation in *Words* in 1964 to make people see the reality; but today the Idealism implicit in the ending of *Nausea*, and in the opening chapter of *What is Writing*, appears all too obvious. Camus reveals his Idealist tendency in the Afterword he wrote for the English translation of *L'Etranger* in 1955, where he speaks of Meursault being driven by 'the passion for an absolute and for truth'. Here he envisions Meursault's philosophic adventure as only a stage in the march towards the goal of 'triumph over the self or over the world'. Camus is here talking Schopenhauerian-Vedantic-Buddhist language, and not the language of one who believed only in one or two truths that can be touched by hand.

If Camus's words quoted above appear not only Idealist but somewhat mystical, it is because the mystical-Idealist element was deeply ingrained in his spirit at an early age. The short texts that Camus put together in 1932 under the Bergsonian title *Intuitions* are described by himself in the opening paragraph: 'They record the desire of a too mystical soul, in search of an object for the fervor and its faith' (*Youthful Writings*, p. 123). Underlining his involvement in Indian Idealist thought, Camus speaks in a review of a book by Brice Parain of his own yearning 'for the masterword that would illuminate everything, for ... this equivalent of 'Aum', the sacred syllable of the Hindus' (quoted by Viallaneix, *Youthful Writings*, p. 30).

In the 1933 essay, 'Art in Communion', Camus celebrates music as the most perfect of the arts, and declares: 'Nothing is more ideal than this art' (*Youthful Writings*, p. 174). He then falls back upon Schopenhauer to arrive at an Idealist definition of art: 'The peculiar quality of Art is to "fix into eternal formulas what flows in the uncertainty of appearances" (Schopenhauer)' (p. 176). Referring to another 1933 text ('Reading Notes', *Youthful Writings*), Paul Viallaneix comments: 'Could he be drawn by the mystical asceticism whose end is to establish a lost unity? He does not deny it' (*Youthful Writings*, p. 61).

From this, it is but a short step to the idea of Art as salvation. It is possible to look upon *The Stranger* as an attempt in that direction. Paul Viallaneix proposes such a reading:

> [Meursault] feels 'ready to start life all over again', and he manages to in telling the story he has just lived through, which will become *The Stranger*. Thus at the most difficult moment of Exile, literary creation holds the power of bringing the Kingdom to life once more. (*Youthful Writings*, p. 78)

The idea that Meursault may have been let off for telling his story so marvellously, which I suggested at the beginning of this essay, might appear whimsical; but it can be taken more seriously. The telling of the story on the part of Meursault/Camus establishes the triumph of Art over life and death. Rescuing his life from the uncertainty of appearances, Meursault has fixed it into an eternal formula. This perspective unexpectedly brings *The Stranger* close to Sartre's *Nausea*, where too, at the end, the writing of a novel is envisioned as a means to achieving permanence and salvation. The strong current of Idealist thought envelops both these key works in the development of modern literature.

The connections I have tried to point out between *The Stranger* and Indian philosophic thought need not be looked upon as an attempt to annex Camus to the Indian world-view, or to take away the originality and individuality of his work. That I have taken for granted. The somewhat objective and 'scholarly' consideration of *The Stranger* that I have attempted in this essay leaves unspoken the deep sense of attachment and kinship that I bear towards this numinous work. The coincidence of the publication of this novel and my own birth within a few days' time in history is the only sign I have chosen to express my feeling towards my brother, the Stranger.

Notes

1. *The Myth of Sisyphus,* Justin O'Brien (trans.) (New York: Vintage Books, 1955), p. 69.
2. 'Afterword' written for the American edition in 1955; included in *The Outsider,* Joseph Laredo (trans.) (London: Penguin, 1983), p. 119.
3. Jean-Paul Sartre, 'An Explication of *The Stranger*', in Germaine Brée (ed.) *Camus: A Collection of Critical Essays* (Englewood Cliffs, NJ: Prentice-Hall, 1962), p. 116.
4. Philip Thody, *Albert Camus 1913–60* (London: Hamish Hamilton, 1962), p. 47.
5. *The Rebel,* Anthony Bower (trans.) (Harmondsworth: Penguin, 1962), p. 224.
6. *The Bhagavad Gita,* vol. II, pp. 27–28, in S. Radhakrishnan and C.A. Moore (eds) *A Sourcebook in Indian Philosophy* (Princeton: Princeton University Press, 1967), p. 108.
7. See Paul Viallaneix's introductory essay in Camus, *Youthful Writings* (Harmondsworth: Penguin, 1980), p. 18; also Herbert R. Lottman, *Albert Camus: A Biography* (London: Picador, 1981), p. 66.
8. Patrick Gardiner, *Schopenhauer* (Harmondsworth: Penguin, 1963), p. 296.
9. *The Outsider,* Stuart Gilbert (trans.) (Harmondsworth: Penguin, 1980), p. 29. My references are to this edition. Only in one case, I have quoted from Laredo's translation, as I felt it was closer to the original.

6

The Impact of *L'Etranger*: Oblique Reflections on an Oblique Novel
K.N. Daruwalla

I came to *L'Etranger* via *L'Exil et le royaume* (*Exile and the Kingdom*), or to be more exact, 'The Renegade', one of the stories that figured in the book. It had been published in 1957, the year Camus won the Nobel Prize. I was taken in by this dark parable on suffering and power and the fascination that power holds for its victims. It had some special insights: 'How can a man become better if he's not bad, I had grasped that in everything they taught me.'[1] Its prose was over-dramatised, raised deliberately to a hallucinated pitch. The characters were straight out of an archetypal nightmare, the sorcerer with his raffia hair and breastplate full of pearls and the Fetish himself with his double axe-head and 'his iron nose twisted like a snake'. The landscape was as exotic as it could be – the fiery sandscapes of the African desert, the city of salt with its streets of mineral whiteness where the protagonist comes to convert the barbarians. (That he had already robbed the Catholic seminary he lived in, and had cast off his habit, was another matter). And there were images of searing heat: 'an endless sea of brown pebbles, screaming with heat, burning with a fire of a thousand mirrors' (EK, 34).

Yet what was really distinguished about the story was its plot and the concept behind it. Once the protagonist was beaten and tortured by the people he had set out to convert, his mouth torn open and his tongue cut out, he started worshipping the Fetish and hating his own people:

the Fetish was there and from the depths of the hole in which I was I did more than pray to him, I believed in him and denied all I had believed up to then. Hail! He was strength and power, he

59

could be destroyed but not converted, he stared over my head with his empty rusty eyes. Hail! He was the master, the only lord, whose indisputable attribute was malice, there are no good masters (EK, 43).

In this kind of a frame of mind he does what he is asked to do, and shoots the missionary, Father Beffort, and his guide as they travel on their camels to the city of salt. His apostasy is complete: 'only evil is present, down with Europe, reason, honour and the cross' (EK, 44).

The result was a poem called 'The Revolt of the Salt-Slaves' which was included in my first book *Under Orion* (1970). An acknowledgement was made beneath the title itself that the poem was written 'after reading Exile and the Kingdom'.

> Truths hung perpendicular here
> like sunlight
> and the only shadow, apart from fear,
> was the night.
> Both were black, the slave-driver and the slaves.
> Only the sun was white
> and salt columns bristling like an infinity of stakes!

I went through the books of Camus in the early 1960s. Sartre one had read a few years earlier. Sartre was a bigger name then, but he didn't come across to me as clearly and sharply as Camus did. Each book of Camus was a statement, the philosophy and the plot going hand in hand, neither overrunning the other completely. For quite a few years in the 1960s I worked on a novel which I later abandoned. It was written in the first person and the story was centered on a large hospital (a figment of the protagonist's imagination) and a real mud fort, and life around its crumbling ramparts. The protagonist, who had been tragically thrown out of a medical college, fantasised about a weird hospital he founded himself in which he was called upon to fight an outbreak of mass impotence that had afflicted the city. Friends suggested I read *La Peste*, which comes off both as allegory and as straightforward description of life in a plague-stricken city. Apart from leaving me a bit depressed (a habitual state of mind when convinced that one can't write half as well as the chap one is reading) I cannot remember the book influencing my work one way or the other. Good books, of course, affect you imperceptibly, their essence getting absorbed into your subconscious, as it were.

To be affected by a work is one thing. To let it influence your work in a weak moment is another. *L'Etranger* was disturbing and unique in that it stripped the reader of certitudes, moral judgements of right and wrong, innocence and guilt and left him with a residue of unease. My response to the novel was ambivalent – it had to be. Reason cannot, or at least should not, sit in judgement over Meursault. The norms for evaluating him have to be different. That is easier said than done.

Any writer would find it very difficult, if not impossible, to carry off the kind of paradox Camus was attempting to fob off on his readers – this paradox of innocent guilt. I found a constant attempt on Camus's part to show that for the judiciary, Meursault's sins of omission were more blameworthy. Hence his utter lack of emotion at his mother's death, his refusal to spurn Raymond Sintès, the pimp, and his indifference to Marie are held against him. It was not just that either marrying her, or not marrying her, were eventualities to which he was equally indifferent. Even if Marie were to die it would have meant nothing to him. 'I couldn't feel interest in a dead girl', says Meursault.[2]

Not that Camus was unaware of the charge of amorality. In *Notebooks, 1935 – 1942* Camus says: 'And how they start to bellow that I am immoral. They must be translated as meaning that I need to give myself a morality. Admit it then, you fool. I do.'

I was conscious of feeling conned into indignation at the way his trial was proceeding. If guilt could be washed away by the bias or stupidity of the prosecutor, or even the judge, then innocence and grace would be within easy reach. To take sides with Meursault went against the grain of a lifetime. I was never impressed with the arguments towards the end of the book. Some debating points were indeed scored by those two young men, Meursault and Camus, but much of all this sounded immature, the kind of talk you hear in a university café frequented by undergraduates. For instance he states 'Also whether I died now or forty years hence, this business of dying had to be got through, inevitably' (O, p. 112), which can't in any seriousness be advanced as an argument in favour of early death through the courtesy of the hangman. When he lashed out against the Chaplain there were other statements equally incoherent. 'And what difference could it make if, after being charged with murder, he were executed because he didn't weep at his mother's funeral, since it all came to the same thing in the end' (O. p. 110). This could be self-delusion on Meursault's part or deliberately obfuscatory. Meursault did not die because he failed to weep at his mother's funeral but because he needlessly shot an aggrieved Arab.

There were other passages which left one scratching one's head. One could understand Meursault, even empathise with him when he said that he had passed his life in a certain way because he felt like it. He could have passed it differently if he had felt like it. But then he talks of a dawn that will justify him. 'From the dark horizon of my future a sort of slow, persistent breeze had been blowing towards me, all my life long, from the years that were to come' (O. p. 118). This was bad windy prose.

As for his relations with Raymond, one felt someone should have grabbed Meursault by the shoulders, shaken him up a bit and told him to give the cold shoulder to that so and so. To me it appeared then, as it does now, that Meursault had abandoned the exercise of all moral choice out of sheer ennui. His first meeting with Raymond, and the entire conversation with him, are appalling. Raymond tells him about the woman he is keeping for a thousand francs a month. He has just beaten up her brother and is highly indignant that she is sleeping with others on the sly, a conclusion he reaches on finding a lottery and a pawn ticket in her handbag. He admits to beating her up 'till the blood came'. Before that he had never beaten her – 'well, not hard anyhow; only affectionately, like. She'd howl a bit, and I had to shut the window' (O. p. 38). He even thinks of having her trapped and registered as a common prostitute. Meursault, however, experiences no revulsion. (In fact he is revolted by nothing throughout the book.) He is quite happy to have his black pudding with Raymond so that he does not have to cook dinner. Raymond plans to go to bed with her, spitting in her face and throwing her out just when she gets all primed up. What does Meursault think of this? He does not think it a bad idea at all. It would punish her all right, he feels, and he writes her a stinker of a letter on Raymond's behalf.

A disconcerting thing about Camus has been his treatment of the Arab. In *L'Etranger* this becomes self-evident. From the first beating which the pimp gives him, the Arab is on the receiving end. He is not dignified by so much as a name. Nor is his much thrashed sister. Nothing gets viewed through their perspective. Since everything is seen through Meursault's consciousness, the Arab and his sister are sidelined into irrelevance.

I had turned to *Le Mythe de Sisyphe*, to search for Camus' own justification of Meursault's act. One discovers only what one wants to find. In that particular frame of mind I found nothing to buttress his arguments in Meursault's favour. There were plenty of digs, among others, at Galileo for abjuring a truth the moment his life was endangered, and at Schopenhauer for praising suicide 'while seated at a well-set table'. Actually it was the wrong book to go to for its preoccupation was with suicide, not homicide. 'The body's judgement is as good as the mind's and the body shrinks from annihilation.'[3] Very fine as long as it was one's own body. But Meursault does not have to shrink from annihilating the Arab. A different scale of values comes into play once the argument switches from suicide to homicide. Camus's argument runs something like this: does the absurdity of existence require one to escape it through hope or suicide? 'Does the absurd dictate death?' he asks. 'Is there a logic to the point of death?' (MS, p. 16). But in all this I found nothing that could justify the needless slaughter of the nameless Arab.

Meursault also has to be seen as a philosophic pawn in an absurd universe. Camus has defined it rather succinctly.

A world that can be explained even with bad reasons is a familiar world. But, on the other hand, in a universe suddenly divested of illusions and lights, man feels an alien, a stranger. His exile is without remedy since he is deprived of a memory of a lost home or the hope of a promised land. This divorce between man and his life, the actor and his setting, is properly the feeling of absurdity. (MS, p. 13)

Discussing moral codes, he says 'As for the others (I mean also immoralism), the absurd man sees nothing in them but justifications and he has nothing to justify. I start out here from the principle of his innocence' (MS, p. 64).

It is this innocence which Meursault exudes. Neither Meursault nor Camus can be judged by a bourgeois value system – it is the very system Camus has been railing against. Writing fiction as philosophic tract is painfully difficult. It is a measure of Camus's triumph that even though the novel is tailored to a philosophy, the characters and landscape are alive and palpable, and the incidents vibrant with the ring of authenticity about them. Of course the chasm between rationality and experience is portrayed for what it is – unbridgeable.

One can't be dismissive about Meursault. His innocence is touching. So is the way he clings to the truth. He does not even think that he needs a lawyer to defend him, his case being so simple and straightforward. When he eventually gets a lawyer and is asked by him whether he felt any emotion on his mother's death, he can only mutter 'I'd rather mother hadn't died' (O. p. 69). At the end of an exhausting session with the magistrate when he is asked if he regretted the killing all that he can admit to is being 'vexed' at the incident (O, p. 74).

Meursault's optimism is both touching and baffling. During the first few days he is hardly conscious of being in prison: 'I had always a vague hope that something would turn up, some agreeable surprise' (O, p. 75) when actually there was never a hope in hell.

He rises in one's esteem not only because he does not give in to self-pity, but also because of the way he rather stoically faces up to his privations and degradations. For instance, his belt, shoe laces and cigarettes are taken away. He misses his cigarettes so desperately that he sucks at splinters, till he feels bilious. Everywhere he comes up against the priggish morality of the system. For instance, Marie is not allowed to visit him in jail for quite a while because she is not his wife. Along with his naiveté, there is a direct matter-of-factness about Meursault which is surprising. Camus always sees life's dualities for what they are. By the end of the book there would be very few people who have not taken to Meursault. Many women readers could have fallen in love with him. The man has grown so much. He thinks, reflects, speculates. A whole new interior life confronts the reader now, like a river flowing through a dark cavern. In the second half of the book he becomes a reflective man, no longer living on the instinctual plane, his feelings dancing 'on the ever-virgin landscape of phenomenon' (O, p. 87).

Both as metaphor and as a work of fiction *L'Etranger* would rank along with Kafka's *The Trial*. The only difference is that while *The Trial*, in parts, bored the pants off you, there was never a dull moment in *L'Etranger*.

Notes

1. *Exile and the Kingdom*, Justin O'Brien (trans.) (Harmondsworth: Penguin, 1962), p. 32 (Further page references are noted EK in the text.)
2. *The Outsider*, Stuart Gilbert (trans.) (Harmondsworth: Penguin, 1961), p. 113 (Further page references are noted O in the text.)
3. *The Myth of Sisyphus*, Justin O'Brien (trans.) (Harmondsworth: Penguin, 1975), p. 15 (Further page references are noted MS in the text.)

7

L'Etranger and *L'Objecteur*
David Bradby

In 1946 in a New York hotel lobby, a young French student was waiting nervously to meet his literary idol, Albert Camus. The student's name was Michel Grinberg, now better known as the playwright Michel Vinaver. Born in France in 1927, he had grown up in Paris, where his mother was a lawyer and his father ran an antiquarian business. The Nazi threat forced the family to emigrate, and the young Michel finished his schooling at the French Lycee in New York, going on to further study at Wesleyan University, Connecticut, where he was admitted as a junior for the summer semester in 1944. He interrupted his studies to volunteer for the French army, and spent a year in barracks in France before returning to the States to complete his course at Wesleyan, finishing with a BA in English and American Literature in 1947. For the student, it was a period of excitement and discovery. He read voraciously and widely, ranging from Hesiod to Kafka, on whom he started, but did not complete, a dissertation. He was particularly excited by the new writing coming out of his home country and had been deeply impressed by *L'Etranger*, so when Camus visited America on a lecture tour, he went straight to his hotel and asked to see him.

Camus was always keen to help young authors; Vinaver had begun to write stories and he spoke of these to Camus, who gave him encouragement and invited him to visit when he returned to France. Vinaver took him up on this offer, and after his return in 1947, he was a regular participant in Camus's literary gatherings. As adviser to Gàllimard, Camus recommended the publication of Vinaver's two novels, *Lataume* (1950) and *L'Objecteur* (1951). Vinaver admits to having been deeply influenced by Camus, and especially by *L'Etranger*, when he was beginning to write; the imprint of Camus's novel can be seen in much of Vinaver's work, most obviously in the figure of the 'objecteur'.

The term 'objecteur' was carefully chosen by Vinaver as the title of his second novel. It suggests a conscientious objector (the French term is *objecteur de'conscience*), but by only including half of the French phrase, it leaves a certain ambiguity, lending the term a more general applicability. The character in question, Julien Bême, refuses to follow orders while on National Service, but he is not strictly speaking a conscientious objector since his behaviour follows no predetermined plan. One day on the parade ground he makes an act of refusal that is as much physical as mental; he simply sits down on the ground and takes no notice of further orders. This does not indicate an incapacity for positive action (he gives proof that he can act decisively elsewhere in the book) but a spontaneous act of passive resistance.

The key to understanding Bême 'l'objecteur' lies in his similarity to Meursault 'l'étranger'. Like Meursault, Bême has a heightened sense of the value of commonplace or everyday events. He responds in a direct way to the physical demands of the moment, unmediated by thoughts of career or the subsequent consequences of his actions. Like Meursault's, Bême's resistance to the established order of things has both its negative and its positive pole. On the negative side, it is instinctive and therefore potentially destructive. On the positive side, it stems from a deeply felt response to lived experience and the sincere attempt to be true to that experience.

Although he shares a fundamental attitude with Meursault, Bême differs from him in his situation. His act of revolt has wider social implications than Meursault's and draws a larger number of other people into its orbit. Vinaver was writing eight years after the publication of *L'Etranger* and five years after the defeat of the Nazis. His novel is very different in structure and purpose from Camus's and his central character is not the only one to give a first-person narrative. *L'Objecteur* can be seen as a novel in which Vinaver is conducting a dialogue with Camus – not only the Camus of *L'Etranger* and *Le Mythe de Sisyphe*, but also with the Camus of the Cold War period, the Camus who was preoccupied with problems of commitment, and was embroiled in the quarrel with Sartre about the political responsibilities of the writer.

Vinaver's novel attempts to get beyond the perspective of its central character so as to present the broad emotional, philosophical and political atmosphere of the period. Through a large cast of characters it grapples with the intellectual movements of the time, the political currents discernible in the beginnings of the Cold War, as the French Communists boxed themselves into rigid, and ultimately untenable positions; with Existentialism and theories of freedom and commitment, the role of the press, the army, the police in post-war

France. Above all it represents an attempt to come terms with ordinary life in a period when the heroic struggles of the Resistance epoch are still remembered but no longer seem a part of people's daily concerns.

One of the characters in the novel is a history professor, named Lecorre, who expounds a cyclical theory of historical change borrowed from Hesiod. According to this theory, history moves through a succession of heroic, adventuring times, when the social structures become unusually fluid, and each of these times is followed by a time of stability, marked by consolidation and establishment of firm social structures. During these latter periods knowledge and self-awareness tend to flourish and this leads gradually but inexorably to a desire to break the bonds of peaceful existence, thus provoking a new burst into a period of heroic adventure. In *L'Objecteur* the France of 1950 is presented as just such a period of consolidation, looking back to the war as a period of heroic testing.

Lecorre attempts to reconcile Hesiod's theory of history with Camus's ideas, using the image of Sisyphus's boulder. In this perspective the boulder represents the level of awareness achieved by any given society:

> les périodes d'héroisme et de conquête sont les périodes où le rocher est tout en bas de la montagne. Et c'est lorsque les hommes sont essoufflés par l'aventure et angoissés par le chaos qui en résulte, qu'ils se remettent à le pousser vers le sommet. Plus il monte haut, plus l'ordre social se parfait et se fige. Plus la société se fige, plus les hommes ont soif de briser ces chaînes, de retrouver leur spontanéité, et ainsi se prépare la prochaine dislocation: le rocher dévale.[1]

> *Eras of heroism and conquest are the eras when the boulder is right at the bottom of the mountain. And it is when men are out of breath and agonised by the resulting chaos that they set out again to push it to the top. The higher it gets, the more social order is perfected and congealed. The more society is congealed, the more men crave to break their chains, to become spontaneous again, and so the next dislocation is prepared: the boulder hurtles down.*

Like Camus, Vinaver frequently makes use of mythical archetypes such as Sisyphus. But he seldom adopts Camus's habit of using them as paradigmatic cases, serving to make an argument more vivid. Their presence is usually not explicitly referred to at all, but is used to shadow an ordinary, everyday situation, setting up parallels and resonances in a poetic manner learned from T. S. Eliot. *L'Objecteur* is the only example of a work in which Vinaver tries to blend fiction with philosophical discussion in the manner of *La Peste* or *La Chute*. As he developed from novelist into playwright, Vinaver's style became progressively less discursive and more poetic. He became convinced that the writer's job was not to account for the world, but to describe it. In 1964 he wrote:

> il ne s'agit pas de montrer où, à coup sûr est le mal et où le bien, où est la réaction et où le progrès, mais de décrire la 'matière' même dont nous sommes faits, de raconter le 'tissu' de l'histoire, et de laisser les ponts se faire, les jugements se former.[2]

> *It is not a question of showing where for certain lie good and evil, where reaction and progress, but to describe the very 'matter' of which we are made, to recount the 'fabric' of history, and then to let bridges be built and judgements formed.*

It is in his vision of this 'tissu' or 'matière' that Vinaver's originality lies. Lecorre remembers that when Julien Bême was a child in his class, he had an unusual approach to history: profound indifference for the 'great events' (battles, invasions, etc.) but a passionate interest in the details of everyday life. Vinaver, writing of his own approach to reality, says something similar, admitting its child-like quality:

> A l'égard du quotidien, j'ai un rapport ancien, un rapport enfantin. Un rapport qui remonte à l'enfance et qui n'a pas changé, et qui est au centre même de mon activité d'écrivain. Je crois bien qu'enfant, j'étais étonné qu'on me permette les choses les plus simples, comme de pousser une porte, de courir, de m'arrêter de courir, etc . . . J'étais étonné, émerveillé de ces droits qu'on me donnait, et j'étais toujours à craindre qu'on me les retire, qu'on me repousse dans la non-existence. De la sorte, le quotidien, c'était quelque chose de très vibrant, au bout de l'interdit, en tout cas précaire, immérité.[3]

> *I have an old relationship toward everyday life, a childlike relationship. A relationship that goes back to my childhood and has not changed. It is at the centre of my activity as a writer. I think that as a child I was*

astonished that I was allowed to do the most simple things, such as opening a door, running, stopping ... I was astonished, full of wonder at the rights I was given and always afraid they would be taken away, that I would be pushed back into non-existence. So, everyday life is something very vibrant, at the edge of the forbidden, in any case precarious, unmerited.

Vinaver is here discussing his approach to writing plays at the end of the 1970s. Twenty years earlier, in 1950, when he was writing *L'Objecteur*, the question of how far the writer should intervene in the world had been a burning issue. The debate between the two camps represented by Sartre and Camus was then at its height: Sartre was trying to establish the absolute political responsibility of the writer, since he was always 'en situation' and that meant he had to accept that, whether he liked it or not, every line he wrote had a political effect. But he never finished the series of novels, *Les Chemins de la liberté*, in which this philosophy was to have found its illustration and justification. Camus had just completed *L'Homme révolté*, and was struggling to set limits on revolt, not denying its necessity, but seeking to avoid the more obvious traps of political commitment, such as the tendency of rebellions simply to replace one tyranny by another, and the abuse of the argument that the end justifies the means.

In *L'Objecteur*, Vinaver suggests a new perspective on the problem of whether the writer should or should not be 'engagé'. In a discussion between Lecorre and a philosopher friend named Barboux, the philosopher claims that, if commitment means anything, it is the necessary consequence of knowledge and is for that reason unavoidable. He calls the whole debate a 'gigantesque rigolade: nécesairement on s'engage à partir du moment où l'on connaît. Inversement, tout engagement qui n'est pas basé sur une prise de connaissance est un acte magique, néfaste à l'organisme.'[4] *'A gigantic joke: you are necessarily committed from the moment you are aware. On the other hand, any commitment not based on awareness is a magic act, harmful to your organism.'* The context of this discussion is the suggestion that 'engagement' must necessarily be part of a dynamic relationship between the individual and his/her situation, and will depend on the individual's 'prise de connaissance'. The situation may be one in which it is possible to intervene effectively; but it may be one in which only a 'negative commitment' is possible – in which the only honest stance available is that of the 'objecteur'.

Vinaver's project of a descriptive rather than a polemical theatre does not imply a belief that writing can remain ideologically neutral. On the contrary, his method as a playwright, developed over the last 35 years, is to juxtapose minutely observed fragments in such a way as to provoke an ironic response and so reveal aspects of social and political relations that would normally remain hidden. In 1950, when he was writing *L'Objecteur*, he was already ᴠeginning to define an approach to the question of the writer's commitment that preserved the social responsibility of the writer while avoiding the dangers of bending truth to fit dogma. Camus found Vinaver's approach had a particular force and commented in his *Carnets* on the position adopted by the young author:

> Vinaver, L'Ecrivain est finalement responsable de ce qu'il fait envers la société. Mais il lui faut accepter (et c'est là qu'il doit se montrer très modeste, très peu exigeant), de ne pas connaître d'avance sa responsabilité, d'ignorer, *tant qu'il écrit*, les conditions de son engagement – de prendre une risque.[5]

> *Vinaver. The writer is finally responsible to society for what he does. But he has to accept (and here he must show that he is very unassuming and undemanding) that he doesn't know in advance his responsibility, that while he is writing he is unaware of how he is committed, that he is taking a risk.*

Because Camus considered the writer to be in a state of dialogue with his society, the act of writing had to be seen as one half only of the dialogue; while writing, the author must listen only to his own voice, and can only guess what reply or what effect his words will provoke.

Camus correctly sees that although Vinaver's view of literature is the opposite of the militant approach adopted by Sartre at this time, that does not mean that he denies the existence of a close relationship between the fictitious world of literature and the real world of everyday experience. Quite the opposite: Vinaver wishes to recreate in his work something of the complexity of the real world, and this is what Roland Barthes admired in his first play, *Les Coréens*, when he wrote: 'The novelty of this work, paradoxically, is because it lies beneath ideological concepts. The achievement of the play was to "lead the audience to a sense of astonishment at a world without trials", thus rejecting the apparent alternatives, "as if there were no other aesthetic solution to human distress except Order or Protest." '6

This note by Barthes was written in 1956 and must be seen in the context of the aesthetic debates of the day, mainly concerned with the recent 'discovery' of Brecht in France and the new definitions of political theatre that were in the process of being articulated. Vinaver's work, as Barthes saw, did not spring from a meditation on Brecht, but somehow succeeded in representing human reality at a fundamental, pre-ideological level.

One way in which he achieves this is by placing characters in situations where they are deprived of the abstract patterns and structures that we habitually use to impose meaning on our lives: many of Vinaver's characters are similar to Meursault in that they experience an instinctive intuition of the Absurd. In *L'Objecteur*, Barboux expresses a theory of what he calls 'le dérisoire' that is very close to Camus's account of the Absurd. He defines 'le dérisoire' as 'l'absence des rapports qu'on voudrait entre les choses', an idea that is clarified in the following exchange:

– Si tout est dérisoire, pourquoi exister?
– Les choses ne sont pas dérisoires; les rapports entre les choses ont un aspect dérisoire qui ne les détruit pas, mais dont l'expérience tient compte quand elle bâtit.
– Qu'est-ce qu'elle bâtit?
– Chaque instant de la vie.[7]

– *And if everything is derisory, why exist?*
– *Things aren't derisory: the relationships between things have a derisory aspect which does not destroy them, but which experience takes into account in building.*
– *What does it build?*
– *Every instant of life.*

This could stand as a comment on the whole of Vinaver's *oeuvre*, in which people and objects are woven into a complex tissue of inter-relationships, often derisory, or marked by their failure to match expectations, but out of which come moments of vivid truthfulness and ironic reflection.

In *L'Etranger*, Meursault has a particularly keen eye for the discrepancies and minor hypocrisies in our day-to-day behaviour. He tries to live without the familiar life props that preserve the safety of daily routines and keep the threat of dangerous sensations at bay. He places the highest value on immediate, physical sensation, as in the excitement of the moment when he runs to catch a lorry with Emmanuel or the sensations of swimming or sunbathing that he enjoys with Marie. In prison, thinking back on his earlier life, Meursault comes to realise that these were the values on which his life was founded and that to preserve his integrity is to be true to these experiences and sensations, not generalising from them, but stating only what he can be certain of by means of direct experience. Belair, the central character of Vinaver's first play, *Les Coréens*, is suddenly cut off from normal routine and habit in the most common-place manner for a soldier: he is separated from his company. For him, the resulting experience is one of finding that the familiar pre-conceptions drop away and new 'prise de connaissance' is achieved because he is freed from the categories habitually imposed on his life. Instead of fighting, regrouping, following the normal imperatives of army discipline, he sits still, looks around, learns from the situation, construes it differently from the way he has been taught to do (in accordance with the mission of the UN force in Korea).

When first performed in 1956, at Planchon's Théâtre de la Comédie in Lyon, the play sparked off violent protests by army supporters who thought that the play was somehow offensive to the French military forces. In a profounder way than they realised, they may have been right, and these demonstrations have more than a hint of the cries of hatred with which Meursault hoped that he would be greeted on the morning of his execution. But on the face of it the play does not take up an anti-militarist position, indeed it takes up no position at all. It is content simply to explore the difference between the isolated Belair on the one hand and the lives and perceptions of the platoon of French soldiers who have remained together on the other. The procedure is ironic and depends on particularly well-observed dialogue among the platoon of soldiers, who display all the usual prejudices and blindnesses of a group of Europeans sent on a 'mission' to a Third World country. In contrast to the scenes of the platoon are the scenes in which Belair begins to experience for himself the humanity of the Korean villagers. His final statement sums up his new sense, both of himself and of the villagers:

Je me sens de plus en plus comme un cheveu sur la soupe, et en même temps de moins en moins ... Votre joie est contagieuse.

(*Il prend d'une main celle de Wen-Ta et de l'autre celle de Wou-Long.*)
Je ne sais pas demain ce qui se passera, mais aujourd'hui, je vais
vous dire, j'ai envie de rester ici, jusqu'à ce que cette guerre soit
finie.[8]

*I feel more and more like a fish out of water, and at the same times less
and less. Your joy is contagious.* (He takes Wen-Ta's and Wou-
Long's hands.) *I don't know what will happen tomorrow, but today,
I'm going to tell you. I want to stay here, until this war is finished.*

After *Les Coréens*, the play most clearly marked by *L'Etranger* is
the only other one of Vinaver's to be set in the 1940s and early
1950s, *Portrait d'une femme*. Written in 1984, the idea for this play
came to the author when he rediscovered a bundle of old newspaper cuttings, reports of the trial of Pauline Dubuisson, a medical
student who murdered her lover and who was sentenced in 1951 to
hard labour for life. On re-reading the accounts of the trial, Vinaver
was struck by the way in which the court authorities failed to draw
the defendant into their linguistic field. She adopted none of the
attitudes expected in such circumstances; she was neither contrite
nor angry – she simply appeared untouched by the proceedings of
the court. Vinaver's play is constructed in order to dramatise this
relationship between the girl and the judicial process. Sophie
Auzanneau, as she is named in the play, exhibits the behaviour of
an 'objecteur'; she does not positively resist, but is recalcitrant towards those who try to draw her into saying more than she wishes.
She never has the kind of violent outburst that Meursault has with
the chaplain, because she never achieves Meursault's level of self-
awareness, but her failure to coincide with the judicial process is
used by Vinaver to achieve just the same kind of ironic effect as that
achieved by Camus in the second half of *L'Etranger*.

In order to remain as truthful as possible to his source, Vinaver
decided that he would limit himself to the accounts of the trial
published in *Le Monde*, and that every word reported as having
been spoken in the court proceedings would be included in the
play. The result is a fragmentary dialogue comprising a multiplicity
of voices. The various witnesses who are called speak a bewil-
dering variety of different idioms, whose ideological presupposi-
tions are gradually revealed through their words and their manner
of speaking them. But Sophie seems untouched by the confronta-
tions in the courtroom; her replies simply do not coincide with the

expectations of her questioners. Her own emotional needs only emerge in the flash-back scenes evoking her childhood with parents, friends, lovers, teachers. But here, too, she is in conflict with other people's expectations of her: each one has a particular idea of what she should be, or an image that each tries to impose on her. When her behaviour or her language fail to coincide with what her interlocutors expect of her, they make no attempt to adapt or adjust (with the partial exception of her lover) and we gradually see how each of these relationships is, to some degree, a power relationship: Sophie is never allowed to take a dominant role.

Her situation in court, as 'accusée', becomes an image of her whole condition: as a woman growing up in the France of the 1940s, she is not permitted to live an independent life (as Meursault could) nor is she able to find an independent voice. If she had been able to impose her view of herself and of social relations on the others, or if she had been able to integrate the different 'selves' that she manifests in her different relationships, then she might have been able to survive. As it is, she can only experience life as a sum of fragmented parts with no centre to hold it together. Her crime is an act of desperation, a protest against the intolerable strain of try-ing to pull together so many separate, subservient selves. It is clear that her predicament is to a large extent the consequence of having to conform to role models proposed by the men in her life. Her lover, her teacher, her father, her boyfriend, all in different ways, cast her in roles that condemn her to passivity.

But in the brief periods when the pressures are off and she is able to make a spontaneous response, Sophie, like Meursault, Bême or Belair, demonstrates the same delight and fulfilment in things that are outwardly ordinary. In developing the figure of 'l'objecteur', Vinaver has identified a particular response to the world. It is not a response that achieves the almost heroic status of Camus's Meursault, but one which takes its place in a more humdrum, everyday perspective. It is characteristic of the person who is searching for solid values in a shifting world, who does not necess-arily find them, but who discovers at the very least a negative commitment: a situation in which s/he objects to the basic data, and maintains this objection, despite being powerless to alter it.

Notes

1. Vinaver, Michel *L'Objecteur*, (Paris: Gallimard, 1951), pp. 259–60. (All translations from the French are by Adele King.)
2. Vinaver, Michel *Ecrits sur le théâtre*, (Lausanne: L'Aire, 1982), pp. 106–7.
3. Ibid., p. 123.
4. Vinaver, *L'Objecteur*, p. 69.
5. Camus Albert, *Carnets*, janvier 1942 – mars 1951 (Paris: Gallimard, 1964), p. 266.
6. Barthes R., 'Note sur *Aujourd'hui*', in Vinaver, *Théâtre I*, Arles: Actes Sud, 1986), pp. 37–40.
7. Vinaver, *L'Objecteur*, p. 217.
8. Vinaver, *Théâtre I*, pp. 118–9.

8

The Reception of *L'Etranger* in the Soviet Union
Hélène Poplyánsky

Albert Camus is one of the Western writers whose work was not available to Soviet readers for many years. As in most such cases, the reason was political. In the dispute between French intellectuals and writers in the Stalinist era, Camus took the anti-Soviet side. In his letter to Emmanuel d'Astier de la Vigerie he expressed his opposition to the concentration camps in the Soviet Union.[1] He was against Soviet interventions in Poland, in Germany and in Hungary.[2] Because of his political opinions Camus was published in the Soviet Union only in 1968, when 'L'Hôte' and *L'Etranger*, translated by Nora Gal', appeared in the review *La Littérature Etrangère*.[3] Since then translations have continued to appear. The review *Le Nouveau Monde* published 'La Femme adultère' and 'Les Muets'. Several months later, the same review published *La Chute*. In the same year a collection of selected works appeared, including *L'Etranger* (translated this time by Nemchinova), *La Peste* and *La Chute*, three stories from *L'Exil et le royaume* ('La Femme adultère', 'Les Muets', 'Jonas'), two essays from Noces ('Noces à Tipasa' and 'Le Vent à Djemila') and one essay from *L'Eté* ('Le retour à Tipasa'). In 1969 *L'Etranger* and *La Peste* were also published in French, for students of French, and specialists in French literature. There was also a Russian translation of *L'Etranger* done in Paris by Georges Adamovitch in 1966.

Criticism of Camus's works considerably preceded their publication, a characteristic of Soviet criticism.[4] The first article devoted to Camus was published in 1947. Until 1959 it was the only study that dealt with his work. Criticism of Camus only appeared after the Cold War, at the end of the 1950s. It seemed to intensify during the second half of the 1960s and especially in the 1970s. Until now there is only one monograph devoted to Camus's work, and twenty-six articles, of which five are devoted only to *L'Etranger*.

However, there are several anthologies, literary collections and encyclopedias with chapters on Camus's work.[5]

I would like to trace the ways in which *L'Etranger* has been introduced in the Soviet Union and to present its reception by 'professional' readers, literary critics. Interpretations of Camus's first novel can be divided into two groups: the first, and much larger, is composed of studies where an ideological interpretation predominates; the second group is criticism of a literary nature. The reaction of critics who use a politico-ideological approach has been almost entirely negative. In most of the studies in this group, the following subjects are considered: the philosophy of the absurd which serves as a point of departure for the novel, the character of Meursault, and the 'bourgeois' society of which Meursault is the victim and the instrument. I. Frid's article, 'Çells for Humanity' is the first Soviet article on Camus. Frid puts Camus in the existentialist line of Malraux and Sartre. He defines *L'Etranger* as 'reactionary and decadent'.

For Soviet critics Camus is the representative of atheistic existentialism. For this reason most of the critics refer first to *Le Mythe de Sisyphe* and interpret *L'Etranger* in the light of this. It is evident that putting these two works together brings out their affinities and helps us appreciate the novel. However, most of the Soviet critics make *L'Etranger* depend upon the philosophical essay, and this leads inevitably to schematic interpretations. Such critics as Karpushin, Kutasova, Grigoliuk among others study in detail the theory of the absurd. They give a brief résumé of the ideas Camus expressed in *Le Mythe de Sisyphe* and interpret the meaning of the categories of the absurd, suicide, and rebellion. They accept the existence of the absurd, but only in the conditions prevailing in bourgeois society. As for the theory of the absurd itself, Soviet authors reject it as lacking any social meaning.

There are very few Soviet critics who analyse the other central aspect of Camus's thought, the 'Mediterranean myth' and the 'pensée de midi'. This is, however, an important moment in Camus's reflections, where he seeks measure and harmony, lost by modern society, and where he expresses his opposition to tyranny.

Very often Camus's and Sartre's works are interpreted together. Camus, whose name is immediately associated with that of Sartre, represents for the Soviets a variation of Sartrean style existentialism. Only a few critics (Erofeev, Velikovskii, Man'kovskaia) make a distinction between the two theories and point out that Camus's theory is based on anguish, born of the confrontation with an indifferent but extremely beautiful world: the confrontation of the human spirit, eager for comprehension, on one hand, and an inexplicable world on the other. Sartre's anguish, by contrast, is born from the hideousness of man and the world, from an absolute absurd.

Meursault is also interpreted in the light of the theory of the absurd. For most Soviet critics, he is the symbol of the absurd. Meursault is far from social conventions or intellectual problems; what counts for him are his own sensations and desires. He is an outsider not only for others but for himself. He looks at himself without trying to analyse his actions and their consequences. At the centre of the book is Meursault's conflict with society, a conflict that ends with his condemnation. In most of the studies, Meursault is represented not only as 'a victim of bourgeois society' but also as 'its instrument, carrying its destructive tendencies', a reading that represents, I believe, a new element in the analysis of the confrontation between Meursault and official society. According to Soviet authors, Meursault's life brings only misfortunes to others. He carries in his blood the same virus as does the society that condemns him: the virus of indifference and cruelty.

There are two critics, Rurikov and Bulanova-Toporkova, for whom L'Etranger seems rather a realistic novel than the reflection of the philosophy of the absurd. These two critics analyse the novel only on the social level. They value especially the scene of the trial, which is written, according to Rurikov, 'in the best traditions of critical realism'.

Opposed to these two critics, many Soviet authors find that L'Etranger has no indication of a temporal setting. Such critics as Lovtsova, Evnina, Andreiev consider that the characters of the novel live in an artificial isolation, with no social or professional points of reference. We might be astonished to find such an affirmation, as the social context is evident throughout the novel. The popular milieu in which Meursault lives is described in the first part of the novel. Details of his daily life, his relations with his friends at work and with his neighbours are given in abundance. Algiers society is described by Meursault himself when, on Sunday, he looks from the balcony of his room on people passing in the street. Official society is described in the second part. Thus Algiers society is represented on several levels, and it is difficult to see why Soviet critics have advanced this suggestion.

There are not many critics who see L'Etranger in relation to the writing of Camus's youth rather then to Le Mythe de Sisyphe, but some do seek to establish that already in *Noces* characteristics of Camus's work can be found: the opposition between happiness and tragedy, the combination of metaphysical and social levels so that the rejection of social values takes on a metaphysical dimension and changes into a rebellion against destiny. Meursault comes from Camus's early writing, and in the light of this writing the 'enigma' of Meursault can be resolved.

Several critics look for Camus's affinities with other writers, most often St Exupery, Hemingway and Dostoievsky.[6] What links Meursault to the characters of St Exupery and Hemingway is feeling deceived by nihilism and feeling confident in the courage of men. As for Dostoievsky, Soviet critics reject any links between the Russian author and such existentialist writers as Kafka, Sartre and Camus. Nevertheless, in comparing *L'Etranger* to *Crime and Punishment* most of the critics find certain coincidences: at the centre of both novels is a murder, or rather the man who has committed the murder and who is judged. If Meursault murders accidentally, Raskolnikov reflects a great deal on his crime, and commits it to free himself, to prove to himself that he has the right to kill. Raskolnikov's crime is only an affirmation of the self. The greatest difference between the two characters can be seen after their crimes: Meursault remains indifferent, whereas Raskolnikov repents. Soviet critics, in spite of certain interesting comments, return at the end of their studies to a preconceived schema and reject analogies between the work of Dostoievsky and that of Camus.

All these studies have in common a neglect of Camus's style. Only a few authors point out the particularities of the structure of the novel or of the narrative technique. Evnina describes the style of *L'Etranger* as 'dry and poor'. She compares Meursault's narrative with the monologue of the hero of Hugo's *Dernier jour du condamné*, and insists on Hugo's superiority. She also expresses her disagreement with the opinion of certain critics about Camus's 'classicism'.

The critical observations of Andreiev and Erofeev are more interesting. Andreiev, in his preface to the French-language edition of *L'Etranger* and *La Peste*, underlines two meanings of the novel – metaphysical and social – and finds them illustrated by the structure of the book. The interpretation of Meursault's daily life in the second part of the novel shows social hypocrisy and expresses the author's mistrust of bourgeois morality. The same critic makes several observations about the narrative technique. Basing his commentary on studies by Western critics, he concludes that the stylistic particularities (monotony, insensibility) characterise not only the character of Meursault but the author of the novel himself. They reveal his pessimism. Probably the critic has let himself be guided here by the principles of critical realism, according to which the literary work should be written with an optimistic perspective and any pessimistic tendency is condemned.

Starting from Roland Barthes's term, 'the zero degree of writing', Erofeev characterises the style of *L'Etranger* as an illustration of Barthes's theory of writing, and underlines the contradiction between the form of the narration and the personality of the narrator.

Even if literary analysis is not always replaced by political interpretation, almost all the Soviet critics rise up against Camus because of the political opinions he expressed in the *Discours de Suède*. Such authors as Evnina, Lovtsova, Grigoliuk, Rurikov emphasise that after the Second World War Camus's position became increasingly anti-democratic. Evnina asserts that the award of the Nobel Prize to Camus was not approved by French intellectuals. She cites Pierre Daix and Anne Uberfeld, who see in this award an encouragement of Camus's political position.[7] Several Soviet writers criticise the *Discours de Suède* because Camus spoke against socialist realism. Finally, his 'ambiguous' comments about the responsibilities of the writer allowed bourgeois criticism to present him as a 'committed' writer, whereas in reality, according to the Soviet critics, Camus is an 'anti-humanist' writer.

The only monograph devoted to Camus's work, *Aspects of Unhappy Conscience*, by Samari Velikovskii, was published in 1973. It is a solid work, and analyses Camus's writing in all its complexity, without separating Camus as thinker from Camus as writer and polemicist. In the first of his eleven chapters, Velikovskii examines the correlation between Camus's philosophical opinions and his literary work, with an accent on the fact that Camus himself did not accept the theories of existentialism and considered himself a moralist, not a philosopher. Velikovskii follows the evolution of the writer and affirms that the contradictions in Camus's work are characteristic of French intellectuals in the post-war period. Criticism of bourgeois society and its political institutions is allied to absurd rebellion, without any larger perspectives.

Velikovskii follows the plan that Camus established and analyses his works as a triptyque. *L'Etranger* belongs to the first series: the absurd. The critic sees in the novel Camus's plea for Meursault, a plea addressed to the reader. Like most Soviet critics, Velikovskii sees Meursault as a primitive man, egotistic, immoral, indifferent to everything except nature and beauty, to which he is very sensitive. The philosophical import of the novel follows the analysis of the character of Meursault. Velikovskii sees the source of Meursault's despair in his solitude (innate, according to Camus, and caused by the problems of capitalism, according to the critic). Here Velikovskii joins other Soviet critics who express their disagreement with Camus's pessimism and reduce the problem of solitude to the faults of the so-called bourgeois society. Like other Soviet critics, Velikovskii pays considerable attention to the second part of the novel, especially to the trial, and shows how the trial brought against Meursault is transformed into a trial against the hypocrisy of the society.

The merit of this book is in its analysis of the style of *L'Etranger*. According to Velikovskii, Camus has found a technique which represents the very conscience of Meursault. Anything that requires intellectual work is absent from the book, as it is from the conscience of the hero. His intellect is so asleep that he cannot explain his own actions. Velikovskii sees Camus's affinities to the surrealists who, in reply to the rationalisation of life, have tried to present to their readers the concept of the unconscious. The critic notes that already in 1932, in his article on Bergson's philosophy, Camus spoke out against reason and opposed it to intuition.

Critics who lay stress on purely literary analysis are less numerous. Semienova's article, 'Camus's novel *L'Etranger* and his early work' is one of the most interesting studies. As the title indicates, the author studies the relationships existing between *L'Etranger*, the essays in *Noces* and *La Mort heureuse*. She underlines the similarity of themes treated in *L'Etranger* and in 'L'Eté à Alger'; it is the same country, the same morality where only the present counts and where life is good only for the young. The heroes of *Noces*, like the hero of *L'Etranger*, live in the presence of nature and admire two forces, the sea and the sun. After considering analogies between 'L'Eté à Alger' and *L'Etranger*, Semienova interprets the crucial episode of the novel: the murder of the Arab. She is interested in showing that at the symbolic level the murder can be explained by the conflict between man and nature, the conflict that appears after man has become conscious of his mortality and of nature's eternity. As the leitmotif of the murder episode is the sun (the supreme force of the cosmos which dooms man to absurd life), Meursault's shot signifies, according to Semienova, the revolt of the hero against death.

In Man'kovskaia's article, 'Problems of style in the aesthetics of Camus', where the author analyses Camus's opinions on art, several paragraphs are devoted to the style of *L'Etranger*. Man'kovskaia also utilises Roland Barthes's term 'zero degree of writing' and describes the grammatical particularities of the narration: the absence of causality, the use of indirect discourse where 'je' and 'il' become almost interchangeable, the use of the *passé composé* instead of the *passé simple*, etc. The author brings out the influence of 'American technique' on Camus's writing, and also underlines Camus's attraction to the themes of confession and trial, an attraction explained, probably, by the influence of Dostoievsky and Kafka. Although the article brings little new to criticism of Camus in general, for the Soviet reader, who reads only Russian or who has not had access to the work of Western critics, it contains many ideas that were previously unknown.

Safronov's article presents an analysis of personal pronouns, used instead of names of characters. Intrigued, like so many critics, by the first-person narration, he examines the particularities of the narration, underlines the characters' absence of personal traits and the large number of third-person pronouns. Safronov gives several examples to indicate the high percentage of personal pronouns, which is responsible for the effect of alienation.

Eliseieva's article is devoted to an analysis of narrative technique in *L'Etranger*. The critic gives a short summary of studies on the use of the *passé composé* in contemporary literature and in *L'Etranger* particular. He shows that the tonality differs in the two parts of the novel. In the first part, events are recounted after a certain lapse of time. Meursault remembers his life without being preoccupied by the logical continuation of the events he narrates; he does it for himself. The *passé composé* employed in this case fulfills the function of a 'perfect', which imitates a spontaneous account. In the second part of the novel Meursault is in prison and the tonality of the narration is different. In the extracts given as examples, the function of the *passé composé* is similar to that of the *passé simple*. The *passé composé* is surrounded by other past tenses: *plus-que-parfait*, *imparfait*. If the narration of the first part is monotonous, narration in the second part contains several commentaries, descriptions, remarks, lyrical digressions. Thus the critic shows how the polysemy of the *passé composé* is used in order to underline two types of narration and characterise the hero.

In *Seminar on French Stylistics* Efim Etkind devotes a chapter to *L'Etranger*. He analyses as an example the beginning of the fourth chapter of the second part, and finds two different stylistic manners, Meursault's and the prosecutor's. Meursault's simple, sincere account is thus opposed to traditional literary form. Rhetorical figures are absent, the syntax is simple. Meursault's tendency to retract what he says is curious; it shows his honesty towards himself. Etkind shows convincingly how throughout the novel Meursault's natural language is opposed to the conventions of official discourse. On this point he enters into a polemical discussion with another Soviet critic, Evnina, who in her study tries to show how the absence of conclusions, explanations, and lyrical passages impoverishes the language. In refuting Evnina's assertion that Camus's style is impoverished, Etkind analyses the eloquent but deceitful discourse of the prosecutor. He concludes that the stylistic opposition between Meursault's discourses and the prosecutor's underlines the conflict between the hero and the formal order of the society.

Criticism is divided into two groups by the date of publication of the novel in the Soviet Union. Typical interpretations of the first period are often characterised by ill-disposed paraphrases of the novel. The writer's work is seen as a direct expression of his political opinions. The aesthetic aspect receives very little attention. Popularisation, superficiality, simplistic explanations are the main characteristics of Soviet criticism of this period. Studies written during the second period are more interesting. Although most critics do not depart from a preconceived scheme, in general a large step forward has been taken. In spite of cliché opinions on Camus's philosophy of the absurd, the character Meursault and the criticism of bourgeois society, several articles contain useful remarks on the demoralising role of judicial power as an example of absolute power and on the alienation of contemporary man, observations, however, that are only applied to capitalism. Criticism becomes more precise, more nuanced, more concerned with the text than with received ideas. Camus is considered as a writer, not as a philosopher. No longer is the technical and stylistic aspect of the novel neglected. Critics base their analysis on Camus's original text and not on a review by other critics, as was occasionally the case.

It is impossible to understand the weaknesses of Soviet criticism without referring to cultural politics after the 1917 revolution. As early as 1905 Lenin wrote: 'Literature must become an integral part of the organised, methodical and unified work of the social-Democratic Party.'[8] Literary life was always organised according to this principle. As soon as the Soviet state came into existence, literature, with the aid of criticism, was supposed to form people according to socialist norms. Obviously the aesthetic values of literary and critical works were not given priority. Commentaries had to be simple to be understood by the general public. Until now, Soviet critics have been requested to undertake tasks of popularisation and formation of public taste; until now, literature has been rigorously supervised by those in power.

After the democratic changes in the Soviet Union, Soviet critics have been able to express themselves openly and explain the inevitable limitations of their work. In a discussion, 'Twentieth-century foreign literature and Soviet criticism',[9] Velikovskii declared that for three decades the goal and justification of Soviet criticism was to give readers access to foreign literatures, especially of the twentieth century. To reach this goal, it was necessary to prove to the bureaucrats that a certain work followed more or less closely the principles of critical realism. Very often, in order to do this critics were obliged to employ all-purpose labels: 'humanist, realist, modernist', etc. As a result, most literary concepts lost their real meaning. Soviet critics now stress the need to free literary concepts from any political nature, the need to resist the method of classification that leads to such oppositions as progressive – reactionary, pessimism – optimism, friend – enemy. They also insist on the need to publish those works that were forbidden in the Soviet Union because of their authors' political opinions, and to reinterpret them in an impartial manner.

According to Emily Tall in 'Camus in the Soviet Union: Some Recent Emigrés Speak',[10] Soviet citizens read the work of critics to know what was published in the West. They understood the critics' desire to show the problems that Camus posed in his work – a desire accompanied by the need to include negative judgements to fool the censors.

It is unfortunate that in spite of the deep links existing between Camus and Russian thinkers (Berdiaev, Dostoievsky, Shestov), his work was forbidden in the Soviet Union for so many years. Obviously, Soviet criticism has not yet expressed all it can about L'Etranger and Camus's other writing. We can hope that its contribution to Camus studies will be much larger in the near future.

Translated by Adele King

Notes

1. 'Deuxième Réponse à Emmanuel d'Astier de la Vigerie', in *Essais* (Paris: Gallimard, Bibliothèque de la Pléïade, 1965), p. 365.
2. 'Poznan', in *Essais*, pp. 1175–7; 'Berlin-Est', in *Essais*, pp. 1771–4; 'Réponse à un Appel', 'Message à un meeting des Étudiants Français en Faveur de la Hongrie', 'Discours de la Salle Wagram', 'Préface à "l'Affaire Nagy" ', in *Essais*, pp. 1978–88.
3. See my bibliography of Camus's works and critical studies on *L'Etranger* published in the Soviet Union.
4. Given the number of literary works published in many languages, it seems normal that the first criticism of a work appears before the first translation. These critical studies can make the thought of the writer available before the work has found a translator. However, in the Soviet Union, the first studies always tend to cast negative judgements on the work, which is not available to Soviet readers, even to those who read French. Even some works written in Russian (for example Solzhenitzyn's novels or those of Pasternak) were not available in the Soviet Union. In such conditions, Soviet readers could not form their own opinions about the literary work.
5. There are also two studies devoted to the reception of Camus in the Soviet Union. Nadine Natov's 'Albert Camus devant la critique soviétique', (*Albert Camus: 8* (Paris, Minard, Lettres Modernes, 1976), pp. 147–66) is a synthesis of Camus criticism in the Soviet Union. She reviews Soviet publications devoted to all of Camus's works, as well as to existentialism, of which Camus is considered a representative. The second article, Emily Tall's 'Camus in the Soviet Union: Some Recent Emigrés Speak' (*Comparative Literature Studies*, no. 3, 1979, pp. 237–49) is based on a questionnaire sent to seventy-five Soviet immigrants to the United States and Canada, and studies the reception of Camus's work in the Soviet Union, primarily from a sociological perspective.
6. It is interesting to see how Western critics treat the same subject – literary relationships between Camus and other writers. See the bibliography in *Albert Camus: 4* (Paris, Minard, Lettres Modernes, 1971).
7. Pierre Daix, 'Albert Camus. Prix Nobel', *Les Lettres Francaises*, 24–30 October 1957; Anne Uberfeld, 'Albert Camus ou la métaphysique de la contre-révolution', *Nouvelle Critique*, 1958, (no pagination).
8. Lenin, 'The Organisation of the Party and the Literature of the Party', *Novaia zhizn'*, no. 12, 1905. (French translation in *Lénine, écrits sur l'art et la littérature* (Moscow: Les Editions du Progrès, 1969), pp. 21–4.)
9. 'Zarubezhnaia literatura dvadtsatogo veka i zadachi sovetskoi kritiki, *Voporsy Literatury*, no. 6, 1988, pp. 3–83.
10. Tall, 'Camus in the Soviet Union' (see note 5).

Bibliography of Camus's Works Published in the Soviet Union and of Critical Studies on Him

Kamiu, A., *Neznakomets*, G. Adamovitch (trans.) (Paris, Editions Victor, 1966).

Kamiu, A., *Postoronnii*, Nora Gal' (trans.) *Inostrannaia literatura*, no. 9, 1968, pp. 117–63.

Kamiu, A., *Gost*, S. Bobrov (trans.) *Inostrannaia literatura*, no. 9, 1968, pp. 163–72.

Kamiu, A., *Zhena*, R. Lintser (trans.) *Novyi Mir*, no. 1, 1969, pp. 100–10.

Kamiu, A., *Nemyie*, R. Lintser (trans.) *Novyi Mir*, no. 1, 1969, pp. 110–17.

Kamiu, A., *Padeniie*, L. Grigorian (trans.) *Novyi Mir*, no. 5, 1969, pp. 112–54.

Kamiu, A., *Izbrannoie* (Moskva, Izd. Progress, 1969).

Camus, A., *L'Etranger. La Peste* (Moskva, Izd. Progress, 1969).

Kamiu, A., Folkner, U., *Rekviem po monakhine*, *Inostrannaia literatura*, no. 2, 1970, pp. 204–61.

Andreiev, L. G., *Frantsuzskaia literatura: 1917–1956* (Moskva, Izd. MGU, 1959), pp. 243–7.

Andreiev, L. G., 'Dve ipostasi Al'bera Kamiu', préface à A. Kamiu, *L'Etranger. La Peste* (Moskva, Izd. Progress), 1969.

Bol'shaia sovetskaia entsiklopediia, 3 éd. (Moskva, Izd. Sovetskaia entsiklopediia, 1973), pp. 291–2.

Borev, Yu. B., 'Ekzistentsializm i iego filosofiia cheloveka' in *Sovremennyie problemy realizma i modernizma* (Moskva, Izd. Nauka, 1965), pp. 458–68.

Bulanova-Toporkova, M. V., 'Progressivnyie tendentsii prozy Al'bera Kamiu' in *Trudy Novocherkasskogo politekhnicheskogo instituta*, 1970, no. 219, pp. 95–103.

Davydov, Yu., 'Pominki po ekzistentsializmu', *Voprosy literatury*, no. 4, 1980, pp. 190–230.

Eliseieva, N., 'Ob odnoi osobennosti povestvovatel' noi manery A. Kamiu v romane *L'Etranger*', *Drevniaia i Novaia Romania*, no. 2, 1978, pp. 114–20.

Erofeev, V., 'Put' Kamiu', *Oktiabr'*, no. 11, 1985, pp. 187–97.

Etkind, E., 'Albert Camus. *L'Etranger*' in *Seminarii po frantsuzskoi stilistike*, Leningrad, Gosudarstvennoie uchebno-pedagogicheskoie izdatel'stvo, 1961, pp. 319–27.

Evnina, E., 'Sud'by ekzistentsialistskogo romana', *Voprosy literatury*, no. 4, 1959, pp. 109–34.

Evnina, E., 'Al'ber Kamiu' in *Sovremennyi frantsuzskii roman: 1940–1960* (Moskva, Iskusstvo, 1960), pp. 97–121.

Frid, I., 'Odinochnyie kamery dlia chelovechestva', *Novyi mir*, no. 8, 1947, pp. 297–8.

Gorbunov, A. M., *Zarubezhnyi roman XX veka* (Moskva, Kniga, 1982), pp. 231–2.

Grigoliuk, T. S., 'Tema istorii v filosofii A. Kamiu', *Sbornik aspirantskikh statei Instituta Filosofii Akademii Nauk SSSR*, no. 3, 1972, pp. 257–8.

Istoriia frantsuzkoi literatury (Moskva, Izdatel'stvo Akademii Nauk SSSR), 1963, vol. 4, pp. 567–73.

Ivashchenko, A. F., *Zametki o sovremennom realizme* (Moskva, Sovetskii pisatel', 1961), p. 222.

Karpushin, V. A., 'Kontseptsiia lichnosti u Al'bera Kamiu', *Voprosy filosofii*, no. 2, 1967, pp. 128–36.

Kushkin, E. P., 'Kamiu i problema bespoleznogo sluzheniia', *Voprosy filologii Leningradskogo universiteta*, no. 4, 1974, pp. 232–41.

Kushkin, E. P., 'U istokov tvorchestva Kamiu', *Zarubezhnaia literatura: Problema metoda*, no. 1, 1979, pp. 119–29.

Kutasova, I. M., 'Al'ber Kamiu: nigilist protiv nigilizma', *Voprosy filosofii*, no. 7, 1975, pp. 96–108.

Kuznetsov, V. N., 'Eticheskie vzgliady frantsuzskikh ekzistentsialistov' in *Protiv sovremennoi burzhuaznoi etiki* (Moskva, Nauka, 1965), pp. no. 60–210.

Kuznetsova, S. N., 'Vzaimootnosheniia cheloveka i obtshchestva v tvorchestve Al'bera Kamiu', *Filosofiia*, no. 1, 1975, pp. 72–80.

Latynina, A. N., 'Ekzistentsialistskaia kontseptsiia cheloveka i problema otnosheniia lichnosti i obshchestva u Dostoïevskogo', *Vestnik Moskovskogo Universiteta: Filosofiia*, no. 2, 1969, pp. 67–76.

Lovtsova, O., *Literatura Frantsii: 1917–1965*, 2 edn (Moskva, Vysshaia shkola, 1966), pp. 142–6.

Malaia sovetskaia entsiklopediia, 3 edn (Moskva, Izd. Bol'shaia sovetskaia entsiklopediia, 1958–1961), p. 453.

Man'kovskaia, N. B., 'Funktsiia iskusstva v estetike Al'bera Kamiu' in *Voprosy istorii i teorii estetiki* (Izdatel'stvo Moskovskogo Universiteta, 1975), pp. 161–6.

Man'kovskaia, N. B., 'Problema chelovek i priroda v filosofii Al'bera Kamiu', *Vestnik Moskovskogo Universiteta: Filosofiia*, no. 4, 1976, pp. 84–9.

Man'kovskaia, N. B., 'Problema tvorcheskogo metoda i stilia estetike Al'bera Kamiu', *Voprosy iazyka i literatury*, no. 3, 1972, pp. 257–78.

Man'kovskaia, N. B., 'Schastlivaia smert' postoronnego', *Vestnik Moskovskogo Universiteta: Filosofiia*, no. 2, 1973, pp. 78–84.

Moskvina, R. R., 'Antropologicheskoie obosnovaniie otchuzhdeniia lichnosti v filosofii Al'bera Kamiu', *Istoriko-filosofskiie issledovaniia*, Ural'skii Universitet, no. 1, 1973, pp. 67–73.

Moskvina, R. R., 'Metod absurda: Al'ber Kamiu kak fenomen neklassicheskogo filosovstvovaniia', *Voprosy filosofii*, no. 10, 1974, pp. 137–43.

Rurikov, B. S., 'Chelovek – odinochestvo i svoboda', *Inostrannaia literatura*, no. 9, 1968, pp. 189–97.

Safronov, M. V., 'Stilisticheskaia rol' lichnykh mestoimenii – zamestitelei imien personnazhei: na materiale povesti A. Kamiu *Postoronnii'* in *Lingvisticheskiie issledovaniia* (Moskva, publisher not known, 1979), pp. 222–9.

Sakharova, N., *Ekzistentsializm i strukturalizm* (Moskva, Izd. Iskusstvo, 1974), pp. 41–9.

Semienova, S. G., 'Povest' Al'bera Kamiu *Postoronnii* i ranneie tvorchestvo pisatelia', *Izvestiia Akademii Nauk SSSR* (Seriia Nauka i Literatura), no. 5, vol. XXXII, pp. 419–29.

Shkunaieva, I. D., *Sovremennaia frantsuzskaia literatura* (Moskva, Izd. IMO, 1961), pp. 153–96.

Tavrizian, G. M., *Problema cheloveka vo frantsuzskom ekzistentsializme* (Moskva, Nauka, 1977), pp. 121–2.

Velikovskii, S. I., *Grani neschastnogo soznaniia* (Moskva, Iskusstvo, 1973).
Velikovskii, S. I., 'K pristanishchu pravednykh bez boga' in *V Poiskakh utrachennogo smysla* (Moskva, Khudozhestvennaia literatura, 1979), pp. 185–250.
Velikovskii, S. I., 'Na ochnoi stavke s istoriiei', *Voprosy literatury*, no. 1, 1965, pp. 109–44.
Velikovskii, S. I., 'Otchuzhdeniie i literatura Zapada' in *Sovremennyie problemy realizma i modernizma* (Moskva, Nauka, 1965), pp. 522–35.
Velikovskii, S. I., 'Posle smerti boga', *Novyi Mir*, no. 9, 1969, pp. 215–32.
Velikovskii, S. I., 'Proza Kamiu', préface à A. Kamiu, *Izbrannoie* (Moskva, Progress, 1969), pp. 5–48.

No known author, 'Istoriiu delaiut drugii', *Inostrannaia literatura*, no. 4, 1959, pp. 237–9.

9

Camus and Algerian Writers
Christiane Achour

8 May 1990: Algeria celebrates in splendour the forty-fifth anniversary of the Sétif revolt, the revolt described by Kateb Yacine in *Nedjma*: 'The people were everywhere, to such an extent that they became invisible, mingled with the trees and the dust, and only the roar of their voices drifted towards me.' On 8 May 1990, the national daily paper, *El Moudiahid*, proposed as the introduction to an article about this key date in national history, a sentence by Camus:

> 'Algeria is plunged into an economic and political crisis. In this admirable country which an incomparable spring is right now covering with its flowers and its light, a people is suffering.' Albert Camus, moved by the suffering of the Algerian people, wrote this beautiful paragraph in the newspaper *Combat* in the first week of May 1945.[1]

It is an unexpected reference for the reader in 1990, but it is familiar; it seems to me symptomatic of the many traces and imprints of Camus's continued influence on Algerian writers, an influence I would like to recall here, as much as possible in their own words.

For or against Camus, Camus silenced or cited; between these two extremes appear the seductive power and the irritation that this intellectual from the periphery, consecrated by the metropolis, exercises on the other community of his native land. Ahmed Taleb evoked, in 1959, the young *lycée* students of 1949, of which he was one, who were 'steeped' in Camus's work:

> If you were certainly not our *'maître à penser'*, Taleb wrote to Camus from the prison of Fresnes where he was incarcerated, at least you represented our model of writing. The beauty of the

language moved us all the more because we considered you one of our own. We were, moreover, proud that this son of Algeria had attained, by himself, the rock of success.[2]

In the works of Algerian writers, both fiction and essays, we can find allusions and quotations, homage and argument, dialogue and rectification. Camus's writing and Albert Camus as humanist have offered writers two poles of attraction. The first is writing linked 'sensually' to a soil, a nature, a country, an expression of the un-solvable conflict between History and Nature that creation, unable to erase, sublimates by emphasising one of the two terms:

> Admirably singing the beauty and the charm of the Algerian land, he contributed, through work that reached a universal audience, to making known and immortalising the gentleness of our shores, 'this vast landscape in which tenderness and glory merge in blue and yellow' (*Noces à Tipasa*), the tenderness of our skys (*Le Vent à Djémila*), the beauty of our cities (*L'Eté à Alger, Le Minotaure où la Halte d'Oran*), or the bewitching fascination of our Sahara (*Le Désert*).[3]

The second pole of attraction is a writing 'committed' to questioning the human condition caught between individual desire and social and historical necessity; an act of questioning that is crystallised in those scenes positing the universe as a prison, a place of murder and judgement:

> If the theme of the absurd gives the work its philosophical and moral character, the spatial-temporal anchoring of the text in the colonial context, as well as the novel's structure (the confrontation coloniser-colonised and the murder of the latter) give the book its ideological dimension and authorise a 'political reading'.[3]

If the impression made by Camus continued after he left Algeria, it is because the potential for finding him a credible witness had been set in motion during the years from 1935 to 1945, years which corre-spond to the maturation and publication of his first works. Those works appear as references in the writing of our Algerian authors, as in that of Taieb Bougerra, who wrote the first post-independence preface, and whom we have just quoted. The texts by Camus that are often cited are: *L'Envers et L'endroit* (1937), *Noces* (1939), 'Misère de la Kabylie' (*Algér-Républicain*, June 1939), *L'Etranger* (1942), *Le Mythe de Sisyphe* (1942).

TRACES

Vue de haut la beauté d'Alger paraît fragile et contradictoire. En face le mur de la mer tout de suite dressé contre l'horizon ... Aux maisons d'Alger en quelque point que l'on se trouve sont imparties des portions mesurées de ciel. Dans la beauté rigoureuse d'une baie ouverte sur la monotonie bleue d'une mer que nul accident n'humanise l'esprit se sent sollicité et comme voué aux tensions extrêmes ... A Alger pour aller à l'air libre il faut toujours monter.[4]

Seen from above the beauty of Algiers seems fragile and contradictory. In front the wall of the sea rising immediately against the horizon ... No matter where you are you find the houses of Algiers are bestowed with measured portions of sky. In the severe beauty of a bay that opens onto the blue monotony of a sea which no chance event humanises, one's spirit seems tempted, as if destined to feel an extreme tension ... In Algiers in order to reach free air, it is always necessary to climb.

These sentences come not from *L'Envers et l'endroit*, but from the opening of *L'Opium et le Baton*, by Mouloud Mammeri, some thirty years later. The rhetoric, rhythm, musicality, and themes of Camus are well integrated into the text.

We can find a reminiscence of Camus in the work of a young Algerian woman writer, in 1964. Her story, 'La Cicatrice' tells of the separation between a militant rebel and the young girl he loves, a separation that is final since death awaits him with the first barrage of the French military. When an officer begins to look at Ali rather suspiciously, Ali decides to use his gun:

puis, subitement, le soleil a pesé lui aussi, tout s'est alors déclenché ... comme une machine sur le bouton de laquelle le destin de Ali a appuyé. Comme une mise en scène prévue mais dont les acteurs ne savent pas tout à fait jouer leur role.[5]

then, suddenly, the sun weighed down on him as well, and everything went off ... as if Ali's destiny had pushed a button on a machine. As if it were an announced stage production whose actors didn't quite know how to play their roles.

The ruins at Tipasa, of course:

la vertu de la ruine romaine c'est le silence. Cela est vrai pour toutes les ruines, mais à Tipasa, le silence est pire qu'ailleurs et les couleurs insupportables. Des qu'on est arrivé, il faut vite partir et quitter ces ruines; car du mutisme de la beauté des vestiges et de la véhémence des couleurs, une terrible émotion se dégage et épuise vite le voyageur hanté par les pierres et les mirages. L'air tremble-t-il de chaleur? Les insectes ... bourdonnent-ils au soleil? Le silence n'en est que plus grand![6]

The power of the Roman ruins is the silence. This is true for all ruins, but at Tipasa the silence is worse than elsewhere and the colours are unbearable. As soon as you arrive you have to leave these ruins quickly; for from the muteness of the beauty of these remains and from the violence of the colours emanates a frightening emotion, which quickly exhausts the traveller obsessed by the stones and the mirages. Is the air trembling in the heat? Are the insects buzzing in the sun? The silence is only greater because of them.

Here again, as for Mammeri, we should quote the whole page that Rachid Boudjedra devotes to Tipasa in order to appreciate the dialogue: the allusion to *Noces* and also a refutation of it. Colours, silence, the world's rhythm, the sun, murmurs, these impressions are condensed by the Algerian writer and only take on their full weight when the two texts are read in relation to each other.

In 1980 Assia Djebar evoked 'Oran', beginning:

The reflections that a visit to Oran inspired in Albert Camus are entitled 'La Halte d'Oran'. As if you could only stop on these shores for a brief instant or two, catch your breath in a slack moment of your journey and leave again. Or, if you cannot, dream of such a journey.[7]

Camus's title is called up and interpreted to begin a different discourse on the city.

In 1984 the novelist Akli Tadjer, a 'beur' (a person of North African descent, born and living in France) speaks of his disillusionment with Algiers:

El Djanzair swarming with a people of robots who don't even take the time to enjoy admiring their sea, who no longer have the curiosity to go to see if Tipasa in the spring is still inhabited by the gods and if the gods still speak to the sun.[8]

This knowing cultural wink is emphasised, then the text turns towards other subjects.

IMPRINTS

If Camus can seem an accomplice when expressing a passionate relationship to the Algerian soil, in a style that still overwhelms a number of readers today, these readers reject him, painfully or brutally, when he introduces the human element. Is this sentence from *L'Eté* the beginning of the misunderstanding? 'Yes, what I love in Algerian cities cannot be separated from the men who inhabit them.' The *lycée* students in 1949, of whom Ahmed Taleb speaks, picked up this sentence. Including themselves among these 'men', they saw it as an affirmation of a community going beyond the exclusion of the colonial system of the time. Camus's series of articles on Kabylie in 1939 confirms this interpretation, an interpretation reinforced by his articles in *Combat* in May 1945:

Camus the Algerian! continues Ahmed Taleb. In this connection which does not seem strange to our ears or in our hearts, we could detect no inconsistency. Such as we imagined you, you could not stay indifferent to the hopes and suffering of Algeria.[9]

At about the same time, Mouloud Feraoun wrote in his diary:

I would love to say to Camus that he is as Algerian as I am and that all Algerians are proud of him ... There is in him the same fraternal warmth which likes to make fun of forms and consequences. His position on the events in Algeria is what I would suppose: nothing could be more human.[10]

If reading this work so sensually linked to the soil is the secret garden of a number of Algerians, who find in Camus a brother of the land, it is the rewriting of the colonial prison universe (murder and judgement) that leaves its imprint on the relationship of Algerian texts to

Camus's. The scene of the murder, 'a condensation of contradictions, the pivot of the novel, and the crossroad of interpretations'[11] represents, in varying degrees, a 'model' for several of the most highly considered Algerian novelists, including as well such novelists from Algeria as Emmanuel Roblès (in *Les Hauteurs de la ville*, 1947) and J. Pelegri (in *Le Maboul*, 1963).

In 1953 Mouloud Feraoun published *La Terre et le sang*, a novel of a return to the native land, a novel both of fantasised violence (that of Marie whom Kamouna imagines killing herself and her son and benefiting from impunity like any colonial who attacks a native), and of actual violence, which occurs not between enemies but between members of the same ethnic group. The murder scene – framework, protagonists, motive – is thus changed from the model of *L'Etranger*. It is no longer the confrontation between colonisers and colonised, but among only the colonised. As Frantz Fanon has written:

> By throwing himself with all his force into the vendetta, the native tries to persuade himself that colonialism does not exist, that everything is going on as before, that history continues. Here on the level of communal organizations we clearly discern the well-known behavior patterns of avoidance. It is as if plunging into a fraternal bloodbath allowed them to ignore the obstacle, and to put off till later the choice, nevertheless inevitable, which opens up the question of armed resistance to colonialism.[12]

In Mouloud Mammeri's *Le Sommeil du juste* (1955), we can find in the dénouement of Arezki's 'commitment' a reworking of Meursault's itinerary. In this way, even if there are no exactly parallel passages, there is a profound influence. A melodic line feeds the text by a sort of osmosis, or contamination. Arezki and Meursault are characterised by the same measured indifference, the same feeling of being 'strangers' to the world which is theirs; their actions have the same apparent gratuitousness. Arezki's long final monologue, in which from his prison he draws up an indictment of society and of his judges, is in many ways related to the ending of *L'Etranger*. Mammeri evades the violent act by suppressing a description of it but insists on the act of accusation of the society and on the inability of the individual to feel a personal interest in the wheels of a society, the mechanisms of which he does not understand, or does not want to understand.

It is especially in the major Algerian novel, Kateb Yacine's *Nedjma*, that the affiliation and the counter-writing of *L'Etranger* appear unambiguously. In Kateb's novel the elements that make up colonial violence are integrated into the story from the beginning: blows, knife, violence, prison, murder.[13] The scene of the murder of Mr Richard appears after a description of the setting that allows no ambiguity. Although chronologically occurring after the fight at the building site between Lakhdar and Mr Ernest, the scene is described earlier in the text, the murder thus appearing, from the beginning, as the unavoidable result of colonial violence. The two scenes of the fight and the murder are complementary and both refer to Chapter 6 of *L'Etranger*. These scenes are completed by other scenes or brief passages where the famous cliché of 'the Arab with a knife between his teeth' is mentioned. The knife, an accepted symbol, is thus present from the beginning to the epilogue, but it is absent from the two scenes of violence: the one where Mourad punches and kicks Mr Richard to death, and the one where Lakhdar butts Mr Ernest with his head. The scene of violence, concentrated at the heart of the story in *L'Etranger* is divided, shared by all the colonised.

This rewriting allows several interpretations: it underlines the violence which is an integral part of the universe evoked – a violence metaphorised by Camus through the hyperbolic effect of the sun, masking the murder itself. With Kateb, the enemy becomes again an historical figure, the coloniser. The necessity of the murder is obvious and anyone else could have done it besides Mourad. Meursault commits an unintentional murder. Mourad comes in, and acts; the murder cannot be erased. There is an inversion of roles. The defeated Arab of *L'Etranger*, the Arab confused with the sun, the Arab who is forgotten as soon as he is murdered, becomes, in *Nedjma*, the conqueror, the actor, present, not forgotten. From victim he becomes aggressor; he takes back the initiative. Thus he can again find his identity. To the anonymity of the stranger, he opposes a multiplicity of names: Mourad, Lakhda, Mustapha, Rachid, Ameziane. And the sun returns to its usual place: 'the sun is now shining on the building site like a theatre set rising from the most annoying banality' (p. 51). When will the colonial setting finally stop?

WHO IS THE STRANGER?

So Camus's words are an unavoidable reference for Algerian writing. Kateb Yacine, recalling his difficult beginnings as a writer, remembers that at the time Camus held the whole scene: 'it is evident that for the French in general, the ideal Algerian was Camus ... But Algerian man was not seen. He was practically "a stranger" in all this litera-ture. There was a whole school called the school of Algiers, the school of Camus, that jealously represented Algerian literature.' Kateb continues by recognising that, if Camus is a great writer, 'his books about Algeria sound a false and hollow note'. And he interprets the murder of the Arab as the inability of the novelist to give fictional existence to an Arab character and, consequently, the necessity he felt to suppress him.[14]

It is more or less in the same way that we can understand the allusion to Camus made by Mouloud Mammeri in a recent inter-view with Tahar Djaout: 'To an internationally known writer, born in Algeria, we can make the reproach that he only introduced an Algerian once in his work, and then as a strange and dangerous handler of a knife.' Mouloud Mammeri judges the trial derisory in so far as the text only becomes a faithful reproduction of colonial reality:

> The two communities ... were complete strangers to one another, I mean in essence ... For a European of Algeria, an Algerian did not exist fully. He was rather a vaguely fantasised model, with a few functions ... sketched rapidly ... against a background of fear. In colonial society he was not an individual; all Algerians were strangers, stranger than the strangest *pied-noir*.[15]

Ahmed Taleb's tone, in 1959, was more violent because the disil-lusionment that Camus's ambiguous position during the fight for liberation provoked was not far distant. The test of the war had tolled the knell of hopes and illusions. Judgement is more brutal the more the idol that is being sacrificed is held in esteem:

> Faithful to an anachronistic vision, you keep on making a distinction 'Arabs' and 'French' ... The revolution forces you to uncover what was equivocal, to take off your mask and to show your true face, which is that of a French Algerian obeying more his reflexes that any reflection, and whose reaction is basically one of fear.

In a 'Letter to Albert Camus', a few months earlier, Mouloud Feraoun clarifies his relationship to the writer:

When I read your articles in *Alger-Républicain*, that schoolteachers' newspaper, I said to myself: 'There's a good guy!' And I admired your tenacity in wanting to understand, your curiosity based on sympathy and perhaps on love. I felt then that you were so close to me, so much a brother, so totally without prejudices!

But the rest of the text expresses important reservations:

But already, I can assure you, I did not believe in you, nor in myself, nor in all those who were interested in us and who were not at all numerous; for all the evil that we could experience from others, no one had been able to prevent.[16]

As a colonised individual, Feraoun cannot, for fear of being caught up in the nationalist struggle, with all the breaks that it entails, express generous and sincere emotions in Camus's fashion! He could not later turn about, or it would be at the price of his own identity and his middle, mediating position.

In a programme on the Algerian war for *France-Culture* in 1987, Kateb said: 'what I don't like about Camus is his way of posing the problem. A revolution is not a moral thought.' Immediately afterwards, a voice recited extracts from Jean Amrouche's poem 'Le Combat Algérien':

nous voulons habiter notre nom
vivre ou mourir sur notre terre mère
    nous ne voulons pas d'une patrie marâtre
et des reliefs de ses festins.[17]

We want to inhabit our name
Live or die on our mother land
    we don't want a stepmother native land
and the outlines of its feasts.

We can perhaps understand better why Algerian writers go back over this 'naming', at the risk of annoying non-Algerian criticism, which sees it as a 'political' obsession. It is however, one of the strengths of Camus's text to be rooted not only in a land but also in the history of this land; this is why it continues to produce reactions in the place where it originated. Three examples of allusions, in post-independence texts, make this clear.

In a recent interview Kassa Houari recalls his reading and notes that he admires Roblès, the *pied-noir*, but that Camus repels him: 'The classic image of the coloniser ... in the works of Camus, the Algerians are non-existent. There is no Arab character (except in *L'Etranger* where several Arabs are criminals).'[18]

Earlier, Rachid Boudjedra notes in his *Journal Palestinien*, after having reread *La Mort heureuse*, which he found in a drawer in his Beirut hotel room:

> what is striking is the absence of Algerians in the novel. They are not even part of the setting ... no Algerians at all – reduced to nothing in the colonial consciousness of the writer, exterminated by the magic of words and fiction. What a great political lapse! Do Israeli writers give life in their books to the rare Palestinians who remain in their country, or do they act like Camus with regard to the Algerians?[19]

Mostefa Lacheraf, analysing the position of the Israelis with regard to the Palestinians, writes:

> We have known, in Algeria, the same semantic ostracism regarding the use of the word 'Algerian' for our compatriots during the French colonial occupation, and even a man as enlightened as Albert Camus – but who was unfortunately influenced by the prejudices of his surroundings – never fails to observe this negative rule about the national identity of others, since in all his novels and articles about our country he spoke of 'Arabs' and never of 'Algerians' ... never associated them with a native land, Algeria, of which they had been the legitimate children for thousands of years.[20]

Thus Camus's texts preceding and accompanying *L'Etranger* are indeed part of the 'intertext' of Algerian literature, because they are all imbued with Algeria, Nature, and History mixed together. For an adhesion to or a rejection of Camus's work, these are the texts which have been and continue either to set reading in motion or to present stumbling blocks. If other readings are possible, useful and desirable, the historical reading must not be smothered under the pretext of cleansing the writer from the rigorous demands of history. An historical reading remains of interest as a means of taking into account the contradictory and conflicting sense of being Algerian that can be found in Camus's work.

Translated by Adele King and Farida Majdoub

Notes

1. Mustapha Talaslimane, report of seminar on the history of 8 May 1945, *El Moudjahid*, 9 May 1990, last page.
2. Ahmed Taleb, *Lettres de prison*, 1957–1961 (Algiers: Société Nationale d'Edition et de Diffusion, Editions Nationales Algériennes, 1966). 'Lettre ouverte à A. Camus', pp. 67 – 83, prison de Fresnes, 26 August 1959.
3. Taieb Bouguerra, Preface to the first Algerian republication of *L'Etranger* (Algiers: ENAG, collection El Aniss, paperback, 1988). Camus was the sixth author published the first year that this collection appeared.
4. Mouloud Mammeri, *L'Opium et le baton* (Paris: Plon, 1965; new edn Paris: Union Générale d'Editions, 10/18, pp. 5 and 6).
5. Hadjira Mouhoub, 'La Cicatrice', in *Alger Républicain*, 1964. The first collection of the stories of this woman writer was published in Algiers by ENAP in 1988.
6. Rachid Boudjedra, *En Algérie* (Paris: Hachette, collection 'Vies quotidiennes contemporaines', 1971), p. 169.
7. Assia Djebar, 'Oran', *Le Monde*, 27 July 1980.
8. Akli Tadjer, *Les ANI du Tassili* (Paris: Le Seuil, 1984), pp. 61–2.
9. Ahmed Taleb, op. cit. (see note 2).
10. Mouloud Feraoun, *Journal* (Paris: Le Seuil, 1962), pp. 204–71.
11. Cf. Isabelle Ansel, *Lectoguide sur L'Etranger* (Paris: Pedagogie Moderne, 1980).
12. Frantz Fanon, *The Wretched of the Earth*, Constance Farrington (trans.) (New York: Grove Press, 1968), p. 54.
13. Kateb Yacine, *Nedjma* (Paris: Le Seuil, 1956). We made a systematic comparison between the two texts in *Un Etranger si familier* (Algiers: ENAP, 1984), pp. 85 ff. Only our conclusions are presented here.
14. 'A Batons Rompus. Kateb Yacine Délivre la Parole', M. Djaider and K. Nekkouri (eds), in *El Moudjahid Culturel*, 4 April 1975, No. 156.
15. *Entretien de Mouloud Mammeri avec Tahar Djaout* (Algiers: Laphomic, 1987), p. 20.
16. Published in *Preuves* no. 91, September 1958, in Paris. Reprinted in *L'Anniversaire*, pp. 35 ff. For an analysis of Camus's reporting on Kabylie, see our study, *Mouloud Feraoun, une voix en contrepoint* (Paris: Silex, 1986), pp. 74 ff.
17. France Culture presents *La Guerre d'Algérie, 25 ans après*, documents recorded on seven cassettes, France-K 5021 AD 035.
18. Kassa Houari, 'Confession d'un Algérien au "Pays des rêves" ', interview with Marie-Jose Protais, *Jeune Afrique Magazine*, no. 51, September 1988.

19. Rachid Boudjedra, *Journal Palestinien* (Algiers: Société Nationale d'Edition et de Diffusion, 1982), pp. 51–2.
20. Mostefa Lacheraf, *Algérie et Tiers Monde* (Algiers: Bouchène, 1989), pp. 171–2. Article written March 1980.

10

History and Ethnicity in the Reception of *L'Etranger*
Alec G. Hargreaves

In the last interview that he gave before his death, Camus was asked what aspects of his works had been unduly neglected by French literary critics. He replied: 'La part obscure, ce qu'il y a d'aveugle et d'instinctif en moi. La critique française s'intéresse d'abord aux idées. Mais, toutes proportions gardées, pourrait-on étudier Faulkner sans faire la part du Sud dans son oeuvre?' '*The obscure part, what I feel blindly and instinctively. French criticism is always first interested in ideas. But, relatively speaking, could you study Faulkner without reference to the South in his work?*'[1] Through this reference to the role of the American South in the writings of William Faulkner, Camus was clearly alluding to the importance of his native Algeria within his own works. While Camus mainly had in mind his emotional attachment to the topographic features of Algeria, other parallels with the American South also suggest themselves. Colonial Algeria, like the southern part of the United States, was characterised not simply by its geographical position in relation to an associated northern territory (which in Camus's case lay in France) but also by an ethnically diverse population and a history of political inequality. As Camus rightly observed, the particularities of Algeria had initially attracted very little attention in critical studies of his works. *L'Etranger* was seen primarily as an exploration of man's universal condition, summed up in the notion of the absurd. Within a year of Camus's death, the French historian Pierre Nora was to publish a radical reassessment of the author's first novel: 'Son roman de l'absurde n'est pas la mise en scène d'une découverte philosophique, mais de l'institution d'une colonie de peuplement raciste; il est l'expression sublimée d'une situation historique réelle, décantée jusqu'à l'épure.' '*His novel about the absurd does not dramatise a philosophical discovery, but the foundation of a racialist colony; it is the sublimated, purified expression of a real*

101

historical situation.'[2] A few years later Ahmed Taleb Ibrahimi, Minister
of Education in post-independence Algeria, made a still more severe
analysis of the novel: 'En tuant l'Arabe [through the intermediary
of Meursault], Camus réalise de manière subconsciente, le rêve du
pied-noir qui aime l'Algérie mais ne peut concevoir cette Algérie que
débarrassée des Algériens.' *In killing the Arab Camus achieves, sub-
consciously, the dream of the* pied-noir *who loves Algeria but can only
conceive of an Algeria without Algerians.'*[3] By 1970, Conor Cruise
O'Brien had produced the first general study of Camus to take as its
pivot the author's colonial roots.[4] Twenty years on, the re-evaluation
of Camus's Algerian origins has continued to feature prominently
in the numerous studies devoted to his work, especially *L'Etranger.*

How are we to explain the diversity of these interpretations, and
how are we to evaluate the significance of the Algerian factor within the fabric of *L'Etranger?* If the first of these questions is slightly
less difficult to answer than the second, the complexities of both are
hinted at by a common thread running through the comments of
Nora and of Taleb Ibrahimi, as well as those of Camus himself. All
three specifically mention the importance of unconscious elements in
the author's depiction of Algeria. The reception theorist Hans Robert
Jauss has emphasised the role of unconscious factors in shaping the
'horizons of expectations' within which texts are written and read.[5]
In producing or interpreting the text, writer and reader create
patterns of meaning which depend on the assumption of certain
types of knowledge, belief and desire. Changes in those assumptions,
which are culturally and historically conditioned, may sharpen the
reader's awareness of aspects of the text which were previously too
self-evident to elicit comment or too deeply buried to be made
manifest. In our analysis of *L'Etranger* and of the divergent interpretations to which it has been subjected, we shall see that variations of
this kind are intimately linked with a tide of historical change at the
heart of which has lain the process of decolonisation. This tide has
stimulated new readings in France and other Western countries. It
has also brought the rise of new groups of readers in what we now
call the Third World. From their different positions in time and
space, Camus's readers have inevitably approached *L'Etranger* with
markedly contrasting horizons of expectations.

The review of *L'Etranger* published by Sartre early in 1943 typified
the line of approach which was to dominate scholarly studies in
France for many years to come. Sartre, like Camus, shared with
many European intellectuals a preoccupation with feelings of cosmic

meaninglessness. In his review, Sartre makes only one reference to the ethnic particularities of Algeria, when he compares Meursault's seemingly arbitrary thoughts in Part 1 of the novel to 'une melopée monotone, [le] chant nasillard d'un Arabe ... un de ces airs dont parle Courteline, qui "s'en vont et ne reviennent jamais" et qui s'arrêtent tout d'un coup, sans qu'on sache pourquoi.' 'A monotonous, nasal, Arab chant ... one of those tunes of which Courteline remarked that "they disappear, never to return" and stop all of a sudden.'[6] The idea of Arab chants being meandering and meaningless is a reflection of Sartre's almost total ignorance of Algeria and its inhabitants. It was not until the Algerian war of independence, which began in 1954, that the inhabitants of metropolitan France began to have anything more than a fitful awareness of the conditions obtaining on the other side of the Mediterranean. Almost three million Frenchmen fought in that war, which for much of its duration ranked as the single most important preoccupation of the French public.[7] Journalists and others turned expectantly to Camus, whose origins seemed to give him an unrivalled basis from which to comment on the conflict. His reluctance to do so puzzled many, and persuaded some that behind Camus's Algerian connections lay some guilty secrets. This shift of horizons among the French reading public prepared the ground for reassessments of *L'Etranger* such as that undertaken by Nora.

The violence through which the French had established and attempted to sustain their presence in Algeria before granting independence in 1962 remains to this day a sensitive area in the self-image of France presented in schoolbooks and official government pronouncements.[8] The continued emphasis given in French textbooks to the philosophical aspects of *L'Etranger* has therefore been viewed with considerable suspicion in Algeria.[9] Far from being an embarrassment, the struggle against French domination is for Algerians fundamental to their sense of nationhood. Government ministers such as Taleb Ibrahimi have helped to create a horizon of expectations in which Algerian scholars have found it natural to interrogate the political credentials of writers who, like Camus, had their origins in the *pied-noir* (settler) community.[10] Within the English-speaking world, the most ambitious attempt at reinterpreting the whole of Camus's *oeuvre* in the light of his French Algerian roots has come from the pen of an Irishman. Situated on the very edge of Western Europe, Ireland may perhaps seem an unlikely position from which to initiate such an analysis. Bearing in mind

the troubled colonial history which has characterised Ireland's relations with Great Britain, O'Brien's interest in parallel aspects of
the Franco-Algerian relationship makes much more obvious sense.

While their historically situated nature helps us to understand
the diversity of the readings to which *L'Etranger* has been subjected,
how are to we to gauge their relative merits? Is there not a danger
of readers simply projecting back onto the novel personal preoccupations devoid of any intrinsic connection with the text? In
assessing the worth of these various interpretations, explanatory
comments made by the author may sometimes help, but it would be
naive to regard external authorial pronouncements as automatically
reliable or exhaustive. The test of any interpretative approach must
ultimately be its purchase on the overall economy of the text itself.

In his review, Sartre shrewdly underlined the paradoxical contrast
between the apparent lack of structure in Meursault's thoughts and
the highly structured form of the text, in which each seemingly
insignificant event in Part 1 is eventually used in the legal case
brought against the narrator-protagonist in Part 2. Meursault's view
of the world and the death sentence which is passed upon him
serve, in Sartre's reading, to make of *L'Etranger* 'une oeuvre d'ordre,
composée a propos de l'absurde et contre l'absurde. Est-ce tout à
fait ce que voulait l'auteur? Je ne sais; c'est l'opinion du lecteur que
je donne.' '*An orderly work, composed about the absurd and against the
absurd. Is this quite what the author was aiming at? I don't know. I am
simply presenting the reader's opinion.*'[11] It is clear from Camus's
notebooks that the formal structure remarked upon by Sartre had
indeed been deliberately designed by the author to articulate the
theme of the absurd:

> C'est un livre très concerté et le ton ... est voulu ... Je voulais
> que mon personnage soit porté au seul grand problème par la
> voie du quotidien et du naturel ... Le sens du livre tient
> exactement dans le parallélisme des deux parties. Conclusion: La
> société a besoin de gens qui pleurent à l'enterrement de leur
> mère; ou bien on n'est jamais condamné pour le crime qu'on
> croit.

> *It is a carefully planned book, with a deliberately chosen tone. I wanted
> my character to reach the only great problem through what occurs daily
> and naturally. The meaning of the book resides precisely in the paral-
> lelism of the two parts. Conclusion: society needs people who cry at*

their mother's funeral; or else you are never condemned for the crime you think you will be.[12]

The absurd – the apparent meaninglessness of life in the face of human mortality and the absence of any transcendent God – is implicit in Meursault's reactions to events in Part 1. The nature of this, '[le] seul grand problème', is cruelly confirmed by the seemingly rational but in fact arbitrary interpretation placed upon his behaviour by the prosecutor in Part 2, and is articulated explicitly in Meursault's confrontation with the prison chaplain in the final chapter of the novel. Meursault has by then become convinced that his is a universal condition shared by all human beings, and this view is clearly endorsed by both Camus and Sartre. In reality, *L'Etranger* is far more culture-specific than the author on Sartre suggests. As Camus notes, the novel leads the protagonist and the reader to its allegedly universal truths 'par la voie du quotidien et du naturel', i.e. through the depiction of spontaneous and seemingly ordinary social experiences. The everyday world portrayed in *L'Etranger* is that of colonial Algeria. Camus's aim was to use self-evident aspects of that world as a peg on which to hang his 'universal' theme. Yet things are never truly self-evident: they only appear so to certain observers. What Camus takes for granted serves in practice to mark the ethnic and historical position from which he speaks.

The very notion of the absurd as a universally–felt human condition is itself indicative of the ethnic divide which stood between Camus and most of Algeria's inhabitants. Had they been able to read Camus's novel, it is highly unlikely that the Muslims who accounted for the overwhelming majority of the Algerian population would have recognised themselves in its picture of cosmic meaninglessness. The godless universe inhabited by Camus was that of a twentieth-century European; it was light years away from the Islamic beliefs adhered to by most Algerians. Few of the Muslims living in Algeria in Camus's day were capable of reading *L'Etranger*, for after more than a century of colonial rule education remained the preserve of the minority settler population, together with a small native elite. Most Muslims therefore remained as ignorant of European thought as did Camus or for that matter Sartre where the ideas and beliefs of non-Europeans were concerned. Sartre's description of Arab chants as meandering and incomprehensible is an obvious mark of this ignorance; such chants would appear wholly

natural and coherent in Arab ears. Sartre was of course a native of
metropolitan France and had never set foot in Algeria, so his lack of
instruction in North African culture is perhaps hardly surprising.
Granted that Camus had been born and lived practically all his life
in Algeria, his ignorance of the Arabic language and of Islamic
culture in general in far more striking.

Camus always claimed to feel a deep affinity with Algerians of
non-European descent (*Essais*, pp. 963, 998, 1865–6, 1883), and was
proud to have campaigned for improvements in their lot during his
early career as a journalist.[13] The road to the improvements which
Camus wished to secure for the Muslims lay through assimilation.
This long-established colonial doctrine meant in theory that the indigenous inhabitants of France's overseas empire would be turned
into fully-fledged Frenchmen, with the same culture, living standards
and political rights as the settler population.[14] In practice, the seemingly generous notion of assimilation was bedevilled by a number
of intractable problems. Firstly, the lofty rhetoric of the civilising
mission was matched on the ground by very few economic resources
(hence the low levels of educational provision in colonies such as
Algeria). Moreover, settlers anxious to retain their privileges were
positively opposed to any moves which would give equal political
status to non-Europeans. Finally, even apparently sincere assimi-
lationists such as Camus implicitly took the view that indigenous
cultures were of lesser value than French civilisation; the arrogance
inherent in that view rather took the edge off the generosity of
spirit often associated with assimilation. Although Camus never
acknowledged his commitment to full-blown cultural assimilation,
his deepest instincts undoubtedly lay in that direction. It is true that
while explicitly supporting political and economic assimilation
(*Essais*, pp. 951–3, 956–7, 959, 1328–9),[15] Camus would sometimes
add that the cultural traditions of non-Europeans merited serious
respect (*Essais*, pp. 938, 942). More commonly, however, he urged
during the 1930s that all of Algeria's inhabitants should come
together in a new Mediterranean culture. Whenever he defined that
culture, it consisted almost exclusively of European ingredients
(*Essais*, pp. 1207–9, 1321–31, 1341–3). Islam was conjured away in a
silent disappearing trick; in Camus's eyes it clearly did not appear
as natural as the European presence in Algeria. Later, during the war
of independence, he would depict Islam as a force fundamentally
irrelevant to the true interests of the Algerian people (*Essais*, pp. 901,
979–80, 1013–14). Wedded as he was to the idea of French sovereignty

in Algeria, Camus simply could not bring himself to accept that Muslims might legitimately define an pursue an entirely independent identity of their own.[16]

Algeria had been brought under French rule during the nineteenth century by military conquest. A people subjugated by force of arms and vastly superior to them in numbers was hardly a reassuring presence from the point of view of the *pieds-noirs*. The beauty of assimilation (in theory, at any rate) was that it appeared to make the 'native problem' vanish: by turning Algerians into Frenchmen, the threat to the French presence in Algeria was removed. In an article published alongside that of Pierre Nora, and which directly anticipates Taleb Ibrahimi's anaylsis, Henri Kréa (a writer of mixed French-Algerian descent) was to see in *L'Etranger* a much more violent version of this disappearing trick:

> Quand Meursault, 'l'Etranger', tire sur 'l'Arabe', il tue magiquement une entité raciale où il a peur de se dissoudre. Cet acte, qu'il croit causé 'par le soleil', est la réalisation subconsciente du rêve obscur et puéril du petit Blanc que Camus ne cessa jamais d'être.[17]

> *When Meursault, 'the stranger', fires on 'the Arab', he magically kills a racial entity in which he is afraid of being dissolved. This action, which he believes is caused 'by the sun', is the subconscious realisation of the obscure, childish dream of the little white man that Camus never stopped being.*

During his trial , Meursault denies that he intended to shoot the Arab, and blames the killing on the sun.[18] While Kréa may doubt the sincerity of these assertions,[19] there is every reason to suppose that Camus intends the reader to believe them. In his preface to the American edition of *L'Etranger* (*TRN*, pp. 1928–9), as in the extract from his *Carnets* quoted earlier, Camus suggests that Meursault is convicted not for having murdered an Arab but for having failed to cry at his mother's funeral. The same point is made by Meursault in his conversation with the priest (*TRN*, p. 1211). The prosecution case against Meursault in Part 2 rests on a monstrous but seemingly rational interpretation of the events depicted in Part 1. The author undoubtedly intends the reader to see in Meursault an innocent man unjustly condemned to death. Within the economy of the novel, this conclusion flows inescapably from both the ideology of the absurd and the narrative structure so carefully thought out by Camus.

It is therefore difficult to substantiate the notion that *L'Etranger* embodies an unconscious genocidal urge, for there appears to be no role for such an impulse within the main fabric of the novel. The story does, however, make significant use of the inter-ethnic tensions which characterised colonial Algeria. Meursault finds himself with a gun in his hand facing a hostile Arab as a consequence of his friendship with Raymond. Raymond's brutal mistreatment of his Arab mistress, which provokes the confrontation on the beach, is surely emblematic of the historical rape inflicted on Algerian Muslims by the settler population in general. While Meursault does not share Raymond's enthusiasm for initiating violence, he has no qualms where self-defence is concerned. In the first of two skirmishes which precede the shooting, it is one of the Arabs who makes the first aggressive move and who draws first blood by using his knife on Raymond. In the second incident, Meursault tells Raymond that he cannot use his gun unless the knife is first drawn once more. When, in the final confrontation, Meursault faces one of the Arabs alone, he does not shoot until after the knife has been has drawn. The obvious inference to draw from all this is that the shots fired by Meursault are a justified response to the threat posed by the Arab.

It is tempting to see in this arrangement of the story evidence of an underlying consent, on the part of the author, to the defence of the French presence in Algeria by force of arms. For many, this commitment appeared to become explicit when, at the height of the war of independence, Camus declared that he would if necessary defend his mother rather than justice in Algeria (*Essais*, p. 1882). Yet while readers of *L'Etranger* may see in the text evidence of legitimate selfdefence, neither Meursault nor his lawyer makes such a case explicitly. Within the overarching framework of the absurd it is important that the killing of the Arab should in fact defy rational explanation; hence Meursault's baffling references to the sun. It is in this sense an arbitrary killing. Implicit evidence of self-defence helps subtly to strengthen the image of innocence attaching to the protagonist, but the primary source of that innocence is shown to reside in the metaphysical absurdity which permeates his existence.

The injustice visited upon Meursault by the court is an image of that which is inflicted on all human beings by virtue of their mortal condition: the death sentence which is imposed on each and every one of us seems as arbitrary and unjust as that to which Meursault falls victim. Yet to sympathise with Meursault the reader must condone or at the very least disregard his equally arbitrary killing of another human being. There seems to be a double standard at work here: the injustice inherent in the shooting of the Arab is implicitly deemed to matter less than that involved in the execution of his killer. It is true that, unlike the prosecutor, Meursault does not intend to kill. Somewhat more disturbingly, however, he seems equally detached from the killing after the event. At no point does he express regret over the death of the Arab. Camus clearly intends his readers to share Meursault's indifference towards the murdered man; otherwise they will find it impossible fully to sympathise with the protagonist when the court orders his execution. In what ways do the killer and his victim differ? Apart from his movements on the beach, we are told practically nothing about the dead man. His only distinguishing feature is that he is an Arab, whereas Meursault is a European. Perhaps it is this that accounts for his lesser worth.

Like Meursault in *L'Etranger*, Patrice Mersault, the protagonist in Camus's early novel, *La Mort heureuse*, feels innocent despite the fact that he has killed a man. The victim in *La Mort heureuse* is a cripple who conveniently describes himself as 'une moitié d'homme',[20] thereby reducing the significance of his death. The murdered Arab in *L'Etranger* hardly seems to qualify as a man at all. The Arabs in Camus's novels are always nameless, shadowy characters, and as a number of commentators have observed, this tends somewhat to depersonalise or even dehumanise them altogether.[21] We have already seen from external sources that although Camus never admitted it, at an unconscious level he took a dismissive view of Algeria's Islamic culture. The assumption that non-Europeans were inferior was so widespread when *L'Etranger* was written that for most white men it literally went without saying. Opinions differ as to whether, in writing the novel, Camus was aiming primarily at a *pied-noir* audience or at readers in metropolitan France.[22] Bearing in mind the virtual non-existence of a Muslim public sufficiently educated to read his works, Camus must certainly have assumed that his readership would consist essentially of Europeans, whether on the northern or the southern side of the Mediterranean. In the colonial period, it seemed self-evident that the death of an Arab was less important than that of a European. Camus may not have consciously thought in those terms when constructing the plot, but the exoneration of Meursault in the eyes of many readers was undoubtedly made very much easier by the ethnicity of his victim.

Among the most recent monographs devoted to *L'Etranger* is that
of Patrick McCarthy. The horizon of expectations within which he
approaches the novel is markedly different from that of Camus's
earliest readers. From his post-colonial vantage point, McCarthy
singles out Camus's treatment of the Arab for special attention. He
finds it 'hard to imagine that the author ... could have chosen to
write a novel where an Arab is murdered, without brooding on his
choice of victim'.[23] Yet there is no evidence in Camus's published
notebooks or correspondence to show that he made such a carefully
considered decision. His main concerns were of a quite different,
philosophical order. In fictionalising them he seems to have drawn
on social attitudes and assumptions which hardly needed thinking
about at all. Within the overall fabric of the novel, the shooting of
the Arab is no more than an instrument through which to set up
Meursault's trial on a charge sufficiently serious to carry the death
penalty. Through this sequence of events, Meursault and the reader
are eventually brought face to face with what, in his *Carnets*, Camus
described as '[le] seul grand problème', namely the absurd. But by
casting an Arab as Meursault's victim, the author approached his
'universal' theme via attitudes and experiences of a much more
localised nature. Camus appears to have assumed that in the eyes
of most readers, the inherent inferiority of Arabs and the threat
which they were felt to pose to Europeans would reduce or even
eliminate any element of guilt attaching to Meursault. As an Algerian
scholar has recently observed, there is a deep irony in the fact that
in emphasising Meursault's innocence, 'Camus cannot universalise
the central problem articulated in *L'Etranger* without ... committing
an injustice against the colonised Arab.'[24]

Notes

1. Interview in *Venture*, Spring-Summer 1960, reprinted in *Essais* (Paris:
    Gallimard, Bibliothèque de la Pléïade, 1965), p. 1925; cited hereafter in
    the text as *Essais*. (Any translations not attributed to a published
    version are by Adele King).
2. Pierre Nora, 'Pour une Autre Explication de *L'Etranger*', in *France-
    Observateur*, 5 January 1961, p. 17.
3. Ahmed Taleb Ibrahimi, *De la Décolonisation à la révolution culturelle
    (1962–1972)*, 3rd edn. (Algiers: Société Nationale d'Edition et de
    Diffusion, 1981), p. 1980; the lecture in which this remark was made
    was originally delivered in 1967.
4. Conor Cruise O'Brien, *Camus* (London: Fontana/Collins, 1970).

5. Hans Robert Jauss, *Toward an Aesthetic of Reception*, Timothy Bahti (trans.) (Brighton: Harvester Press, 1982), esp. pp. 22–8.

6. Jean-Paul Sartre, 'Explication de *L'Etranger*' in *Situations I* (Paris: Gallimard, 1947), pp. 111–12 and Jean-Paul Sartre, *Literary and Philosophical Essays*, Annette Michelson (trans.) (New York: Collier, 1955), p. 43.

7. Charles-Robert Ageron, 'L'Opinion Française devant la guerre d'Algérie', in *Revue française d'histoire d'outre-mer*, vol. 63, no. 231, 1976, esp. pp. 260, 265.

8. This sensitivity is illustrated particularly clearly by Robert Frank, 'Amnisties, anniversaires et commémorations depuis 1962', in Jean-Pierre Rioux (ed.), *La Guerre d'Algérie et les Français* (Paris: Fayard, 1990).

9. See, for example, the analysis of French textbooks conducted by Ouahiba Hamouda, 'Une Lecture d'Albert Camus: *L'Etranger – La Peste*. Fonctionnement Social dans l'appareil scolaire', DEA thesis, University of Algiers, 1979.

10. The most valuable study to approach *L'Etranger* in this way is that of Christine Achour, *L'Etranger si familier: lecture du Récit d'Albert Camus* (Algiers: ENAP,1985).

11. Sartre, 'Explication de *L'Etranger*,' p. 112 and *Literary and Philosophical Essays*, p. 44.

12. Camus, *Carnets, Janvier 1942–mars 1951* (Paris: Gallimard, 1964), pp. 29–30.

13. Most notably in the newspaper articles which he wrote during the late 1930s, now collected in Jacqueline Lévi-Valensi and André Abbou (eds), *Fragments d'un combat: 1938–1940* (Paris: Gallimard, Cahiers Albert Camus, 1978).

14. The standard work on this doctrine is Raymond F. Betts, *Assimilation and Association in French Colonial Theory 1890–1914* (New York: Columbia University Press, 1961).

15. See also the following uncollected articles: 'Le Général Catroux . . .', in *Combat*, 28 October 1944 and 'C'est la Justice qui Sauvera l'Algérie de la Haine', in *Combat*, 23 May 1945.

16. For a fuller discussion of these issues, see Alec G. Hargreaves, 'Camus and the Colonial Question in Algeria', in *Muslim World*, Vol. 77, Nos 3–4, July–October 1987, pp. 164–74.

17. Henri Kréa, 'Le Malentendu Algérien', in *France-Observateur*, 5 January 1961, p. 16.

18. Camus, *Théâtre, récits, nouvelles* (Paris: Gallimard, Bibliothèque de la Pléiade, 1962), pp. 1188, 1198; cited hereafter in the text as *TRN*.

19. As do Algerians such as Mahfoud Benanteur: 'Neither his [i.e. Meursault's] deliberately false testimony to the police in favour of his friend Raymond, nor his murderous act can be considered as accidental. Rather, both of these (testimony and violence) are determined by a specific historical situation (occupied Algeria) which imposes on the individual (Meursault in the novel) a self-definition according to the racial parameter that supersedes any other consideration'. (Benanteur, M., 'On Three Readings of Albert Camus's *L'Etranger*', MA thesis, University of Essex, 1986, p. 42.)

20. Camus, *La Mort heureuse* (Paris: Gallimard, 1971), p. 27.

21. The point is made forcefully by O'Brien, *Camus*, pp. 25, 46; cf André Elbaz, 'Albert Camus l'Algérien?', in *Cahiers de littérature générale et comparée*, no. 5, Autumn 1981, pp. 105–6.
22. Garth St Omer, 'The Colonial Novel: Studies in the Novels of Albert Camus, V.S. Naipaul and Alejo Carpentier', PhD thesis, Princeton University, 1975, pp. 34–57, argues that *L'Etranger* was written for *pied-noir* audience. St Omer supports this view through a linguistic analysis of Part 1, together with Edmond Charlot's assertion that Camus originally tried to publish the novel in Algeria: 'Interview accordée à Eric Sellin par Edmond Charlot', *Albert Camus: 3* (Paris, Minard, Lettres Modernes, 1970), pp. 157–8. By contrast, Hubert Gourdon et al., 'Roman colonial et idéologie coloniale en Algérie', in *Revue algérienne des sciences juridiques, économiques et politiques*, vol. 11, no. 1. March 1974, esp. pp. 90, 92n. 21, 97, 121–3, argue that the main audience at which *L'Etranger* was aimed lay in metropolitan France.
23. Patrick McCarthy, *Albert Camus: The Stranger* (Cambridge: Cambridge University Press, 1988), p.11.
24. Azzedine Haddour, 'Camus: The Other as Outsider in a Univocal Discourse', PhD thesis, University of Sussex, 1989, p. 99.

Part Three
Textual Studies

11

Telling Stories: Narrative Reflections in *L'Etranger*
Rosemarie Jones

il avait eu une bagarre avec un type qui lui cherchait des histoires[1]

L'Etranger is of course 'l'histoire de Meursault'. However sharply divided critical opinion may be on other aspects of the novel, in this case there is unanimity, no cause for *bagarre*: Meursault is the prime narrative subject of the book. So glaringly obvious, so unworthy of comment is this fact that its tacit, constant recognition obscures the place held by other story-tellers and story-subjects in Camus's text.

'J'ai raconté à Marie l'histoire du vieux et elle a ri' (p. 1151). Meursault is referring to Salamano, and the story he tells Marie must be the one we have recently read (p. 1144): the description of the indissoluble couple formed by the old man and his dog and of the ritual of their twice-daily walk. No sooner, however, has this seemingly definitive account been related and reacted to, than Salamano appears in another guise: as the narrator of a story about the disappearance of his dog. So the notion of *histoire* which will operate in this novel acquires, on introduction, its two different senses: referring to a story told about a character, and to a story told by that character. We shall see that each of these senses is developed in its own terms but that at the same time, in a characteristically Camusian both/and scheme, full understanding of each is gained only when the two are combined to form a 'whole truth' or complete story.

Salamano, then, tells Meursault and Raymond what has just happened to him. For one whose verbal utterances are normally limited to the ejaculations *salaud* and *charogne*, the start of narration is uneasy: 'il n'a pas répondu tout de suite'; 'il murmurait'; 'il m'a répondu brusquement'; once launched, however, 'il a parlé avec volubilité' (p. 1153). The story he tells, about the loss of his dog, is

114

in direct opposition to the story told about him, according to which man and dog are inseparable. The manner of the telling of each *histoire* also displays contrarieties.

The story about Salamano, narrated by Meursault, shows a quite remarkable adherence to, and insistence on, a strict temporal order. The beginning and the end are clearly marked out by the use of the same clause: 'il y a huit ans qu'on les voit ensemble' ... il y a huit ans que cela dure' (p. 1144). In the brief space occupied by the story, temporal indications form a dense constellation:

> il y a huit ans qu'on les voit ensemble ... deux fois par jour ... à onze heures et à six heures ... depuis huit ans ... jusqu'à ce que ... alors ... à ce moment ... quand ... de nouveau ... de nouveau ... alors ... tous les jours ... quand ... ne lui en laisse pas le temps ... alors ... encore ... il y a huit ans que cela dure.

This *tic* of time serves to place the couple squarely within the space of public law and order, since chronology, supreme instance of the general law, rules all. Their itinerary and their progress can be calculated and timed, their every action is predictable in a chain of stimulus-response: the dog pulls, the man beats him, the dog then has to be pulled along. Displayed to the public gaze, bound together in appearance as well as in reality, their very illnesses visible with repugnant skin disorders, Salamano and his dog issue forth from and return to their little room as though governed by some monstrous horological mechanism.

In marked contrast to the precise concision with which the story about him is related, the story Salamano tells is fragmented. It occupies three narrative spaces: the initial telling of the dog's disappearance (p. 1153), the request for reassurance from Meursault (p. 1153–4), the 'conclusion' that the dog is lost because it has not been taken to the pound (pp. 1157–8), itself no very satisfactory ending. The unity the story reveals is not the uniformity of external measurement, but the plausibility of internal coherence, depending on intertextual mirroring and ironic reflection. That the dog should make off while Salamano was watching 'le Roi de l'Evasion' is pleasantly humorous; more sober is the realisation that *charogne* is defined by being unable to *partir*; sombre, finally, is the fulfilment of Salamano's youthful ambition to go on the stage: in old age he provides the comedy of the *quartier*, provoking the laughter of Marie and Raymond. Fortunately unaware of these ironies, Salamano has one conscious purpose: to find the dog, to put an end to the story. In the interim uncertainty he appeals to Meursault for his pronouncement, or judgement, on the likely outcome: 'Ils ne vont pas me le prendre, dites, monsieur Meursault' (p. 1154). In the light of Salamano's interpretative blindness, it is hardly surprising that he should fail to penetrate to the deeper level of meaning which informs both his story and the story about him. 'Qu'est-ce que je vais devenir?' (p. 1154), applied to the loss of the spaniel, is a grotesque over-reaction. This device of textual jamming, whereby the place of the predicted response is taken by an intrusion from another context, obscuring and deforming the clarity of reading-reception, itself serves to alert the reader to the possibility that all is not as it appears. Owning the dog not only provided companionship; it was also a *divertissement*: a means of concentrating on the present which deflected energy from thought of the future – a future which for Salamano will be the same as for his wife. Meursault's story about Salamano, in its obsession with time, provided a different angle on the the same question, and emphasises how the passage of the days brings us ever nearer the end of life. Putting the two stories together reveals that both, in fact, relate to the same underlying theme. The apparent irreconcilability of the stories, the language of their narration, Salamano's question: all receive meaning in the light of the coming of death.

The story Raymond tells precedes the story told about him. Initially irresolute: 'il hésitait d'abord un peu. "J'ai connu une dame ... c'était pour autant dire ma maîtresse"' (p. 1146), Raymond proves to be more voluble a raconteur than Salamano; as a man who can refer to 'mon histoire' (p. 1146), he is more self-confident a narrator also. Having told his story, he too solicits Meursault's opinion on it (p. 1147); like Salamano again, Raymond is anxious to finish the story and bring it to a satisfactory conclusion. Indeed when he first sees his ex-mistress's brother on the day of the murder, his reaction is 'c'était maintenant une histoire finie' (p. 1161). Later that day, Meursault is surprised to find the Arab on the beach the third time he walks there. Echoing Raymond, a stage later, he too thinks 'c'était une histoire finie' (p. 1167).

Raymond's is a tale of deceit and of affronted honour. In his eyes his mistress has broken the contract between them according to which he provided everything on the assumption that she possessed nothing in her own right. The obligations of this contract are rehearsed in Raymond's speech, which for all its poverty and repetitiousness, is steadfastly ethical in tone: 'tromperie ... j'ai bien agi ... tu me le rends mal ... tromperie ... je lui ai dit ses vérités ... punie' (pp. 1146–7); 'Tu m'as manqué, tu m'as manqué. Je vais t'apprendre à me manquer' (p. 1151). The woman's brother, having in Raymond's view no cause to defend, impugns his honour: 'Il m'a dit que je n'étais pas un homme' (p. 1145).

This is not how the court judges the 'histoire de Raymond' (p. 1196). For the prosecution 'il s'agissait d'un drame crapuleux de la plus basse espèce ... une affaire de moeurs inqualifiable' (p. 1193). 'They had before them the basest of crimes ... an affair of unspeakable vice' (pp. 95–96).) Once again, there is disjunction between *histoire* and *histoire*, an unbridgeable gap between the public view of Raymond and his private vision. Whatever comment were to surface from Raymond's interior monologue would be contradicted in the forum. *Magasinier/souteneur* – Raymond is unaware of his vulnerability in any altercation with authority, as he is oblivious of the ironies inherent in his position. Chief among these is the disparity between his ethical expression and his perception of the world, which is primarily physical and normally violent. If his mistress deceives him over money and jewellery, it is likely that she will be unfaithful sexually: 'tout ce qu'elle voulait, c'était s'amuser avec sa chose' (p. 1147); a letter is capable of conveying 'coups de pied' (p. 1148); *tendrement* is defined in terms of *taper* (p. 1147).

It is not a case of reconciling high morals and low life, nor of imposing the one and erasing the other. The main issue lies elsewhere, as Raymond's words, unbeknown to him, indicate. Demonstrating to Meursault the woman's shameful deception, Raymond establishes a careful balance sheet. On the credit side – his – he details his disbursements: 'Trois cents francs de chambre, six cents francs de nourriture, une paire de bas de temps en temps, ça faisait mille francs' (p. 1146). The woman is capable of no such stock-taking, and Raymond's anger flares because her assets are subtilised, volatile, abstracted. The real commerce in which Raymond is engaged, though he knows it not, is accountancy: a precise reckoning must be made, figures must tally perfectly: it is the exercise of the latter-day demand for an eye for an eye. Where Salamano was bewildered, helplessly dependent, Raymond acts with assurance. His principle is the knock-for-knock, as blind and mechanical in its application as Salamano's regulated appearances. The stories of Raymond are compounded of instalments of score-settling between himself and the Arab, and the pay-off is fatal for the man who becomes embroiled in the tale.

Inevitably: and here one glimpses the source from which Raymond's working principle ultimately derives: the only aspect of life which illustrates his ideal of total accuracy is the advent of death.

Even Raymond's *histoire* is used by him as a commercial token. His telling of it to Meursault functions as advance payment for the letter he anticipates asking Meursault to write; this in turn will be rewarded by the bestowing of Raymond's *copinage*. Fiction itself may give mimetic expression to this notion of computability, and *L'Etranger* offers an instructive example of a narrative equation established in advance and worked out exactly. Meursault reminds the over-excited Raymond of the obligation to fight fair: 'Prends-le d'homme à homme et donne-moi ton revolver. Si l'autre intervient ou *s'il tire son couteau, je le descendrai*' (p. 1166; italics mine). *'take him on man to man and give me your gun. If the other one moves in, or* if he draws his knife, I'll let him have it' (p. 56).

In court Raymond, with the casual bonhomie of the *copain*, dismisses Meursault's 'guilt' and insists on the random nature of the events leading to the Arab's death. The prosecution's 'histoire de Raymond' is elaborated in stated contradistinction to this account and stresses intentionality, bringing about logical and irrevocable consequences. In that respect, it carries the same accent on the ineluctable, and exhibits the same underlying concern with death as does Raymond's own *histoire*; more openly even, since it is designed to explain murder and secure the death penalty.

Both the stories concerning Raymond, and the 'histoires de Salamano', then, converge upon death. Whereas in the case of Salamano the emphasis lay on the extinction of individual life, with Raymond it falls on the general law. Clearly, these formulations echo *Le Mythe de Sisyphe*'s analysis of the twofold aspect under which death appears to us. In telling and giving rise to stories which reaffirm the scandal and bloody mathematics of the human condition, Salamano and Raymond at the same time reformulate the paradox expressed by the nurse which functions as *cogito* of the novel:"Si on va doucement, on risque une insolation, Mais si on va trop vite, on est en transpiration et dans l'église on attrape un chaud et froid." Elle avait raison. Il n'y avait pas d'issue' (p. 1137). '"*If you go slowly, you risk getting sunstroke. But if you go too fast, you work up a sweat and then catch a chill inside the church." She was right. There was no way out*' (p. 17).

The spaniel, however, escapes the tyranny of its treatment, and Raymond's mistress vanishes from view. Both examples, though,

ıre evasions beyond the boundaries of the stories, and the un-
esolved problem of collusion with the force that destroys has
ɔerhaps to be pursued in terms of the narrators and protagonists of
ıistoires. Salamano and Raymond are not the only reflections of
Meursault in this respect. Masson appears at first to designate
ıimself with some conviction as story-teller: his mannerism 'et je
dirai plus' foregrounds speech and promises that supplement in
which the development of a story consists. But his *plus* never
epresents an advance; he remains in the slough of synonym, in
:ontrast to the principal narrative which, as we have seen, moves
ɔorward and redeems its pledge, at the risk of death. The concierge at
he old people's home, likewise, is unencumbered with narratorial
doubt. Not only does he speak a great deal: 'Pendant tout ce temps
ɛe concierge a parlé (p. 1128); 'il a beaucoup bavardé' (p. 1130), but
ɛe shows none of the hesitation displayed by Salamano and
Raymond: 'Immédiatement il a répondu: "Cinq ans" – comme s'il
ıvait attendu depuis longtemps ma demande' (p. 1130). So facile
ınd luxuriant is his speech that his wife feels the need to adopt the
ɛole of censor: 'Tais-toi, ce ne sont pas des choses à raconter à
Monsieur' (p. 1130).

Neither Masson nor the concierge has a story told about him.
However, the novel contains examples of stories told of people who
do not themselves tell stories. Clearest among these is the 'histoire
du Tchécoslovaque' (p. 1182), exemplary in the further sense that it
has taken on a quite independent life; having appeared in the
papers, it has emerged fully into the public domain, and is thereby
subject to temporal laws. Yellow with age, the cutting is also transparent, which suggests that the story, become *fait divers*, has shed
the opacity and recalcitrance of 'le vécu' and is henceforward open
to any interpretation: 'D'un côté, elle était invraisemblable ... D'un
ıutre côté, elle était naturelle' (p. 1182). Equally certain to be reported
ıs the 'histoire ... du parricide' (p. 1185). Meursault's story is
ıntrinsically not so interesting but, as the journalist suggests, blown
ıp, it might compare. The details selected for enlargement would
of course be those of Meursault's relationship to his mother. By
ɛeliance on the trope of metonymy, if Meursault's story can be
ɔresented from the angle of matricide, this would ensure sensational
diffusion. Moreover, a satisfying narrative grouping would be formed: the text would then present the cardinal points of parricide,
matricide, infanticide (the 'histoire du Tchécoslovaque') and a form
of fratricide in which Meursault, symbolic brother of Raymond,[2]

kills the brother of Raymond's mistress. The resulting model is too
neat, but it is typical of the kind of plausible connection suggested
by the law, that expert in fabulation. Meursault's assumption that a
story can stand on its own is shown up as naive by his barrister: 'Je
lui ai fait remarquer que cette histoire n'avait pas de rapport avec
mon affaire, mais il m'a répondu seulement qu'il était visible que je
n'avais jamais eu de rapports avec la justice' (p. 1173). *'I pointed out
to him that none of this had anything to do with my case, but all he said
was that it was obvious I had never had any dealings with the law'* (p. 65)
     The salient point about these latter stories is that each presents
only one side of the double story about/story by, that collision
between private and public, internal and external, which prompts
consciousness, at least on the reader's part, of the misery of the
human condition. There is therefore no problem, which is perhaps
why the concierge and Masson can remain so unflaggingly cheerful
and the pronouncements of the law so triumphant. Imaginative
writing can function in this respect as catalyst to that consciousness
in its tendency to write out the other side of the story: *Le
Malentendu* provides the private perspective on 'l'histoire du
Tchécoslovaque', while *La Peste* reminds the reader of the public
aspect of the story of Meursault: 'une arrestation récente qui avait
fait du bruit à Alger. Il s'agissait d'un jeune employé de commerce
qui avait tué un Arabe sur une plage'; *'a recent arrest that caused a
stir in Algiers. It concerned a young office worker who had killed an Arab
on the beach'*.[3]
     It is to the stories of and about Meursault that one must now turn
in conclusion. He tells his story first, to the examining magistrate,
and of course it carries no mention of his mother, being composed
of: 'Raymond, la plage, le bain, la querelle, encore la plage, la petite
source, le soleil et les cinq coups de revolver' (pp. 1173–74). Not
only is he tired of the telling: 'j'étais lassé de répéter ainsi la même
histoire' (p. 1174), but the story does not, for the 'juge d'instruction'
"add up": he seeks the link which will explain why Meursault fired
five shots, not one. Altogether more convincing and acceptable are
the stories about Meursault, rival versions. The prosecuting barrister
tells of 'cette âme criminelle' (p. 1195), of 'un visage d'homme où je
ne lis rien que de monstrueux' (p. 1198) and of premeditation; the
counsel for the defence counters with the portrayal of 'un honnête
homme, un travailleur régulier, infatigable, fidèle à la maison qui
l'employait, aimé de tous et compatissant aux misères d'autrui ...
perdu par une minute d'égarement' (p. 1199); *'an honest man, a*

steadily employed, tireless worker, loyal to the firm that employed him, well liked, and sympathetic to the misfortunes of others ... [who] had lost control of himself for one moment' (pp. 104–5).) Contrary to what one might have expected, it is the first version that Meursault finds clear and plausible (p. 1196), the second that troubles him, principally because of his barrister's substitution of himself for Meursault by appropriating the narrative *je* (p. 1198). In referring to his *affaire* (p. 1171 twice; p. 1176, p. 1184) and his *cas*[4] (p. 1176) Meursault recognises his fundamental role as actor, if not as author; he has indeed some difficulty in coming to terms with himself as a criminal, or 'auteur de son crime'.

The division between private and public spheres is written out clearly with respect to the stories concerning Meursault. His private 'motive': 'c' était à cause du soleil' (p. 1198) is poorly received in contrast to the alternatives of killing 'en pleine connaissance de cause' (p. 1196) or in 'une minute d'égarement'. Moreover, one can see how private individuals, 'des hommes qui changent de linge' (p. 1203), who might be bald or wear starched shirts, agree to transform themselves into representatives of the public order who decree in the name of the 'peuple français (ou allemand ou chinois)' (p. 1203) that a man shall be beheaded on the 'place publique' (p. 1201). Again, quite explicitly, the stories end in death: the death of the Arab leading, presumably, to Meursault's. Yet the underlying concern is not quite so apparent. Meursault's meditation in the final chapter makes manifest that it is not 'just' death that is at issue: 'd'être abattu au coin d'une rue, en pleine course, et d'une balle à la volée' (pp. 1202–3) *'being cut down on some street corner, as you ran like mad, by a random bullet'* (p. 109); is not only not a problem; it is the kind of end one might hope for. The problem lies in the coming to terms with approaching death, considered from the double angle of the man in the condemned cell and of the setting in motion of the death machinery.

The concluding chapter of the novel begins with Meursault considering the second, public angle, and significantly, he starts from stories. There are 'récits d'exécution'; in specialised works which would give more details than the newspaper accounts one might perhaps find examples of the other side: 'des récits d'évasion' (p. 1202). But despite Meursault's projects of law reform, his imagined modes of execution which would give even the slightest chance of escape to the 'patient', he has to conclude that there is no way of evading 'la mécanique'. This seems to designate primarily the process set in motion by the death sentence, but which perhaps also refers to the precision mechanism of the guillotine, image and culmination of that process.

Meursault then reviews his own responses, and these have no more satisfactory outcome: his thoughts can only oscillate between 'l'aube' (dawn) and 'le pourvoi' (the appeal), and the only possibility of escape lies in the unlikely success of the latter. The reasons for his failure are inscribed, however, in the very process of his reflection. Thought simply retraces the 'chemins familiers' marked out by 'la mécanique'. More lucid and resilient a narrator than either Salamano or Raymond, Meursault realises that one is seemingly obliged to 'collaborer moralement' (p. 1204), but still he endeavours to 'détourner le cours de [ses] pensées' (p. 1205), to avoid becoming an accomplice in the mechanism which will destroy him, in the manner of Salamano emerging into the street dead on time, or of Raymond and his bloody encounters. Again, in vain: 'l'aube ou mon pourvoi étaient là' (p. 1205).

In fact Meursault has forgotten his own story, abandoned long before in the office of the examining magistrate by its weary narrator. The measure of his acceptance of, and collusion in, the stories told about him is given by the development of his reflective competence as narrator, following the fatal shot. He is able to separate out the different stages in his experience since the murder: 'c'est là ... que tout a commencé' (p. 1168); 'c'est à partir de ce moment qu'ont commencé les choses dont je n'ai jamais aimé parler' (p. 1180). '*And the things I've never liked talking about began*' (p. 76). It was the prosecution and defence who transformed and deformed his *je* and abstracted him from his *affaire*, but Meursault comes to view his own case with the same detachment with which he listened to Raymond's story, finding the pleadings now interesting, now tedious. All this while his own story is not entirely written off, and occasionally reminders of the continuing monologue rise to the surface of the narrative: 'j'ai entendu distinctement le son de ma voix ... j'ai compris que pendant tout ce temps j'avais parlé seul' (p. 1183). '*I distinctly heard the sound of my own voice ... I realized that all that time I had been talking to myself*' (p. 81). But Meursault is now able to censure his own speech, and his impulse to interrupt the court proceedings and say 'j'ai quelque chose à dire' is immediately corrected: 'réflexion faite, je n'avais rien à dire' (p. 1195).

Fortunately, at this *impasse* of reflection, the chaplain enters. He employs the same device as has been used against Meursault ever since his entry into prison: the non-acceptance of his story and its replacement by a story about him. This proposed, revised version is not one which appeals to Meursault: 'ce dont il me parlait ne m'intéressait pas' (p. 1207), but it affects him once its parameters become clear. It is a story in which Meursault is 'le fils', the chaplain 'le père', and it would only be a matter of time before another father figure would be introduced. And Meursault does not let the story get that far. Suddenly he remakes contact with the old story, and all its characters crowd into the cell. He rediscovers himself as teller of that story, whose expression, in comparison with that of the legal records, may be impoverished and repetitive: 'j'avais eu raison, j'avais encore raison, j'avais toujours raison' (p. 1220), but it is his own. Sticking to his own story will not make the stories about him redundant, but they will no longer be definitive, only partial. 'La mécanique' still operates, but one need no longer engage with it.

Meursault will be remembered through story, like his father before him: 'une histoire que maman me racontait à propos de mon père ... Tout ce que je connaissais de précis sur cet homme, c'était peut-être ce que m'en disait alors maman' (p. 1203). '*a story Maman used to tell me about my father ... Maybe the only thing I did know about the man was the story Maman would tell me*' (p. 110). Ironically, the story with which Meursault re-engages now also goes back to, and includes, his mother. If he had to start all over again, echoing his mother's wish, it would be in the terms with which he began. It is always 'aujourd'hui'.

Notes

1. He said he'd been in a fight with some guy who was trying to start trouble (Ward, p. 28). *Théâtre, récits, nouvelles* (Paris, Gallimard, Bibliothèque de la Pléïade, 1962), p. 1145. Future references are to this edition. Translations are from *The Stranger*, Matthew Ward (trans.) (New York: Alfred A. Knopf, 1988).

2. The narration of the evening Meursault and Raymond spend together is marked by blood. Raymond describes how after he had punched his mistress's brother the latter 'avait la figure en sang' (p. 1146) and how he had beaten the girl herself 'jusqu' au sang' (p. 1147). He envelops his – presumably bleeding – right hand in a bandage, and he and Meursault consume blood-sausage together. These elements constitute, I think, sufficient evidence for considering the two men as 'frères du même sang', especially since in writing the letter Meursault substitutes himself for Raymond.

3. *Théâtre, récits, nouvelles*, p. 1262. Translation by Adele King.

4. I think it is important that, during the trial, Meursault should use these
    terms and not the potentially more personal *histoire*, which he jettisons,
    like the story itself, in the examining magistrate's office. During the
    trial period, the term *histoire* is used by others to refer to Meursault's
    'case'; in the narrative, as we have seen, it refers to the stories of
    Raymond and of the Czech; it is used by the narratively scrupulous
    Meursault to isolate one – for him discrete – element in a more general
    structure: 'cette histoire n'avait pas de rapport avec mon affaire'; and
    his reference to 'l'histoire du café au lait et celle de la cigarette'
    (p. 1189).

12

Narrative Desire in
L'Etranger
Gilbert D. Chaitin

Le présent et la succession des présents devant une âme sans cesse consciente, c'est l'idéal de l'homme absurd. (*Le Mythe de Sisyphe, Essais*, p. 145.)

The present moment and the succession of present moments confronting a mind that always remains conscious, that is the ideal of the absurd man.

Since its inception in the seventeenth century, the modern French novel has repeatedly struggled to develop the implications of the primal scene performed in *La Princesse de Clèves*, the confession of an illicit desire.[1] In that novel as in many others, the confession plays a pivotal role in an otherwise third person narrative. In quite a few cases, such as *Manon Lescaut* or *Adolphe*, the confession expands so forcefully that it occupies almost the complete space of narration, compressing alternative modes – letters, commentaries, other narratives – into the frame of the story, or squeezing them out of existence entirely. By its narrative form, *L'Etranger* would seem to fall into the last category, but consideration of its structure brings to light its relation to another variety of Romantic novels, those such as *Le Rouge et le noir*, *Notre-Dame de Paris*, or *Mauprat*, in which the confession emerges in the context of a criminal trial. This variety is not restricted to France or to Romanticism, however, and Camus was an acute and passionate reader of Dostoyevsky's *Crime and Punishment* and *The Brothers Karamazov*, and of Kafka's *The Trial*. Just recently, another 'source' has been uncovered, a short novel called *Die Ursache* (*The Cause*) published by the German author Leonhard Frank in 1915 and translated into French in the 1920s (see Grimm, 1986).

The peculiar strength of the trial novel is of course its ability to present questions of guilt and innocence, of desire and law, of truth

125

and justice, in heightened form. In these novels we soon understand that the protagonist is not on trial for the commission of a
specific act but for her entire life, no doubt because her life is
literally at stake in a procedure whose outcome may be the death
penalty. More often than not, at least in works tributary to
Romanticism, the conviction of the hero becomes the implicit
condemnation of society with its legal and political system, or even
a source of doubt about the very possibility of justice.

Trial novels generally share with confessional novels another
attribute, the use of retrospective narration in which the hero reviews,
evaluates and interprets his past life from the new-found perspective attained through some radical change in circumstances –
the death of the loved woman in *Manon Lescaut* or *Adolphe*, Marcel's
discovery of his vocation, the need to testify or to confront death in
trial novels. However painful the experiences related, the location
of the moment of narration beyond the boundaries of those events
has the reassuring effect of removing the narrator – and reader –
from the flux of time.

By incorporating the trial into the first person narrative of
L'Etranger, Camus produced a new configuration of the relation
between confession and desire, one which has intrigued and
puzzled readers from the time of its publication. Starting with
Sartre, critics have taken the bipartite structure of the novel as the
point of departure for their explanations of its meaning. According
to these views, in Part 1 Meursault lives on the level of 'immediate
experience', in an unthinking or pre-reflective state. For humanist
critics who, wittingly or unwittingly, parrot the attitudes of the
prosecutor in the novel, this state is pre-human, even animalistic
(Solomon). For others, the claim to portray such a state is evidence
of Camus's romantic belief in self-presence (Eisenzweig), or of
artistic cheating in that language cannot be divested of the meanings
it inevitably attaches to experience (Sartre). During the course of
Part 2 Meursault supposedly becomes more and more reflective, a
condition which culminates in the paroxysm of self-awareness he
attains in and just after his dispute with the prison chaplain. In this
part, Meursault increasingly remembers, summarises, synthesises,
abstracts and judges; thus he connects one thing to another in a
meaningful web of interpretation which makes it possible for him
to experience and understand higher thoughts and emotions.

A corollary to this theory holds that in each part of the book the
narrator uses a distinctive style, the one geared toward sensation

and immediacy, the other toward emotion and self-consciousness. The narrator's use of the present tense and the *passé composé* (perfect tense) supports the impression of immediacy, of a lack of distance between the narrator and the events he recounts. If Part 1 contains many instances of the present tense and of temporal shifters – 'today', 'now', 'yesterday', 'tomorrow' – while in Part 2 their use is restricted almost completely to the final chapter, that is because the day-by-day presentation of the first part is reduplicated by the retrospective narrative of the second, which constitutes a kind of interpretation of the earlier events and experiences, filling in the gaps between them.

One problem with this sort of theory is that is fails to account for the fact that, in Part 2, Meursault never thinks about his crime except when being interrogated by officers of the court, or when confronting reactions of the persons in the courtroom. His mind is preoccupied with thoughts about his friends, his lover, life, and his own death. Only the court insists on formulating a coherent reconstruction of the past, of the circumstances leading to and explaining the murder. One way of reconciling this disparity is to conclude that the object of inquiry is not the crime, but the question of who Meursault is. On this account, the hero's view of himself is totally at odds with that provided by the court, and the basic thrust of Part 2 is an ironic rejection of the humanist style of retrospective definition and explanation (Fitch, 1982).

A more serious flaw in these theories is the patent falsity of the claim that in the first part, the protagonist lives only on the level of sensation and immediate experience. Recent critics have shown that Meursault is interested in questions of meaning. Merad lists over one hundred uses of verbs of thought such as 'penser', 'trouver', 'sentir', 'avoir 1' impression' (p. 55), although he does not specify in which part of the novel these examples occur. Showalter explicitly points out that, from the start Meursault has 'problems of interpretation', worrying about what his boss, or the people at the old-age home expect of him (p. 99); and the critic concludes that the 'desire for meaning is implicit in many of Meursault's remarks' (p. 101). In fact, careful scrutiny of the text shows that, from the very first paragraph, Meursault uses expressions of thought and interpretation: 'cela ne veut rien dire', 'peut-être', 'ainsi', 'il n'avait pas l'air content', 'j'ai pensé', 'en somme', 'sans doute', 'parce que', 'à cause de', all occur on the first page (*TRN*, p. 1127). The first metaphor of the novel appears as early as page three: 'On aurait dit d'un jacassement assourdi de perruches.' Such expressions are rampant not only in the narrative of the wake and funeral in the first chapter, but throughout Part 1. The first few pages of Chapter 2, for instance, provide the following terms: 'j'ai compris pourquoi', 'pour ainsi dire', 'tout naturellement', '[il] avait l'air mécontent', '[il] a pensé', 'bien entendu', 'ma faute', 'comprendre', 'j'ai pensé', 'je crois', 'parce que', 'j'ai trouvé', 'comme une promesse de pluie' (pp. 1137–38).

Part 1 does not lack synthesising, summarising, or retrospective passages either. During the funeral procession: 'Tout cela, le soleil, l'odeur . . . , celle . . . , et celle . . . , la fatigue . . . me troublait le regard et les idées' (p. 1134). 'J'ai encore gardé quelques images de cette journée: par exemple' (p. 1135). The retrospective summary of Salamano and his dog:

> Il y a huit ans qu'on les voit ensemble . . . A force de vivre avec lui . . . le vieux Salamano a fini par lui resembler . . . Deux fois par jour . . . le vieux mène son chien promener. Depuis huit ans, ils n'ont pas changé d'itinéraire. On peut les voir . . . Il bat son chien alors et il l'insulte . . . C'est ainsi tous les jours (p. 1142).

> *The two of them have been inseparable for eight years . . . After living together for so long, the two them alone in one tiny room, they've ended up looking like each other . . . Twice a day . . . the old man takes the dog out for a walk. They haven't changed their route in eight years. You can see them . . . Then he beats the dog and swears at it . . . it's the same thing every day.*

The introductory portrait of Raymond is vaguer and more concise, but it follows the same general format.

Perhaps Champigny summed it up best in his brilliant study, *Sur un héros païen*: 'Meursault présente les phénomènes comme ils lui sont apparus, c'est-à-dire en faisant une part implicite ou explicite à sa réaction' (p. 83). (*Meursault presents phenomena the way they appeared to him, that is, with implicit or explicit reference to, his reactions.*) Meursault does include his subjective reactions to the events of his life; he simply refuses to add on to the phenomena any broad meanings not justified by the facts of his experience. Unfortunately, Champigny goes on to repeat the notion that the narrator's style denotes an avoidance of connections among those facts: 'Les phénomènes, les phrases se succèdent, mais ne se lient pas, ne s'organisent pas. La subordination et même la coordination sont évitées, sauf dans le cas de brefs raisonnements' (p. 87). (*Phenomena and sentences come one after another, but they are not linked together, they are not organized. Subordination and even coordination are avoided except for brief argumentative passages.*) Once again, simple inspection proves the incorrectness of this assertion. The first sentence of Chapter 2 (p. 1136) includes a participial phrase, a main clause, a noun clause, an adverbial clause, and a second independent clause in apposition. The second (pp. 1136–7) has two coordinate clauses joined by the conjunction 'but', and a participial phrase. It is true that these sentences form part of a 'brief argument'; but even in the next paragraph, when Meursault is describing his visit to the port, the first sentence has a subordinate clause with 'because', and the second contains two subordinate clauses and two coordinate clauses, each introduced with its conjunction. In fact, of the thirty-two sentences in this paragraph, only ten have a single main clause with no coordinate or subordinate clauses.

How then is it possible for these acute readers to overlook such obvious evidence? In part, no doubt, they are striving to account for the effect of strangeness Meursault's narration produces in its readers, especially those accustomed to the introspective style of practitioners of the so-called psychological novel like Proust. In part they are misled by the desire to substantiate their main theses about the meaning of the novel. But some of the burden must fall on the legitimate attempt to explain the overall development of the novel culminating in Meursault's 'prise de conscience', or what Champigny labels 'le moment extatique où cesse la scission entre présent et passé' (p. 149). (*The moment of* extasis *when the split between past and present is abolished.*) In the face of his imminent death, Meursault has realised that 'nothing has any importance', that only life itself has value. Having noticed the retrospective force of many of the remarks couched in the present tense in Part 1, and wanting to assign full weight to the hero's moment of truth at the end of the novel, Champigny and the Fitch of *Narrateur et Narration* come to the conclusion that the entire narrative is effected from the vantage point of Meursault's new understanding of his life. Specifically, it is the latter's willingness to 'relive his life' which the critics take to be the key to understanding the narrative stance and perspective of the whole novel, Meursault's desire to confess.

In a sense, then, the whole novel would be the story of the formation of Meursault's narrative desire, the development of his literary vocation. He uses the present tense in the first three chapters, for the most part, in order to intensify the sense of presence implied in the notion of 'reliving', as when he announces, 'Aujourd'hui, maman est morte'; or 'c'est aujourd'hui samedi'. The real present of the narration, however, appears only in those retrospective judgements he occasionally makes contrasting his thoughts at the time events transpired to the opinions he holds 'now', at the time of writing while in prison awaiting the guillotine. At the wake, for instance, as the old people file into the room:

> Lorsqu'ils se sont assis, la plupart m'ont regardé et ont hoché la tête avec gêne ... sans que je puisse savoir s'ils me saluaient ou s'il s'agissait d'un tic. *Je crois plutôt* qu'ils me saluaient.

> *When they'd sat down, most of them looked at me and nodded awkwardly ... I couldn't tell if they were greeting me or if it was just a nervous tic.* I think *they were greeting me.*

And a few moments later:

> J'avais même l'impression que cette morte ... ne signifiait rien à leurs yeux. *Mais je crois maintenant* que c'était une impression fausse (p. 1130).

> *I even had the impression that the dead woman ... didn't mean anything to them.* But I think *now that was a false impression (p. 11).*

Here again, the simple textual evidence contradicts the claim that there are two present tenses in the narrative, that of the (intensified) time of experience, and that of the time of writing. The retrospective presentation of Salamano and his dog in Chapter 3, clearly has nothing to do with heightening the intensity of an experience, nor is it a matter of reliving an experience as completed and thus closed, since this account describes a series of events that is repeated every day and continues into an indeterminate future. Nor can the present tense be attributed to the time of writing while in prison, for at that time, as Meursault's subsequent narration explains, Salamano's dog had run away. Therefore, when the text says: 'Deux fois par jour ... le vieux mène son chien promener. Depuis huit ans, ils n'ont pas changé d'itinéraire. On peut les voir.' '*Twice a day ... the old man takes the dog out for a walk. They haven't changed their route in eight years. You can see them.*' (p. 20) and so on, the time designated by the present must be prior to the end of Chapter 4, before the murder and Meursault's imprisonment. Moreover, this is not an isolated occurrence; Meursault often gives retrospective accounts or judgements whose present tense refers to a time well before his final stay in prison.

Of course, both Fitch (1972, p. 119) and Champigny (1959, p. 197) readily acknowledge that there are defects in their thesis, but from these deficiencies they merely draw the conclusion that the point of view of Meursault's narration is inconsistent. What they do not do is renounce the claim that his narrative is primarily retrospective throughout the novel, and that the specific character of this retrospection results from Meursault's final discovery. And this view still predominates among the critics. Thus Soelberg, who recognises that Meursault 'thinks' in Part 1 and that the time referred to by the present tense varies, nevertheless strives to explain these narrative features on the assumption that Meursault recounts the entire novel while in prison, after his appeal has been refused. He argues that the interview with the chaplain must have taken place in Meursault's first cell, whereas the narrator relates the story of the visit while in the second cell, at a later time. In order to support his contention, he adduces three pieces of textual data from the last chapter: first, Meursault states that he will see the chaplain soon (p. 1200), an obvious reference to the guillotine and thus a strong indication that Meursault already knows that his appeal has been refused; second, the chaplain tells him at the beginning of his visit that he knows nothing about the outcome of the appeal (p. 1205); third, during his confrontation with the chaplain, the hero declares that he has been looking at the prison walls for months (p. 1207), an impossibility if it were in the second cell.

As ingenious as this theory is, it does not seem to be the most plausible explanation of the textual facts. At the beginning of the last chapter, Meursault informs us that, in his new cell, 'lorsque je suis allongé, je vois le ciel et je ne vois que lui' (1200), and that he spends his days there lying on his back, looking at the sky and thinking about the guillotine, dawn, and his appeal. The description of the original cell indicates that he could see the sky only by standing up; 'La prison était en haut de la ville et, par une petite fenêtre, je pouvais voir la mer. C'est un jour que j'étais agrippé aux barreaux, mon visage tendu vers la lumière ....' (p. 1175). *'The prison was on the heights above the town, and through a small window I could see the sea. One day as I was gripping the bars, my face straining toward the light ...'* (p. 73). Now, Meursault specifically explains that, on the evening of the chaplain's unwanted intrusion: 'J'étais étendu et je devinais l'approche du soir d'été à une certaine blondeur du *ciel'* (p. 1204). *'I was lying down, and I could tell from the golden glow in the sky that evening was coming on'* (p. 115). It is difficult to imagine why he would stress precisely the two details that establish a continuity with the description at the beginning of the chapter, were it not in order to indicate that he has now returned to that point of departure, the present tense of the opening sentences: 'Pour la troisième fois, j'ai refusé de recevoir l'aumônier. Je n'ai rien à lui dire, je n'ai pas envie de parler, je le verrai bien assez tôt' (p. 1200). *'For the third time I've refused to see the chaplain. I don't have anything to say to him; I don't feel like talking, and I'll be seeing him soon enough as it is'* (p. 108). Indeed, the introduction that immediately precedes the visit echoes this passage:

C'est à un semblable moment que j'ai refusé une fois de plus de recevoir l'aumônier. J'étais étendu et je devinais l'approche du soir d'été à une certaine blondeur du ciel. Je venais de rejeter mon pourvoi et je pouvais sentir les ondes de mon sang circuler régulièrement en moi. Je n'avais pas besoin de voir l'aumônier. (p. 1204)

It was at one such moment that I once again refused to see the chaplain. I was lying down, and I could tell from the golden glow in the sky that evening was coming on. I had just denied my appeal and I could feel the steady pulse of my blood circulating inside me. I didn't need to see the chaplain. (p. 115)

As for Meursault's alleged knowledge that his appeal has been denied, despite the chaplain's disclaimer at the beginning of their meeting, Meursault already knows he will be executed *immediately after the confrontation.* He tells us that he must have fallen asleep after the priest's departure, that he wakes up that same night, and, at that time: 'il me restait à souhaiter qu'il y ait beaucoup de spectateurs le jour de mon exécution.' (p. 1210). *'I had only to wish that there be a large crowd of spectators the day of my execution and that they greet me with cries of hate'* (p. 123).

One can then explain the textual facts in the way I imagine readers have always done: whether Camus made a mistake or was not concerned with supplying a realistic account of the moment when Meursault was informed that his appeal was rejected, the crucial point is that the hero has come to accept his own death before the chaplain's third visit; when Meursault insists that he's been contemplating 'ces murailles' for months, he refers to the walls of the prison in general, not to those of this or that particular cell.

The phenomenon Soelberg has noticed and rightly emphasised is slightly different from what he supposes it to be. Dazzled like his predecessors by the brilliance of the retrospective hypothesis, he seems convinced that there can only be two basic frameworks for Meursault's uses of the present tense, two static states joined and separated by the watershed experience of his revelation that 'nothing has any importance'. But what happens in the last chapter of the novel is that *the time denoted by the present tense, the time of narration, changes in the middle of the chapter*. When Chapter 5 begins, the time of narration is the moment before the chaplain's visit, just after Meursault declines to see him; when Meursault describes that same visit, imposed upon him despite his wishes, the narrative present is some time afterwards, that night perhaps or a few days later.

The narrative technique employed here is no different from that of the first chapter of the novel; I would even argue that it is an exact parallel to what occurs there. No reader can forget that the narrative begins with the present tense signifying the day Meursault receives the telegram informing him of his mother's death. Yet his conversation with his boss that same day, requesting permission to take two days off, is already recounted *half in the present (and future) tense (s) and half in the past*. 'J'ai demandé'; 'il n'avait pas l'air'; 'je lui ai dit'; and so on. 'Il le fera ... après-demain'; 'il me verra'. 'Pour le moment, c'est'; 'ce sera'; 'tout aura revêtu' (p. 1125). And his departure for the old-people's home, as well as the subsequent wake and funeral, are related in past tenses. The time of narration must therefore have moved forward, even though, as in the last chapter, there is nothing in the text to signal this change.

The divergence between the time of narration and the time of the events narrated is no doubt significant, but nowhere does the retrospective space span the entire distance from the time of Meursault's revelation to that of his past life. Nor does the time of narration ever cease its relentless advance toward its inevitable limit. In truth, *L'Etranger* follows the *journal* (diary) format from start to finish.[3]

Since the publication of the novel many readers have challenged this view and many others have simply acted on the premise that at least the second part consists of retrospective narration, but neither the objections nor the assumption, I think, hold water. When Champigny argues, for instance, that the final page of the novel marks the moment of *extasis* when the split between past and present is abolished, he ignores the fact that Meursault chooses to narrate that final experience in the past tense. Why not recount it in the present, unless he wanted to retain the separation between the time of narration and that of the narrated even in this (non-) final moment? Indeed, he does employ the present tense just once in this passage, in order to introduce the account of his 'awakening': 'Je crois que j'ai dormi parce que je me suis réveillé avec des étoiles sur le visage' (p. 1209). '[I think] I must have fallen asleep, because I woke up with the stars in my face' (p. 122). But the present tense here has precisely the effect of emphasising the distance between narrator and narrated, not of closing the gap. Thus, unlike in Proust, there is never a time, even as an ideal virtuality, when past and present coincide.

Many critics have pointed to the type of example first isolated by Fitch, in which the present tense is used to make retrospective judgements. We have already shown that the present time of several of these retrospective passages cannot possibly be the last days of Meursault's imprisonment (e.g. Salamano and his dog). Moreover, even those passages in which the present tense marks a change in Meursault's judgement about an event, as when he decides that his dead mother really did have significance for the people gathered at her wake, can be plausibly taken to refer to the 'near future', a day or two after the event rather than a full year later.[4]

A more compelling argument has focused on the alleged disparity in narrative styles between the two parts of the novel, the first progressing linearly, on the principle of chronology, the second summarising whole series of events organised according to theme (Noyer-Weidner, 1980). In reality, Meursault often utilises summaries organised on a thematic basis in Part 1 as well. Yet there is a noteworthy, albeit more subtle, difference between the two parts on this score. The summaries in the first part either concern Meursault but cover a brief duration, or involve others and span a lengthy period of time; whereas, in Part 2, each chapter consists of Meursault's synthesis of his own experiences while in prison – interrogations (1), getting used to being a prisoner (2), the trial (3 and 4), thinking about death (5). Thus, although his general mental capacity has not changed significantly while in prison, he has developed a new willingness to group together long segments from his own life.

Nevertheless, it is clear that, even in these synthesising retro-spectives, the time of the events narrated does not reach the last days of his imprisonment until the last chapter. It is therefore impossible to ascertain the precise time of narration here as in the very first chapters of the book. In Chapter 2 of Part 2, for instance, Meursault informs us, in the present tense: 'Je peux dire que, dans les derniers mois, je dormais de seize à dix-huit heures par jour' (p. 1180). *'In fact, during the last few months I've been sleeping sixteen to eighteen hours a day' (p. 79).* The temptation to read this as a statement about his last days in prison must give way before the assertion in Chapter 5 that, while awaiting the outcome of his appeal, he slept very little during the day and not at all at night (p. 1203). The 'last months' in question therefore probably designate the end of the period covered in Chapter 2, the first five months of his stay. At most, they stretch to the moment when the succeeding chapter resumes the narrative, eleven months after his arrest (Viggiani, p. 867). In short, this chapter could well have been composed before the trial; it can be read as coming from a temporal perspective in the relatively 'near future' of a few months.

Of course, this sort of evidence does not constitute definitive proof that the time of narration for Part 2 is not fixed at the time of Meursault's 'prise de conscience'. If there were any such evidence to be found in the novel, someone would have long since produced it and put an end to the controversy. What it does show is that there is nothing in the novel to support the claim that the time of narration is so fixed, and that all the textual data are compatible with the thesis that the journal style is employed from beginning to end of the novel. The impression that Part 2 is more retrospective than Part 1 derives not from any fundamental change in style or mentality, but from the omission of temporal shifters and the relative paucity of uses of the present tense. These phenomena prevail in the text as early as Chapter 5 of Part 1, well before murder or the imprisonment (Pariente, 1968, p. 59); and, as we have seen, they govern most portions of every chapter in the novel, starting with the first.

The text does contain one very powerful indication that Meursault does not narrate his story retrospectively from a single vantage point just before his death. In the heat of his confrontation with the priest, the latter asks him to explain his conception of the afterlife: 'Alors, je lui ai crié: *"Une vie où je pourrais me souvenir de celle-ci"*, et aussitôt je lui ai dit que j'en avais assez' (p. 1208). *'Then I shouted at* him, *"One where I could remember this life!" and that's when I told him I'd had enough'* (p. 120). To Meursault, the hope for an afterlife is therefore equivalent to the desire to become a retrospective narrator, one who thinks back on his past life from the vantage point of total self-consciousness. But he violently rejects this desire as an idle wish: 'cela [the wish for an afterlife] n'avait pas plus d'importance que de souhaiter d'être riche, de nager très vite ou d'avoir une bouche mieux faite' (p. 1207). *'It [the wish for an afterlife] didn't mean any more than wishing to be rich, to be able to swim faster, or to have a more nicely shaped mouth'* (pp. 119–20).

In 'La création absurde', Camus establishes a specific link between conceptions of an afterlife, retrospection, and narration. In an effort to distance himself from Dostoievsky, one of the writers he admired most at this period, he analyses the ending of a major intertext for *L'Etranger, The Brothers Karamazov*. The boys ask Alyosha if they will meet after death; he replies: 'Certes, nous nous reverrons, nous nous *raconterons* joyeusement tout ce qui s'est passé' (*Essais*, p. 186). (*'Certainly, we shall see one another again, we shall joyfully tell one another everything that has happened'* (O'Brien, 1969, p. 110).) For Camus, it is precisely this promise of an afterlife makes of Dostoievsky an existential rather than an absurd novelist: 'ce qui contredit l'absurde dans cette oeuvre, ce n'est pas son caractère chrétien, c'est l'annonce qu'elle fait de la vie future' (*Essais*, p. 188). (*'What contradicts the absurd in that work is not its Christian character, but rather its announcing a future life'* (O'Brien, 1969, p. 112).)

In the novel, only the prosecutor and the defence attorney are guilty of practicing the retrospective narration so often attributed to Meursault. As both Champigny and the Fitch of *The Narcissistic Text* admirably demonstrate, *L'Etranger* puts the court on trial for indulging in the 'theatre' of Christian-humanist reinterpretation. But the impact of *L'Etranger*, today as well as a half-century ago, stems as much from its unflinching display of the inexorability of the temporal process as it does from its Nietzschean repudiation of the violence of interpretation. From beginning to end, the narrator is plunged into a present which sweeps him irrevocably onward in the flow of time. The confessional form prevents the narrator from effecting closure, when the event to be recounted is his own death.

If Meursault does not tell his story from a fixed point, then that story cannot possibly recount the process of the development of his narrative desire. The impetus to narrate does not arise at the conclusion of the narrative; there from the start, it makes possible the birth of the subject[5] which constitutes its end point. It is the very process of narration which allows Meursault to come to terms with his mother's death, by helping him to accept the necessity of his own death. Far from finding himself and his vocation in a final revelation like the Proustian hero, Meursault comes to recognise that he must lose himself. His 'prise de conscience' consists of the rejection of self-consciousness. He can mourn the loss of his mother only when he has mourned his own.

Like a slap in the face, the experience of this realisation strikes readers of *L'Etranger* today as it did fifty years ago.

Notes

1. This is the first of two articles on confession and desire in *L'Etranger*. References to Camus's works are to the edition listed in the Works cited.
2. Translations are from *The Stranger*, Matthew Ward (trans.) (1988).
3. My thesis is of course similar to those of Viggiani (1956) and Pariente (1968), and to the more recent argument of Magyar (1985). Unfortunately, space is lacking here to discuss fully the many points of agreement and disagreement among us. Suffice it to say that I mean by 'journal format' not a literal diary but a stream of consciousness narration that constantly moves forward in time, but which is not constrained by a realist or formalist concern with justifying when and how the narrator supposedly spoke, or wrote down, his narrative.
4. I have looked at all examples of retrospective judgements made in the present tense and can find none that exclude reading them as referring to a near future.
5. See Eisenzweig, 1983, pp. 37, 48–9. However, Eisenzweig uses this Lacanian term in a very different sense from that of Lacan. It is the latter meaning that I will develop in the second article of this study.

Works Cited

Camus, Albert, *Essais* (Paris: Gallimard, Bibliothèque de la Pléiade, 1967).

Camus, Albert, *The Myth of Sisyphus and other Essays*, Justin O'Brien (trans.) (New York: Knopf, 1969).

Camus, Albert, *The Stranger*, Matthew Ward (trans.) (New York: Knopf, 1988).

Camus, Albert, *Théâtre, récits, nouvelles* (Paris: Gallimard, Bibliothèque de la Pléiade, 1965).

Champigny, Robert, *Sur un héros païen* (Paris: Gallimard, 1959).

Eisenzweig, Uri, *Les Jeux de l'écriture dans 'L'Etranger' de Camus* (Paris: Lettres Modernes, 1983).

Fitch, Brian T., *'L'Etranger' d'Albert Camus: un texte, ses lecteurs, leurs lectures, étude méthodologique* (Paris: Larousse, 1972).

Fitch, Brian T., *The Narcissistic Text: A Reading of Camus's Fiction* (Toronto: Toronto University Press, 1982).

Fitch, Brian T., *Narrateur et narration dans 'L'Etranger' de Camus* (Paris; Lettres Modernes, 1960).

Frank, Leonhard, *Die Ursache. Gesammelte Werke*, vol. 3 (Berlin: Aufbau-Verlag, 1957) pp. 7–118.

Grimm, Reinhold. 'Die Deutsche "Ursache" des Camus'schen "Frem-den", *Jahrbuch der Deutschen Schillergesellschaft*, vol. 30 (1986) pp. 594–639.

Magyar, Miklos, 'Technique narrative dans *L'Etranger* d'Albert Camus', *Acta Litteraria Academiae Scientiarum Hungaricae*, vol. 27 (1985) pp. 61–73.

Merad, Ghani, '*L'Etranger* de Camus vu sous un angle Psychosociologique', *Revue Romane*, vol. 10 (1975) pp. 51–91.

Noyer-Weidner, Alfred, 'Structure et sens de *L'Etranger*', in Raymond Gay-Crosier (ed.) *Albert Camus 1980*: (Gainesville: Florida University Press, 1980), pp. 72–85.

Pariente, Jean-Claude. 'L'Etranger et son double.' *Albert Camus*: 1 (Paris, Minard, Lettres Modernes, 1968) pp. 53–80.

Sartre, Jean-Paul, 'Explication de *L'Etranger*', *Situations I*, (Paris: Gallimard, 1947), pp. 99–121.

Showalter, English Jr '*The Stranger*': *Humanity and the Absurd* (Boston: Twayne Publishers, 1989).

Soelberg, Nils, 'Le Paradoxe du JE-narrateur: Approche narratologique de '*L'Etranger* de Camus'. *Revue Romane* vol. 20 (1985) pp. 68–97.

Solomon, Robert C. '*L'Etranger* and the Truth', *Philosophy and Literature*, vol. 2 (1978) pp. 141–59.

Viggiani, Carl A., 'Camus' L'Etranger', PMLA , vol. 71 (1956) pp. 865–87.

13

The Rhetoric of the Text: Causality, Metaphor, and Irony
Peter Schofer

Vous ne voulez pas? . . . Pourquoi? . . . J'ai dit 'Je ne sais pas.[1]

Meursault explains why he did not want to view his mother's corpse.

J'ai pensé qu'ils allaient aux cinémas du centre. C'était pourquoi ils partaient si tôt et se dépêchaient vers le tram en riant très fort. (p. 1139)

Meursault explains why people in the street were hurrying.

Il m'a semblé que le ciel s'ouvrait sur toute son étendue pour laisser pleuvoir du feu. (p. 1166)

Meursault describes the instant before he killed the Algerian.

Why does he kill? How does he explain it? Those are two questions that the reader is left with upon completing *L'Etranger*. Conventional wisdom explains the book by appealing to the notion of the absurd: we cannot really understand why he kills the Arab, and his manner of telling the story seems only to confirm this explanation. The *Petit Robert* defines the 'absurd' as 'contraire à la raison, au sens commun'. There is little question that Meursault's crime was unreasonable and goes against common sense. He did not know his victim, he was thrust in front of him almost by chance, and he is condemned for the wrong reasons. Yet is it all that absurd? Does not the text reveal something more than a vacuum around such important questions?

A close examination of the rhetoric of the story can dissipate much of the ambiguity surrounding the murder and can answer the two questions above. Words such as 'reason' and 'explain' imply the notion of causality – if we can see chains of cause and effect, we can then understand the event as being 'reasonable'. Although murder in itself is not a reasonable act, if we knew that Meursault hated the Algerian and that the Algerian had threatened him several times, the murder would seem 'reasonable'. It is that series of links which Meursault is incapable of supplying in his narrative and which leads us to seeing his act as 'absurd'.

Yet Meursault is quite capable of observing, understanding, and inferring causes. One of the best examples is the famous scene when Meursault spends a Sunday afternoon, immediately after the funeral, sitting on his balcony and observing activities in the street. Not only does he demonstrate that he has an acute sense of the smallest details, but he also deduces what the people are like, what they are doing, and where they are going.

Of a family man carrying a cane and wearing a bow-tie and boater, Meursault concludes 'j'ai compris pourquoi dans le quartier on disait de lui qu'il était distingué '(p. 1138). In the same passage, he sees people dressed up and running for the tram, concluding that they are going to the movies. The streets are than empty because 'les spectacles étaient partout commencés, je crois' (p. 1139). Later, he explains that the sudden outburst of people on the trams indicates that the soccer game is over. When the films are over, Meursault can even deduce that the spectators, by their forceful gestures, have seen an adventure film. He concludes his observations by noting that 'c'était un dimanche de tiré' (p. 1140). Based on past experience and the habitual activities of a typical Sunday afternoon, Meursault can take pleasure in watching the streets and feel assured that he understands what *other* people are doing. Where there is an action, there is also a cause or motivation.

If he can draw conclusions seated on his balcony, at a distance from the participants, he does not show the same abilities when it comes to his own feelings and emotions. The passage in question ends rather astoundingly when he writes that 'c'était un dimanche de tiré, que maman était maintenant enterrée, que j'allais reprendre mon travail et que, somme toute, il n'y avait rien de changé '(p. 1140). 'It occurred to me that anyway one more Sunday was over, that Maman was buried now, that I was going back to work, and that, really, nothing had changed' (p. 24). His mother's death is absorbed into the routine of weekly life, where his motivations and feelings become part of impersonal actions and activities. One might say that her death has not brought on any effects in his life.

This pattern is obvious throughout the book. Sometimes Meursault does put together cause and effect, but after the fact. On the first page of the book, when he asks his boss for time off, the latter does not seem happy with the request. It is not until the beginning of the following chapter that Meusault understands 'pourquoi le patron avait l'air mécontent quand je lui ai demandé mes deux jours de congé: c'est aujourd'hui samedi ... Mon patron, tout naturellement, a pensé que j'aurais ainsi quatre jours de vacances et cela ne pouvait pas lui faire plaisir' (p. 1136); '*why my boss had seemed annoyed when I asked him for two days off: today is Saturday ... And, naturally, my boss thought about the fact that I'd be getting four days' vacation that way, including Sunday, and he couldn't have been happy about that*' (p. 19). But at other times he has no answer, as when he is asked directly why he does not want to see his mother's body.

At moments when one could expect him to examine motives, he is satisfied with accepting the sequence of events without questioning them. For example, after he learns that Salamano has lost his dog, he goes to his room and hears the old man crying. He writes: 'je ne sais pas pourquoi j'ai pensé à maman. Mais il fallait que je me lève tôt le lendemain (p. 1152). '*For some reason I thought of Maman. But I had to get up early the next morning*' (p. 39). Nowhere does he associate Salamano's loss with his own, nor does he see a causal link between Salamano's tears and his own repressed grief. He does write that he was not hungry and went to bed, but he does not ask himself why he is not hungry.

This same pattern of repression of causal links is clearly established from the moment he learns of his mother's death. One could expect that he would think of his mother while taking the bus to Marengo. Instead, he falls asleep and gives a clear reason: 'Cette hâte, cette course, c'est à cause de tout cela sans doute, ajouté aux cahots, à l'odeur d'essence, à la réverbération de la route et du ciel, que je me suis assoupi' (p. 1126). '*It was probably because of all the rushing around, and on top of that the bumpy ride, the smell of gasoline, and the glare of the sky and the road, that I dozed off*' (p. 4). The accumulation of material causes almost acts as a sort of overkill to suppress any thinking and any introspection. As we will see later in an examination of the funeral procession, observation precludes any reflection about the effects of his mother's death on him directly.

This relative absence of causal links is intimately tied to the narrative style, where Meursault provides sequences of events but no causal links about his personal feelings. The following passage, during the wake, is typical:

> Quand elle est partie, le concierge a parlé: 'Je vais vous laisser seul.' Je ne sais pas quel geste j'ai fait, mais il est resté debout derrière moi. Cette présence dans mon dos me gênait. La pièce était pleine d'une belle lumière de fin d'apres-midi. Deux frelons bourdonnaient contre la verrière. Et je sentais le sommeil me gagner. (p. 1132) *When she'd gone, the caretaker said, 'I'll leave you alone.' I don't know what kind of gesture I made, but he stayed where he was, behind me. Having this presence breathing down my neck was starting to annoy me. The room was filled with beautiful late-afternoon sunlight. Two hornets were buzzing aginst the glass roof. I could feel myself getting sleepy.* (p. 17)

Although he says that the man's presence 'bothers' him, he does not explain why. As in the rest of the text, we are given a series of observations and actions without motivations. And, as in the bus, sleep overtakes him. Thus the scene of the murder is not at all exceptional except that it is a murder, not a narrative of banal events.

Causality does play an important role in the book however, particularly in the second half, which might be labelled 'displaced' or 'misplaced' causality. By its very nature, a trial not only seeks to establish facts, but it also establishes motives. Obviously, it is the function of the prosecutor, not the accused, to ascertain guilt and to assign motives; in other words to find reasons for the crime. As is well known, Meursault is condemned because he did not cry at his mother's funeral: he did not show the proper reaction to her death. According to society's conventions, death should be followed by its 'natural' effect, grieving. On a deeper level, Meursault's inability to grieve indicates that he has no heart, thus explaining his crime. Put another way, a lack of heart leads to the insensitivity toward his mother and towards the murder victim. One can read the second part of the book as a sort of double narrative, where Meursault continues to write directly of events and people, and where we try to figure out why he committed the murder. Specifically, at the trial most of the events from the first part of the book return, but now they are used to illustrate Meursault's heartlessness. Two examples suffice. In the first, the prosecutor summarises Marie's testimony: 'Messieurs les jurés, le lendemain de la mort de sa mère, cet homme prenait des bains, commençait une liaison irrégulière, et allait rire devant un film comique. Je n'ai rien de plus à vous dire' (p. 1190). *'Gentlemen of the jury, the day after his mother's death, this man was out swimming, starting up a dubious liaison, and going to the movies, a comedy, for laughs. I have nothing further to say'* (p. 94).

Meursault would not have seen the events in that light, just as he only understands the following events through others:

Il [le concierge] a dit que je n'avais pas voulu voir maman, que j'avais fumé, que j'avais dormi et que j'avais pris du café au lait. J'ai senti alors quelque chose qui soulevait toute la salle, et, pour la première fois, j'ai compris que j'étais coupable. (p. 1187) *He [the concierge] said I hadn't wanted to see Maman, that I had smoked and slept some, and that I had had some coffee. It was then I felt a stirring go through the room and for the first time I realized that I was guilty.* (p. 90).

It is worth noting that Meursault deduces his guilt from the reaction of the audience, not from the words of the concierge, nor from figuring out what he had actually done. As in the rest of the trial, actions which had been narrated as neutral, unmotivated events are transformed into indices of guilt. There is little question that a trial in which such evidence is admitted is an absurd trial, where reason is deflected into judging acts unrelated to the crime. Because of the way the second part of the novel folds back on the first part and imposes 'reasons' on Meursault's actions, and because of the way Meursault refuses to provide his own justification and motivations, the book apparently can be read in only one of two ways. Either we just accept the narration of sequential events or we throw up our arms and declare that it is all too absurd.

In novels, the 'best read' is perhaps the mystery story, where the reader is presented with a crime and is pushed along in his or her reading to discover who the criminal was, how the crime was committed, what instrument was used, and what the motivation was. A mystery writer teases the reader with false leads and mis-information as the reader seeks to tie up the chain of causal effects before the end of the book. In a good book, the answer does not come before the last page. *L'Etranger* is a mystery book gone askew. The criminal is known, the weapon is known, but motivation has to be contrived. The basics of a crime novel – discovering cause and effect – do not apply to this work.

If readings by causality produce no results, a metaphorical reading of the text can bear fruit. By metaphor, I mean metaphorical relationships, where semantic traits are shared by unlike words.[2] They may be pure metaphors ('My flame') or comparisons, where terms are spelled out ('My love burns like a flame'). Metaphorical relationships can be found in the same sentence, in contiguous sentences, or on the same page. They can also be established between passages separated by many pages.

John Cruickshank has pointed out that the style in *L'Etranger* is very unrhetorical and that there are very few metaphors in the book.[3] We can therefore assume that the presence of metaphors anywhere in the text is significant. The very first sentence, 'Aujourd'hui maman est morte', read in context alerts the reader to a metaphorical reading of the novel. Within the first paragraph, it is clear that the narrative does not capture the immediate present, because the second paragraph switches to the past tense, and the rest of the novel remains for the most part in the past. We are further warned that we should not take the first sentence literally when in the first paragraph the narrator says twice that the death was perhaps 'hier'. Logically we might deduce that the narrator does not know where he is, or we can look on his statement metaphorically: he is writing *as though* he were in the present, and he is reliving the experiences as though they were happening. In a sense, then, he is out of time and can put the events together. If we as readers ask 'Why did he do it?' and 'how does he explain it?', the narrator asks simply 'What happened?'. One thing happened: his mother died, and the memory, as he sits in prison, is as though it were today or yesterday.

The first metaphorical gesture is a subtle indication that under the broken causal strands there lurks a metaphorical reading of the entire novel. This reading has little to do with crimes, morals, or misdirected motives. It sees the novel in light of the first sentence, the death of a mother. As the narrator relives the past as though it were the present, he creates a double text. As we read the text before our eyes, we are asked to perceive the events in light of the mother's death '*today*', as though today were yesterday and yesterday were today. The link between present and past, and between life and death, is metaphor.

Where do we go in the search of concrete metaphors in order to see how the double text is joined? According to Cruickshank,

The very restrained character of Camus' vocabulary in *L'Etranger* leads to another interesting feature of his prose which was first pointed out by W. M. Frohock. There is one particular situation – Meursault's experience just before he shoots the Arab – which is described, not in severe and sober prose, but in a passage packed with metaphorical expressions. (p. 156)

Cruickshank explains this exceptional passage as an economical use of language to create a double purpose:

He [Camus] uses the same set of words both to carry forward the narrative and to convey the psychological reasons for it. The accumulation of metaphors ultimately turns into a clever economy by which he dispenses with the necessity of treating narrative and motivation as two separate operations. He narrates in such a way that the motivation is implied without being explicitly formulated. (p. 157)

Cruickshank argues that the double structure of narration and metaphor can be explained as Meursault's hallucination:

It is at this moment that Meursault suffers the final hallucination, and his mental confusion becomes complete. The reader is encouraged to assume that he mistook the flash of light on the blade for the blade itself. Thus it seems as if Meursault really shot the Arab through an instinct for self-defense, an automatic reflex. (pp. 157–8)

Cruickshank is quite right in seeing the double level of the passage, but by limiting his analysis to the passage itself, he fails to see the power of metaphor which permeates the entire text. At the moment that Meursault confuses the effect (the flash of light) and the cause (the Algerian holding the knife), causality is shattered and metaphor appears out of the rhetorical ruins. A comparison between the scene of the murder and the mother's funeral reveals strong metaphorical relationships. Let us first look at the vocabulary of the murder scene, presented here in a very schematic form and classified according to categories that the metaphors fall into:[4]

le soleil: écrasant . . . se brisaient en morceaux . . . a glissé . . . sous la pluie aveuglante . . . le même éclatement rouge . . . cette ivresse . . .
qu'il me déversait . . . se pressait . . . cymbales.

la chaleur: s'appuyait.
l'air: enflammé.
le ciel: s'ouvrait sur toute son étendue pour laisser pleuvoir du feu.
le rocher: entouré d'un halo.
le couteau: glaive éclatant.
la mer: la poussière.
la journée: avait jeté l'ancre dans un océan de métal bouillant.

While the metaphors are marked by extreme violence, they also represent a radical reversal of the natural order. The sea, which earlier represented a kind of rebirth when Meursault was swimming, is now dust. The sun and the air become driving, blinding rain; the knife itself is transformed into an exploding sword.

All the elements around him – the sun, the sky, the sea, and the rocks – are transformed into metaphors, but the Algerian, his presumed enemy, remains a literal entity, calm and 'content'. In no way, except for the presence of the knife, is he aggressive or actively threatening. If there is an absurdity in the passage itself, it resides in the situation before the killing: Meursault has a pistol and the Algerian has only a knife. It is the Algerian who is being menaced, whereas Meursault feels threatened, not by the Algerian, but by the intense heat and the inhuman sun. Meursault seeks refuge in the cool shadows and the murmur of the spring. He does not seek the Algerian, who is backing up. The Algerian is little more than a barrier to his need to find the shadows.

Since his mother's death, Meursault has encountered no barriers until he finds himself face-to-face with the Algerian. His has been in a flight from death and mourning. Upon his return to Algiers, he found Marie, went swimming with her, made love with her, resumed work, saw friends, etc. Now the order and sequences of everyday life are broken, and he finds himself confronting what he has sought to escape:

C'était le même soleil que le jour où j'avais enterré maman et, comme alors, le front surtout me faisait mal et toutes les veines battaient ensemble sous la peau. A cause de cette brûlure, que je ne pouvais plus supporter, j'ai fait un mouvement en avant. (p. 1166)

The sun was the same as it had been the day I'd buried Maman, and like then, my forehead especially was hurting me, all the veins in it throb-

*bing under the skin. It was this burning, which I couldn't stand any-
more, that made me move forward.* (pp. 58–9)

Meursault clearly establishes a metaphorical relationship between
the scene of the murder and the funeral when he says that it was
the 'même soleil'. One might reply that it is obviously the same sun,
since the earth has only one sun, but he explains that 'like then, my
forehead especially was hurting me'. While he provides a link for
the reader to the passage of the funeral, he also establishes causal
parallels between the two scenes: the sun beats down and gives
him an unbearable headache. In both cases, he moves forward.

Movement becomes a key. With all the differences between the
funeral scene and the murder (the lack of the sea at Marengo, the
prevalence of black, the flat surface), the most important is that of
movement. At the funeral, he was in constant movement as he
walked from the retirement home to the church. Now, he moves
toward the blackness of the shadows. But the two movements are
radically different: in the first scene, he walked toward the church,
where his mother's death would be consecrated by the church, and
where he would be faced with its finality. In the second, he walks
toward the inverse of his mother's funeral, because he must kill in
order to reach the security of the water (the source of life) and the
shadows (the site of repose and the hint of death). In the first case,
movement is like life – we move on. In the second, Meursault
causes death when he can go no further.

If there are differences between the two passages, they remain
tightly woven together, not just by the explicit quotation cited above,
but by the similarity of key descriptive words. Let us look at the
vocabulary to describe nature and Meursault's reaction to it:[5]

le soleil: pesait, débordait, faisait trésaillir, inhumain, déprimant.
le ciel: un éclat.
le front: des gouttes perlaient.
la terre: couleur de sang.
le chapeau: semblait avoir été pétri dans cette boue noire.
la campagne: gorgée de soleil.

As in the scene of the murder, the oppressive heat overwhelms
him: 'me troublait le regard et les idées ... Moi, je sentais le sang
qui me battait aux tempes'. The expressions are highly metaphorical and suggest nature's violent effect on him: the sun 'weighed

down', the sky was a 'flash', the earth takes on the color of blood, the countryside was 'filled'. Unlike his reaction at the murder scene, Meursault states that: 'je ne me souviens de rien'. Thus we are faced with similarities and differences. In the two scenes, the sun beats down so violently that he literally loses his head. At the funeral, there are signs of death everywhere, in the form of blackness – the black hats, the black of the road, and of course the black clothes. It would seem that objects became mud or sticky in the blazing heat. In both scenes, nature is alive and humans act as though they were dead. Meursault acts as though he were dead at the funeral, because on a real level he does not come to terms with death; it remains no more than signs. This realisation only comes to the surface at the instant that he shoots the Algerian, transforming his repressed grief into violence. In one case he forgets (represses), and in the other, he murders an innocent man. Both scenes represent a dead-end or an impasse, as is stated during the funeral, where 'il n'y avait pas d'issue' (p. 1135). The murder provides a double passage out of the sun and also out of the repressive bind, where his grief turns finally to violence.

For the reader, the metaphor of the sun can provide a way out of the impasse created by the movement of repressed grief to the violence of murder. Whereas the midday sun is represented in both passages as inhuman and maddening, on two other occasions, it stands for peace and tranquility. At the beginning of the funeral march, Meursault observes:

A travers les lignes de cyprès qui menaient aux collines près du ciel, cette terre rousse et verte, ces maisons rares et bien dessinées, je comprenais maman. Le soir, dans ce pays, devait être comme une trêve mélancolique. (p. 1133)

Seeing the rows of cypress trees leading up to the hills next to the sky, and the houses standing out here and there against that red and green earth, I was able to understand Maman better. Evenings in that part of the country must have been a kind of sad relief. (p. 15)

The setting sun marks an end to the war of everyday life and provides a respite, a truce. Conventional symbolism associates the setting sun with the approach of death, here that of his mother which Meursault interprets as a peaceful moment. Exactly the same words appear in the final paragraph of the book, where for the first time Meursault brings together his mother's death, his crime, and hiw own death. Appropriately, the passage occurs at night:

Des odeurs de nuit, de terre et de sel rafraîchissaient mes tempes. La merveilleuse paix de cet été endormi entrait en moi comme une marée. Pour la première fois, j'ai pensé à maman. Il m'a semblé que je comprenais pourquoi à la fin d'une vie elle avait pris un «fiancé», pourquoi elle avait joué à recommencer. Là-bas, là-bas aussi, autour de cette asile où des vies s'éteignaient, le soir était comme une trêve mélancolique. Si pres de la mort, maman devait s'y sentir libérée et prête à tout revivre. Personne, personne n'avait le droit de pleurer sur elle. Et moi aussi, je me suis senti prêt à tout revivre. Comme si cette grande colère m'avait purgé du mal, vidé d'espoir, devant cette nuit chargée de signes et d'étoiles, je m'ouvrais pour la première fois à la tendre indifférence du monde. (p. 1209)

Smells of the night, earth, and salt air were cooling my temples. The wondrous peace of that sleeping summer flowed through me like a tide. Then, in the dark hour before dawn, sirens blasted. They were announcing departures for a world that now and forever meant nothing to me. For the first time in a long time I thought about Maman. I felt as if I understood why at the end of her life she had taken a 'fiance', why she had played at beginning again. Even there, in that home where lives were fading out, evening was a kind of wistful respite. So close to death, Maman must have felt free then and ready to live it all again. Nobody, nobody had the right to cry over her. And I felt ready to live it all again too. As if that blind rage had washed me clean, rid me of hope; for the first time, in that night alive with signs and stars, I opened myself to the gentle indifference of the world. (p. 122)

The above passage rewrites the previous ones referred to. The absent sun is replaced by the indirect sensations of smells of the night, the earth, and the sea. Metaphorically, the revitalising sea returns to him as a 'marvelous peace' (not a truce, as before), and enters him like a tide. He is now like his mother, united with her over time and death, and, like his mother, he is free to live again. For the two of them, the world is no longer violent, but rather 'indifférent'. However, Meursault achieves this indifference only because he had become angry with the priest and had purged himself. Significantly absent from this passage is any direct reference to the murder, because the crime now has significance only as part of the progression from negation to reconciliation with his birth and death. Murder stands as an intermediary between repression and acceptance of the void. The crime itself has been transformed into society's battle with Meursault.

If he is reconciled with his mother, he remains nonetheless alone and alienated by the injustices of his trial. To the end he has refrained from pronouncing the word 'amour', and the text ends on its opposite, 'haine'. A Lacanian might well point out that the two words are one. In any case, the unarticulated private love is transformed and deformed into its opposite and directed toward the crowd as it will observe his execution. Hate depends upon love, and love recalls hate.

While metaphor brings meaning out of the absurd, the text leaves open a number of ironies and unanswered questions. The most obvious, which Meursault broaches in his conclusion, is that he could not cry at his mother's funeral, because it would not, according to him, have been appropirate. No one had the right to cry. He could 'understand' his mother, yet he could never express his love directly, and his narration ends on hate. At the same time, the narrative itself is ironical, particularly for a person who relished the sea, sensuality, and the simple moments of life, all signs of a vital life. Ironical, because he learns to live in an enclosed cell, and he starts to live life only when he starts to write of it. Only through writing does he live. Writing brings deliverance where unarticulated love and hate of society have brought disaster. His new life through writing is also ironical because he had such difficulty talking with people. He tells us that he and his mother seldom talked. Now, only through writing can he speak of death and reconciliation.

The above reading of *L'Etranger* is ironical in the larger context of traditional readings of the text which emphasised the philosophical bent in Camus's thinking. To be sure, all texts contain a philosophical reading, but from the beginning to the end, *L'Etranger* is a highly personal confession in which the narrator arrives at self-knowledge while denying the validity of others in society, those Others beyond the Mother. Between birth and death is the Algerian, the Arab, the Other, the murder, and finally the hate of the Others. Toward the end of his life, Meursault notes that his execution will occur at sunrise: 'C'est à l'aube qu'ils venaient, je le savais' (p. 1203). He is secure in his knowledge that he will die when the sun is precariously balanced between black (hate) and light (love and understanding).

Notes

1. Camus, Albert, *Théâtre, récits, nouvelles* (Paris: Gallimard, Bibliothèque de la Pléiade, 1962), p. 1127. All future references to the Pléiade edition of *L'Etranger* will be given in the text unless otherwise indicated. Translations are from *The Stranger*, Matthew Ward (trans.) (New York: Knopf, 1988).
2. For a more detailed explanation, see Peter Schofer and Donald Rice, *Rhetorical Poetics* (Madison: University of Wisconsin Press, 1973), pp. 198–23 and 35 to 55.
3. John Cruickshank, *Albert Camus and the Literature of Revolt* (London: Oxford University Press, 1959), p. 156. All future references will be given in text.
4. All quotations are from pp. 1165–6 of the Pléiade edition.
5. All references are to the Pléiade edition, pp. 1133–5.

14

Mama's Boy: Reading Woman in *L'Etranger*
Vicki Mistacco

In his last interview, when asked what he felt critics had most neglected in his work, Camus replied: 'La part obscure, ce qu'il y a d'aveugle et d'instinctif en moi.'[1] Many have since sought to approach this dark, enigmatic side from the perspective of psychoanalysis, emphasising, as Freudian and Lacanian orthodoxy requires, the oedipal moment, and in so doing repressing or devaluing the maternal bond, giving primacy to the phallus and the threat of castration. To my knowledge, however, no sustained effort has been made to view Camus's writing from the perspective of psychoanalytic *feminism*, stressing rather the importance of the *pre-oedipal* stage in which the primary figure is not the father but the *mother* and the primary relationship is a dual not triangular one, between mother and child.[2] Feminist critics have most often adopted this approach to study the mother/*daughter* dyad in *women* writers. Shifting the context, I propose here to effect a kind of 'naive' reading, to 'overread' Camus, as if he were a woman writer, for traces of the relationship between the feminine and text production, bracketing psychoanalytic orthodoxy to allow the 'underread',[3] the feminine maternal, to emerge from the shadows of critical repression and be seen in Meursault's revolt in *L'Etranger*, the text' ambiguities, and the author's concept of the Absurd. By referring positively to Meursault as a 'mama's boy', I am drawing upon the hero's infantile vocabulary to suggest the transgressive potential in this relationship and to question the term's pejorative cultural connotations of a somehow 'effeminate' boy whose excessive attachment to the mother extends scandalously beyond the 'normal' time.

It is difficult to appreciate the consequences of this critical move without a sense of the constraints of previous masculinist psychoanalytic interpretations. These have instituted and reinforced a kind of *doxa*, a rigid hermeneutic grid that only permits repetition of the same, phallocentrism, and generates the greatest degree of critical excitement around the ideas of incest and castration.[4]

The standard procedure among the Freudian critics is to interpret all of Camus, and especially *L'Etranger*, in the light of *L'Envers et l'endroit*, a collection of autobiographical essays first published in 1937 just prior to the composition of *L'Etranger*, then republished in 1958 with an all-important preface in which Camus points to the childhood world of poverty they evoke – and above all the silent mother – as the source of his work. These critics then focus on two features of the mother/son relationship as portrayed in one of the essays, 'Entre oui et non,' the boy's ambivalence toward maternal silence and an incident in which the mother is attacked by a male intruder and the son, called in to tend to her in her state of shock, ends up spending the night on her bed watching over her. Camus uses the third person to refer to the son in the recollected past, distancing himself from what may in fact be fiction or fictional transposition of lived experience for aesthetic ends, something most Freudian critics tend to overlook, keen as they are to (re)discover the 'events' determining Camus's psyche and writing that will allow them to replay the usual gynophobic Freudian scenarios.

Let us first consider maternal silence. Camus's mother as depicted in *L'Envers et l'endroit* was nearly deaf, practically mute, inarticulate, feeble-minded, illiterate. Conversation between mother and son was sparse as the mother withdrew into a solitary, immobile, and unreflective world of silence. On the one hand, her silence is described in positive terms as a form of presence and plenitude (' "A quoi tu penses?" "A rien," répondait-elle. Tout est là, donc rien,' II, p. 25), timelessness ('un temps d'arrêt, un instant démesuré,' II, p. 26) and knowledge ('A se taire, la situation s'éclaircit. Il est son fils, elle est sa mère. Elle peut lui dire: "Tu sais" ' II, p. 29). On the other hand, it inspires fear and pain in the young boy and is presented negatively as 'mutisme', 'irrémédiable désolation', 'silence animal' (II, p. 25) and as a form of indifference reinforced by deprivation of maternal caresses and linked with feelings of estrangement and strangeness ('*L'indifférence de cette mère étrange!*' II, p. 26).

According to Costes, Gassin, Lazere, and other Freudian critics, this ambivalence and the frustrations that the mother's seeming indifference 'must have' (a key phrase in these analyses) caused the child, led to a splitting of her imago as a defence mechanism. She thus becomes both Good Mother and Bad Mother and is endowed with both maternal (good) and paternal (bad) characteristics, including in the latter instance, a phallus. What is interesting is that although Camus stresses in these essays ambivalence and tension *maintained* between opposing notions which ultimately revert back to the mother ('Entre cet endroit et cet envers du monde, je ne veux pas choisir, je n'aime pas qu'on choisisse,' II, p. 49), for all these critics the scales definitely tip toward the Bad or Phallic Mother whose phallus is her silence. Costes goes so far as to say that the Phallic Mother presides, 'en maîtresse absolue' (p. 221) over the early cycle of the Absurd. Clearly, this type of simplification is commanded by the critic's own desire for unity, an unproblematised unity which, unlike the one I see at work in Camus, enables interpretive mastery of the author's psyche and writings and a repetition of the same, the masculine, the valorised term. The Good Mother and the positive attributes of her silence are essentially dismissed as an idealisation, a defence wrought by castration anxiety. The persecuting phallus (Costes, p. 119) turns out to be nothing but a mask for the mother's lack and her silent mouth none other than a castrating *vagina dentata* (Gassin, p. 183; Lazere, p. 89). Critical gynophobia is transformed into the hermeneutic key that will unlock the secrets of Camus's work protecting us all (all of us men) from the enigmatic Sphinx who devours young men (Costes, p. 92): 'l'oeuvre entière de Camus n'avait d'autre fonction – de son seul point de vue inconscient, évidemment – que de combler ce silence maternel, véritable gouffre à fantasmes' (Costes, pp. 118–19). The threatening hole must be filled, repressed, covered up with a phallus, lest the 'nothing' be acknowledged to harbour a something and the 'admirable silence' that Camus sets forth in the preface as the centre of his work and an ethical model (II, p. 13) be viewed positively. Contradictions must be swept aside by the 'symbolisme latent et négatif' of the Mother (Gassin, p. 215) psychoanalysis relentlessly rediscovers.

The second critical move, involving slippage from the pre-oedipal to the oedipal, from positive symbiosis to incest, and from maternal discourse to 'incestuous language', may be discerned in the standard Freudian interpretations of the scene of the attack on the mother and the ensuing night with her son. Gassin and Costes are essentially in agreement that this is Camus's version of the primal scene fantasy – that of the child's witnessing of parental intercourse – with its accompanying panoply of sadism, masochism, and guilt. It is an anxiety-inducing scene in which the mother appears to castrate the father and incorporate his penis. The son's identification with the aggressor, here seen as his taking the place of the aggressor/father in his mother's bed, yields guilty incestuous feelings as well as anxiety about his own potential castration by father and mother combined. Only Lazere suggests that the night shared by mother and son on the same bed may be interpreted as a fantasy of the womb, a pre-genital fantasy of symbiotic union with the mother, although, retrospectively, he too shifts to a negative oedipal interpretation in analysing the remainder of the essay. Incest is clearly but one possible interpretation of the scene which may also be read in a way that highlights pre-oedipal union where vivid memories of the womb subsist and where the simultaneous breathing, the solitary bonding of mother and child against the rest of the world ('Seuls contre tous. Les "autres" dormaient, à l'heure où tous deux respiraient la fièvre'), even abolishing the outside world ('Le monde s'était dissous'), and 'les liens qui l'attachaient à sa mére', (II, p. 27) are most important. To view *L'Etranger* 'dans son ensemble' (Costes, p. 71), not to mention all of Camus's *oeuvre*, in the exclusive light of an oedipal and primal scene interpretation of this one episode is to blind oneself to the workings of the maternal in Camus and to foreclose all possibility of a hermeneutics of the feminine. It is hardly surprising, then, that Costes should fail to recognise a crucial distinction in his own terminology when he conflates 'la langue maternelle' with 'le langage incestueux' (p. 132) as the aim of Camus's literary discourse.

Barthes pondered in *The Pleasure of the Text*, 'Doesn't every narrative lead back to Oedipus?'[5] I suggest we reformulate the question, asking 'does every narrative *have to* lead back to Oedipus, even if the subject is male?' Perhaps the oedipal perspective is not, as Freud would have it, 'the only angle on the pre-oedipal'.[6] Freed from the oedipal grid, would we not also be freed from the requisite remarks about Camus's fear and hostility toward the mother and therefore toward women in general?[7] Would we not then be able to see beyond obvious thematics – Meursault's treatment of Marie, his participation in Raymond's sordid scheme of revenge, his apparent indifference to his mother – and come to a more nuanced appreciation of the novel's ambiguities? And as feminists, to escape repetition of the same, must we not propose a feminist reading that is first and foremost a reading of the feminine?

What does this mean? To read the feminine is not primarily to psychoanalyse the hero or the author, but rather to draw attention to traces of maternal discourse, to the workings of the pre-oedipal in the signifying system of the novel. This frame of reference makes it possible to recontextualise previous critical findings and illuminate the text otherwise. Take, for example, the famous opening paragraph:

> Aujourd'hui, maman est morte. Ou peut-être hier, je ne sais pas. J'ai reçu un télégramme de l'asile: 'Mère décédée. Enterrement demain. Sentiments distingués.' Cela ne veut rien dire.

> *Maman died today. Or yesterday maybe. I don't know. I got a telegram from the home: 'Mother deceased. Funeral tomorrow. Faithfully yours.' That doesn't mean anything. Maybe it was yesterday.*[8]

This text represents the first cut, a disruption of undifferentiated pre-narrative existence that sets the story in motion. As such, it figures not so much a death as a birth, the cutting of the umbilical cord which precipitates the child into a first, pre-oedipal, signifying process not structured by the phallus, into a *process of differentiation* between self and other (Julia Kristeva on maternity, discussed in Jacobus, pp. 137–93). The first emblem of this process is lexical: 'maman'. In the absence of a father he never knew, Meursault seems to prolong into adulthood the pre-oedipal phase and the early linguistic relationship to the mother. Whether or not this is by choice, as his remark about abandoned studies suggests (I, p. 1154), is not immediately relevant. Many have noted Meursault's childish, simple vocabulary, his elementary syntax, his childlike attitudes, and infantile occupations (the games he plays to pass the time, his long hours of sleep). What interests me here is that, by ironic juxtaposition with the formal, stilted language of the telegram, a first incursion of the symbolic, the language of patriarchy, Meursault's infantile vocabulary and syntax reinscribe the pre-oedipal in much the same way as feminist theoreticians such as Kristeva, as both a marginal space and a space of dissidence, projecting into meaninglessness language as we know it: 'cela ne veut rien dire'. The feminine maternal thus becomes the vantage point for the crisis in language that is evidenced throughout the novel and for the crisis in meaning it engenders. The pre-oedipal archaic mother presides over a narrative of non-mastery, of meaning decontextualised and deferred, of unresolved enigmas: 'peut-être ..., je ne sais pas'.

At the threshold and in the margins of the narrative, the mother's body unsettles the border between absence and presence, inside and outside, beginnings and endings, perturbing, by this liminality, identity, representation, and truth. We never actually 'see' the mother's body: 'J'ai voulu voir maman tout de suite. Mais le concierge m'a dit qu'il fallait que je rencontre le directeur' (I, p. 1126). Paternal figures intervene to screen it. The concierge explains: 'On l'a couverte, mais je dois dévisser la bière pour que vous puissiez la voir' (I, p. 1127) Later the director reiterates the invitation to view the body in the casket. What this amounts to is maternal repression. From the point of view of the Symbolic Order, to look at the mother can only mean to see death – or lack, as the director's expression 'veiller la disparue' (I, p. 1127) suggests. Above all, for patriarchy to function smoothly, the maternal body must simply be *buried*, for it is only after the burial, Meursault concludes, that 'tout aura revêtu une allure plus officielle' (I, p. 1125).

Situating the mother's absence differently, Meursault's refusal to view the body draws attention to society's repression of the maternal and rewrites feminine lack as dissidence. This is the real crime for which he is punished by the judicial system, the most ostentatious manifestation of the Law of the Father in the novel. In the words of the prosecutor: 'j'accuse cet homme d'avoir enterré une mère avec un coeur criminel' (I, p. 1192). This symbolic 'matricide' turn out to be in society's eyes the equivalent of patricide: Meursault has threatened patriarchy by killing its body-effacing image of the mother.

The pre-oedipal attachment to the mother is not without contradiction and attempts at distancing, however, just as her procreating body itself marks a space of differentiation. By putting her in an old-people's home, Meursault has re-enacted an infant's primal distancing from the mother as not-yet-object. To explain his impassiveness at the funeral, he tells his lawyer: 'Tous les êtres sains avaient plus ou moins souhaité la mort de ceux qu'ils aimaient' (I, p. 1170). We need not invoke the oedipal drama, incest, maternal indifference or rejection to account for these apparently negative moments in the son's relationship to the mother. They are part of the self-differentiating process that brings about subject-formation and therefore a pre-symbolic type of signification, a process Julia Kristeva has called 'abjection': 'A massive and sudden emergence of uncanniness, which, familiar as it might have been in an opaque and forgotten [pre-natal?] life, now harries me as radically separate, loathsome.'[9] The 'abject' or maternal pseudo-object represents a first attempt to distinguish ourselves from the maternal entity even before we exist outside her through the autonomy granted by language (Kristeva, p. 20). The mother in this perspective is same-but-different and the mother/child relationship is one of estrangement as well as union. It seems difficult not to recognise in these the ambivalent terms of the mother/son relationship in *L'Envers et l'endroit* also, and not to read a reference to abjection in that *ur*-text of the maternal in Camus, the first entry in the *Carnets*: 'le sentiment bizarre qu'un fils porte à sa mère constitue *toute sa sensibilité*. Les manifestations de cette sensibilité dans les domaines les plus divers s'expliquent suffisamment par le souvenir latent, matériel de son enfance (une glu qui s'accroche à l'âme).' *'The bizarre feeling that a son has for his mother constitutes all his sensitivity. The expressions of this sensitivity in the most varied spheres can be sufficiently explained by the latent, material memory of his childhood (a glue that sticks to the soul).*[10] Union and estrangement/abjection at once, not only are these the basis of Camus's art, they also anticipate the fundamental contradiction of the Absurd.

Neither fully absent nor present, dispersed and disseminated, the mother's body returns with insistence throughout the novel. During the vigil, Meursault unconsciously discerns its eery presence everywhere, from the Arab nurse with her back to him whom he imagines knitting and whose face is covered except for her eyes, to the silent old women with their huge, bulging stomachs protruding under their aprons. These are all anonymous, marginal figures of subordinate otherness with respect to the dominant white, French male colonialists represented here by the paternalistic director and to a certain degree by the concierge – both refer to the old people as 'the others' (I, pp. 1126, 1128). But seen through the eyes of Meursault these enigmatic characters recast difference as differentiation rather than polar opposition reducible to the dominant term, just as they multiply and disperse, same and different, the body of the mother – silent, gazing, or pregnant – from whom the child has been severed. Similarly, the old woman's crying and the toothless old people's bizarre sucking sounds displace the infant's instinctual behaviour after being torn from the womb.[11] In this entire episode of the vigil, Camus is calling attention to the originary trauma of birth which creates a space at once separating and linking mother and child where otherness and dissidence may eventually find a voice. The mother's body and her body language – her silence, her gaze ('Quand elle était à la maison, maman passait son temps à me suivre des yeux en silence' I, 1126), replicated in the judgemental looks and silent intimacy of the old people – become the potential site of an alternative non-symbolic discourse of vigilance, repressed anger, and truth that would unsettle the institutions of patriarchy.

A less obvious attack originating in the maternal takes place on the level of naming. 'Maman' may be buried, but her name surfaces everywhere confounding identity and blurring gender distinctions. The already reduplicated 'ma' reappears in the names or designations of other female characters: *Marie*,[12] 'la *Ma*uresque', 'l'infir*m*ière *a*rabe', 'la petite femme auto*m*ate', 'la femme de *M*asson'. But, more importantly, the infant's rhythmic, pre-discursive signifier is disseminated in the names of practically all of the *male* characters as well: Em*m*anuel, *M*asson, Sala*m*ano. In the case of R*a*y*m*ono, as if to compensate for the reversal of phonemes, the maternal is inscribed in Sintès, Camus's own mother's maiden name. The feminine maternal surfaces as non-expressive rhythm, word-play,[13] traversing the symbolic and displacing the founding opposition of female to male upon which the entire oppressive dialectics of patriarchy rests. Summing up this subversive gesture by which sexual difference and the categories it supports are confused and exceeded is the name of the mother's fiancé: Tho*m*as Pérez, 'maman/père', mama/father.

An apparently marginal figure, Thomas Pérez is nonetheless present at two strategic moments: the beginning where Meursault's lingering fascination yields perhaps the most elaborate, if repugnant, physical portrait in the novel and the climactic final revelation in which he comes to understand why, on the eve of death, his mother had taken a fiancé. This and the fact that a substantial portion of the opening chapter is devoted to Thomas Pérez suggest that this figure merits even more scrutiny than his name alone would warrant. The director's embarrassed dismissal of his relationship with Mme Meursault as 'childish' intimates that here too we might look for subversive traces of the feminine maternal or, more generally, Woman. What is 'embarrassing' to the director and fascinating to Meursault is the intimation by way of Pérez of the mother's sexuality, her existence as woman, both sexual and maternal.

Beyond the surface, in between or outside the categories of the symbolic, the most deeply repressed figure of the orgasmic mother points enigmatically to a truth other than man's, the half-heard truth of woman's *jouissance*. Thus, the text forges an elusive link between the mother, Pérez, the landscape, and truth. Meursault observes Pérez while the director explains that often Pérez and Meursault's mother would take evening walks to the village.

Je regardais la campagne autour de moi. A travers les lignes de cyprès qui menaient aux collines près du ciel, cette terre rousse et verte, ces maisons rares et bien dessinées, je comprenais maman. Le soir, dans ce pays, devait être comme une trêve mélancolique (I, p. 1133).

I was looking at the countryside around me. Seeing the rows of cypress trees leading up to the hills next to the sky, and the houses standing out here and there against that red and green earth, I was able to understand Maman better. Evenings in that part of the country must have been a kind of sad relief. (p. 15)

Access to maternal truth-*jouissance* will be indirect, via the landscape and/or Pérez. The mother earth figure, which others have discussed in Camus, is actually not a figure, a substitute for the mother's body that erases it. The conjoining of mother and earth is, in my view, a manifestation of the confusion of boundaries, of the mingling of same and other in non-contradictory synthesis, that Lacanian and feminist psychoanalysis attributes to feminine *jouissance*. The feminist psychoanalyst Luce Irigaray analogises this feature of woman's *jouissance* from her body:

As for woman, she touches herself in and of herself without any need for mediation, and before there is any way to distinguish activity from passivity. Woman "touches herself" all the time ... for her genitals are formed of two lips in continuous contact. Thus, within herself, she is already two – but not divisible into one(s) – that caress each other.[14]

In this light, the mother earth connection represents the insistence in the text of the mother's body as the locus of a non-figural truth beyond meaning and mastery. Thus, Meursault's final revelation, precipitated by sense impressions from the landscape, reconvenes the same elements, including some of the same phrases, that are linked in this passage:

J'ai pensé à maman. Il m'a semblé que je comprenais pourquoi à la fin d'une vie elle avait pris un 'fiancé', pourquoi elle avait joué à recommencer. Là-bas, là-bas aussi ... le soir était comme une trêve mélancolique. Si près de la mort, maman devait s'y sentir libérée et prête à tout revivre' (I, p. 1209).

I thought about Maman. I felt as if I understood why at the end of her life she had taken a 'fiancé,' why she had played at beginning again. Even there ... evening was a kind of wistful respite. So close to death, Maman must have felt free then and ready to live it all again. (p. 122)

Mersault's reading of Woman justifies his refusal of patriarchy and culminates in rejection of the binary oppositions that support it. Endings, of novels and of lives, are also beginnings, and in this non-hierarchical imbrication of opposites lie truth, freedom, and the real unity sought in Camus's writings. As we shall see, these are not the only traces of the feminine in the last pages of the novel.

Truth is in neither term of the opposition, but in between, 'entre', 'inter-dit'. Unlike the lighting at the vigil described by the concierge as 'tout ou rien' (I, p. 1129), 'she-truths' burst forth where contradiction is maintained. In 'Le vréel' ('she-truth' or 'true-real') Julia Kristeva theorises that in this space where the symbolic falters the pre-oedipal archaic mother surfaces and reclaims her right to language, pointing to ineffable *jouissance* and causing the real to appear as a jubilant enigma.[15] This perspective is strikingly close to Camus's when he meditates on truth in 'L'Enigme' (1950):

Tout se tait ... De nouveau, une énigme heureuse m'aide à tout comprendre ... Le soleil ... coagule l'univers et ses formes dans un éblouissement obscur ... cette clarté blanche et noire qui, pour moi, a toujours été celle de la vérité (II, p. 861).

Everything grows quiet ... Once again, a happy enigma helps me to understand everything ... the sun ... coagulates the universe and its forms into a dazzling darkness ... the white and black clarity that, for me, has always been the sign of truth (pp. 154–5).

In the inscrutable, unimaginable space between alternatives in Camus's writing may be glimpsed an elusive 'mother's truth' whose roots are buried in childhood:

Si ce soir, c'est l'image d'une certaine enfance qui revient vers moi, comment ne pas accueillir la leçon d'amour et de pauvreté que je puis en tirer? Puisque cette heure est comme un intervalle entre oui et non, ... recueillir seulement la transparence et la simplicité des paradis perdus: dans une image (II, p. 28).

If, this evening, the image of a certain childhood comes back to me, how can I keep from welcoming the lesson of love and poverty it offers? Since this hour is like a pause between yes and no ... only to capture the transparency and simplicity of paradises lost: in an image (p. 37).

'She-truths' or the lost paradise of maternal *jouissance*, these represent both the source ('image') and the aim ('image') of Camus's thought and art.[16] When it refuses to repress otherness, when it affirms non-hierarchically both elements of an opposition ('oui et non'; 'Il n'y a pas d'amour de vivre sans désespoir de vivre' II, p. 44), the discourse of the Absurd approximates a discourse of the feminine. By the same token, Meursault's celebrated indifference – apparent in such formulas as 'cela m'était égal', 'dans un sens ... dans un autre', 'd'un côté ... d'un autre côté' – may be understood not as difference annulled but rather as an illustration of this 'feminine' kind of difference.

Most important for their implications of alterity and for Meursault's evolution with respect to otherness are the Arabs. In much the same way as the mother the Arabs contribute to Camus's myth of utopian otherness. 'Ils nous regardaient en silence, mais à leur manière, ni plus ni moins que si nous étions des pierres ou des arbres morts' (I, p. 1159). These are the same silent looks as the mother's, looks of the oppressed/repressed whose silence may signify anger. They recall the alternative discourse of dissidence suggested in the attitude of the old people during the vigil and the blend of familiarity and estrangement we have traced to the pre-oedipal relationship to the mother. Marginalised, colonised, depersonalised, presented anonymously as 'Arabes' or 'groupes d'Arabes' or more exotically as 'Mauresques', from an abstract semiotic point of view – though not, as many of Camus's critics have observed, a pragmatic, political one – they serve in *L'Etranger* to critique Western notions of identity and the self. In Part 2, the murmured communication between the crouching Arab prisoners and their visitors beneath the din of their French counterparts forms a 'basso continuo' that suggests the repressed semiotic subtext of the symbolic, a non-figural (hence the musical comparison to convey the impression their Arabic makes on Meursault) and more authentic form of communication ('malgré le tumulte, ils parvenaient à s'entendre en parlant très bas' I, p. 1176).

Camus reinforces the association with the semiotic or dissident maternal discourse by juxtaposing the Arabs' conversation with the silent communication between two other characters, an old woman and her son, who stare intensely at each other. At parting their silent looks are seconded by gesture and the pre-discursive 'maman', the only time it does not refer to Meursault's own mother: 'Il a dit: "Au revoir, maman"' et elle a passé sa main entre les deux barreaux pour lui faire un petit signe lent et prolongé' (I, p. 1177). Meursault describes the son as 'un *petit* jeune homme *aux mains fines*' (I, p. 1177, italics mine) as if to emphasise his childlike relationship to the mother and a feminine trait that evokes the sameness-in-difference preceding the oedipal cut and the constitution of sexual difference.

If the Arabs carry all these positive, maternal connotations, then what does it mean to murder an Arab? As others have noted, this is the oedipal moment. Raymond has progressively dragged the passive Meursault into man's world: 'il m'a déclaré ... que moi, j'étais un homme', 'Raymond ... m'a dit qu'entre hommes on se comprenait toujours' (I, pp. 1144, 1146). Reflecting the Symbolic Order, this world of the white Western colonist grants Arabs and women existence only as subordinate others. Thus, Meursault is becoming more 'normal'. He agrees to marry Marie and recognises in the conventional Masson couple an image of his own conjugal future. In the murder chapter there is strong emphasis on traditional gender roles: the men go for a walk while the women do the dishes, the men get into fights and the women cry. Furthermore, Meursault is uncharacteristically patronising: 'Là, nous avons trouvé *nos* deux Arabes' (I, p. 1163, italics mine).

This process culminates in the murder. Raymond's revolver, itself emblematic of his phallocentric world, is symbolically related to the sun, the primary paternal symbol in the episode. The sun glints on the gun when he hands it to Meursault (I, p. 1164). But in this second encounter with the Arabs Meursault remains poised in a quasi-maternal world of equilibrium and suspended choices, of silence and water: 'tout s'arrêtait ici *entre* la mer, le sable et le soleil, le double silence de la flûte et de l'eau. J'ai pensé qu'*on pouvait tirer ou ne pas tirer*' (I, p. 1164, italics mine). '*Everything came to a stop there* between *the sea, the sand, and the sun, and the double silence of the flute and the water. It was then that I realised that* you could either shoot or not shoot' (p. 56). When he returns to the beach alone, he is both rejecting Raymond's world with its stereotyped femininity and trying to shake off the 'blinding' sun which opposes his advance to the shade, repose, and the cool maternal spring ('je me tendais tout entier pour triompher du soleil' I, p. 1165). The play of the sun on the Arab's knife becomes more obviously a metaphor for the threat of castration.[17] The paternal sun in fact *prevents him from turning back* and pushes him toward the constitution of the Arab – and Woman – as polar Other. The associations between the Arab and Woman are numerous. Not only does the Arab occupy a space connoted maternal, he is lying in a 'feminine', almost seductive pose. And he is there to exact revenge on behalf of his sister. Finally, the sun here recalls the primal separation from the mother's body at the funeral: 'C'était le même soleil que le jour où j'avais enterré maman' (I, p. 1166). With the passive firing of the first shot under the influence of the sun, Meursault has destroyed 'l'équilibre du jour' (I, p. 1166) and happy silence. He now fully enters the Symbolic Order, firing four more shots with Raymond's gun to complete the repression of Arab and Woman as Other.

Cut from the pre-oedipal by this act, Meursault will (re)discover in it a positive rhetoric of dissidence. The prison visit represents an important turning point in this development. Camus builds on the implications of maternal semiosis in the scene by devoting the rest of the chapter to Meursault's infantile regression. The prison cell becomes a womblike environment returning him to maternal wisdom ('C'était d'ailleurs une idée de maman ... qu'on finissait par s'habituer à tout' I, p. 1178) and unsettling adult temporality, antinomy, fixed boundaries, as well as language: 'Je n'avais pas compris à quel point les jours pouvaient être *à la fois longs et courts* ... ils finissaient par *déborder* les uns sur les autres. Ils y *perdaient leur nom*. Les mots hier et demain étaient les seuls qui gardaient un sens pour moi' (I, pp. 1180 – 81, italics mine). '*I hadn't understood how days could be* both long and short at the same time ... *they ended up flowing into one another. They lost their names. Only the words "yesterday" and "tomorrow" still had any meaning for me*' (p. 80). But these pages also suggest the dangers of pure silence through the cautionary tale of the Czech who fails to speak his identity when he returns to his village after twenty-five years and ends up being killed by his mother and sister who have not recognised him.

Not until the final chapter, however, does Meursault emerge from his characteristic 'rien à dire' to speech. Before his outburst against the priest, his efforts at symbolisation are striking. He tries, for example, to represent the unrepresentable, the moment his heart will stop beating. More importantly, there is a long meditation on the guillotine, the core of which is the memory of a story his mother used to tell about the father he never knew. Access to the father occurs only via the mother who does not embody here the 'feminine' stereotype of a mute presence whose silence may be rich with meaning. She assumes rather the 'masculine' role of speaking subject, of storyteller (I, p. 1201), and in her story the father, unlike all the other paternal figures in the novel, appears in a positive light. For in his openness to the man whose execution he witnessed, in his refusal to perceive the assassin as absolute Other, in his bodily protest against death and the horror of the guillotine–he vomits, a reaction not unlike the body language of female hysterics – the father transcends traditional gender roles. Like Thomas Pérez, he mingles the maternal and paternal, the feminine and masculine, just as by speaking the mother embodies both masculine and feminine. In playing out sexual differentiation rather than difference, in suggesting a process, a back-and-forth movement between same and other rather than rigid divisions, the mother's discourse opens a space for the unrepresentable and offers in its form as in its content a model for an authentic language – and literature – of dissidence.

Assuming a feminine maternal posture, Meursault puts this discourse of dissidence into effect against the priest and in his climactic nocturnal vision. His revolt against the priest turns a passionate outcry into a reasoned rejection of the hierarchised world of Fathers and Others. The pre-oedipal origins of this revolt are suggested in the introduction to his tirade: 'Alors, je ne sais pas pourquoi, il y a *quelque chose qui a crevé en moi. Je me suis mis à crier à plein gosier* et je l'ai insulté' (I, p. 1208, italics mine). '*Then, I don't know why, but* something inside me snapped. I started yelling at the top of my lungs, *and I insulted him*' (p. 120). Meursault identifies with the self-differentiating mother's body. He is both mother and child. The waters break and he gives birth to the cry, the semiotic of the infant converted into the language of protest of the adult. 'J'étouffais en criant tout ceci . . .' (I, p. 1209). '*All the shouting had me gasping for air*' (p. 122).

By far the most spectacular feminisation of Meursault and the most far-reaching identification with the mother occur after the priest's departure in the closing paragraph of the novel. Calling upon those elements of nature already connoted maternal, Camus presents Meursault's revelation as an opening up to the mother: 'Des odeurs de *nuit*, de *terre* et de *sel* rafraîchissaient mes tempes. La merveilleuse paix de cet été endormi entrait en moi comme *une marée* . . . Je m'ouvrais pour la première fois à la *tendre indifférence* du monde' (I, p. 1209, italics mine). '*Smells of* night, earth, *and* salt air *were cooling my temples. The wondrous peace of that sleeping summer flowed through me like* a tide ... *I opened myself to the* gentle indifference *of the world*' (p. 122). If in the scene with the priest he identifies with the *procreating* mother, here his identification is with the *orgasmic* mother. Opening up to the maternal brings understanding of the mother's taking a fiancé and experience of the limitlessness and confusion of boundaries in maternal *jouissance*: 'maman devait s'y sentir libérée et prête à tout revivre ... Et moi aussi, je me suis senti prêt à tout revivre' (I, p. 1209). '*Maman must have felt free then and ready to live it all again ... And I felt ready to live it all again too*' (p. 122). The world allows Meursault to reenact this positive movement between same and different, self and other: 'De l'éprouver si pareil à moi, si fraternel enfin, j'ai senti que j'avais été heureux, et que je l'étais encore' (I, p. 1209). '*Finding it so much like myself – so like a brother, really – I felt that I had been happy and that I was happy again*' (pp. 122–3). Maternal and fraternal, the world confounds feminine and masculine, just as Meursault figures in non-contradictory synthesis his mother, his mother's son, and his mother's daughter. Rather than a reversal of the sexual hierarchy with Woman in the dominant position, feminisation entails the displacement of opposition and 'results in an excess, a spilling over of categories and an ambiguous surplus of meanings' (Mistacco, p. 79).

Meursault has learned to 'read' ambiguous maternal signs – 'cette nuit chargée de signes et d'étoiles' (I, p. 1209) – and in dying commits to turning his own body into an equally enigmatic Woman-sign capable of inciting revolt: 'il me restait à souhaiter qu'il y ait beaucoup de spectateurs le jour de mon exécution et qu'ils m'accueillent avec des cris de haine' (I, p. 1210). With death imminent, Meursault can never really translate feminisation and reading Woman into effective action in his own life. This can lead one to interpret the ending as a death-wish signifying pre-oedipal escapism rather than heroic dissidence. But if Meursault is viewed as *a sign to be read* and not just a character to be psychoanalysed, then like Janine in 'La Femme adultère' – a more explicit figuration of Woman who also identifies with the orgasmic mother in a nocturnal ecstasy (Mistacco, pp. 81, 84) – he can be interpreted as an expression of Camus's own repressed feminine and as the positive outcome of his concerted effort to symbolise the maternal in art and praxis. However surprising it may seem to those who view him chiefly as the proponent of virile fraternity, Camus appears in fact to be one of those rare male writers of whom Héléne Cixous writes, who are 'able to venture onto the brink where writing, freed from law, unencumbered by moderation, exceeds phallic authority, and where subjectivity inscribing its effects becomes feminine'.[17]

This gesture is not without its own ambiguity and I wouldn't be much of a feminist reader if I didn't end by problematising it. For in the long run we have to ask ourselves some questions. Does Meursault/Camus speak *for* or *with* the mother? Is the mother effaced as usual as subject and her discourse finally appropriated by man? Is this yet another instance of symbolic 'matricide' and a male fantasy of self-engenderment after all? But ambivalence toward the mother as enabling/engulfing, as eliminated subject yet object of a sustained quest, is as much a feature of women's writing (see, among others, Hirsch, pp. 133, 138). Camus's artistic dilemma, so poignantly voiced in the preface to *L'Envers et l'endroit*, namely, to find a discourse of love that would 'balance' yet incorporate admirable maternal silence, reflects many women writers' entanglement with the maternal. Not until we approach the writing of men with the insights into the maternal and the critical tools gained from studying women writers will we begin to appreciate the primordial role played by Woman in the generation of literary texts.

Notes and Works Cited

1. Albert Camus, *Essais* (Paris: Bibliothéque de la Pléïade, 1965), 1925. Future references to this volume will be given in the text as II, followed by the page number. This practice of giving initial documentation in a note with subsequent page references in the text will be followed throughout. Translations are from *Lyrical and Critical Essays*, P. Thody (ed.), Ellen Connay Kennedy (trans.) (New York: Alfred A. Knopf, 1969).
2. See Vicki Mistacco, 'Nomadic Meanings: The Woman Effect in "La Femme adultère"', in *Albert Camus' 'L'Exil et le royaume': The Third Decade* Anthony Rizzuto (ed.) (Toronto: Les Editions Paratexte, 1988), pp. 71–84, for a study informed by psychoanalytic feminism that briefly examines the importance of the pre-oedipal in Camus.
3. Nancy K. Miller proposes a poetics of the underread and a practice of 'overreading' women writers in *Subject to Change: Reading Feminist Writing* (New York: Columbia University Press, 1988), p. 83.
4. My remarks are based on an overview of this vast body of literature. For the sake of economy, however, I refer the reader only to the studies I consider the most representative and/or most influential: Alain Costes, *Albert Camus ou la parole manquante, étude psychanalytique*

(Paris: Payot, 1973); Jean Gassin, *L'Univers symbolique d'Albert Camus. Essai d'interprétation psychanalytique* (Paris: Minard, 1981); Donald Lazere, *The Unique Creation of Albert Camus* (New Haven: Yale University Press, 1973); Ben Stoltzfus, 'Camus's *L'Etranger*: A Lacanian Reading', *Texas Studies in Literature and Language*, vol. 31, no. 4 (Winter 1989), pp. 514–35. All except for the latter are classic Freudian analyses.

5. Richard Miller (trans.) (New York: Hill & Wang, 1975), p. 47. Cited in Marianne Hirsch, *The Mother/Daughter Plot: Narrative, Psychoanalysis, Feminism* (Bloomington and Indianapolis: Indiana University Press, 1989), p. 52. Similarly, Stoltzfus generalises Meursault's guilt toward his mother as 'residual feelings of guilt that *we all* share. Are *we* not guilty of coveting our mothers and wishing for the death of our father?' (p. 530, italics mine).

6. Mary Jacobus, *Reading Woman: Essays in Feminist Criticism* (New York: Columbia University Press, 1986), p. 193.

7. Camus's misogyny has been amply documented. In addition to passing remarks about the author's and his characters' inability to advance to adult sexual relationships in Lazere, Costes, and Gassin, for interpretations of women and the feminine and especially for compilations of misogynist quotes by Camus, see Anthony Rizzuto, 'Camus and a Society without Women,' *Modern Language Studies*, vol. 13, no. 1 (Winter 1983), pp. 3–14, and Edouard Morot-Sir, 'L'Esthétique d'Albert Camus: logique de la limite, mesure de la mystique,' *Cahiers Albert Camus*, vol. 5 (1985), pp. 93–112. For a feminist approach quite distinct from mine that arrives at the opposite conclusion that the Absurd is a discourse of racial and sexual repression, see Louise K. Horowitz, 'Of Women and Arabs: Sexual and Racial Polarization in Camus,' *Modern Language Studies*, vol. 17, no. 3 (Summer 1987), pp. 54–61. Working within a pre-feminist theoretical framework, Pierre Nguyen-Van-Huy underscores the importance of the mother and presents maternal love as an ideal and basis for revolt in *La Métaphysique du bonheur chez Albert Camus* (Neuchâtel: La Baconnière, 1968).

8. *L'Etranger* in *Théâtre, récits, nouvelles* (Paris: Gallimard, Bibliothèque de la Pléiade, 1962; 1963 printing), p. 1125, hereafter cited as I, followed by the page number; *The Stranger*, Matthew Ward (trans.) (New York: Alfred A. Knopf, 1988), p. 3. Further quotations are from this translation.

9. Julia Kristeva, *Powers of Horror*, Léon S. Roudiez (trans.) (New York: Columbia University Press, 1982), p. 2. 'Surgissement massif et abrupt d'une étrangeté qui, si elle a pu m'être familière dans une vie opaque et oubliée, me harcèle maintenant comme radicalement séparée, répugnante.' *Pouvoirs de l'horreur* (Paris: Seuil, 1980), p. 10.

10. *Carnets* (Paris: Gallimard, 1962), p. 15, entry dated May 1935. Translation by Adele King.

11. In 'Le Quotidien et le sacré: introduction à une nouvelle lecture de *L'Etranger*,' André Abbou refers to the sucking sounds and 'l'arrachement au ventre maternel' and makes some pertinent remarks about

the importance of the Arab nurse in this episode: "Présence muette, indice d'un monde reclus et condamné à l'invalidité sociale, porteuse d'une relation au monde faite de silence et d'observation, la "mauresque" mutilée ... semble être le premier jalon dans la quête qu'inaugure Meursault.' Gay-Crosier, Raymond and Jacqueline Lévi-Valensi (eds), *Albert Camus: oeuvre ouverte, oeuvre fermée* (Paris: Gallimard, Cahiers Albert Camus: 5, 1985), pp. 248–9.

12. Marie is obviously a mother substitute, as Costes, Lazere, and Stoltzfus, among others, have noted. Meursault's relationship to her may be viewed as a regressive one that replicates the infant's need for contact with the mother's body. In particular, the scene in which Meursault and Marie swim together in Part 1, Chapter 2, is easily read as an effort to return to the womb (the maternal sea with its amniotic fluid) in the pre-genital phase.

13. Julia Kristeva calls this pre-oedipal signifying system the semiotic, theorising that it both precedes and traverses the sign, syntax, denotation, and meaning. She views it as a provisional articulation of movements and their traces, as non-expressive rhythm. While she relates it to the maternal *chora* which precedes the One in Plato, she contends that it is not limited to the cries, vocalisation, and gestures of infants; the semiotic is in fact also operative in adult discourse in the form of rhythm, prosody, word-play, nonsense, and laughter (*Polylogue* (Paris: Seuil, 1977), p. 14). By bringing heterogeneity into the symbolic, the semiotic, according to Kristeva, functions politically as a revolutionary mechanism for change.

14. *This Sex Which Is Not One*, Catherine Porter (trans.) with Carolyn Burke (Ithaca, NY: Cornell University Press, 1985), p. 24. 'La femme, elle, se touche d'elle-même et en elle-même sans la nécessité d'une médiation, et avant tout départage possible entre activité et passivité. La femme "se touche" tout le temps ... car son sexe est fait de deux lèvres qui s'embrassent continûment. Ainsi, en elle, elle est déjà deux – mais non divisibles en un(e)s – qui s'affectent.' *Ce Sexe qui n'en est pas un* (Paris: Minuit, 1977), p. 24.

15. In *Folle vérité*, Julia Kristeva and Jean-Michel Ribettes (eds) (Paris: Seuil, 1979), pp. 11–35. I am here paraphrasing Kristeva (pp. 24, 31). The term 'she-truth' is also borrowed from this essay.

16. 'On ne pense que par image. Si tu veux être philosophe,. écris des romans', *Carnets*, p. 23.

17. 'Sorties', in Hélène Cixous and Catherine Clément, *The Newly Born Woman*, trans. Betsy Wing (Minneapolis: University of Minnesota Press, 1986), p. 86. 'qui peuvent s'aventurer au bord où l'écriture libérée de la loi, débarrassée de la mesure, excède l'instance phallique, où la subjectivité qui inscrit ses effets se féminise.' 'Sorties', in Catherine Clément and Hélène Cixous, *La Jeune née* (Paris: Union Générale d'Editions, 1975), p. 160.

15

Humanism and the 'White Man's Burden': Camus, Daru, Meursault, and the Arabs
Michel Grimaud

In *The Stranger* (1942), a French Algerian named Meursault murders a nameless Arab. In 'L'Hôte', the central story of *Exile and the Kingdom* (1957), a schoolteacher named Daru feeds the hungry bodies and souls of young Arab children; he is sentenced to death by Arab freedom fighters because of a misunderstanding related to his handling of a nameless Arab criminal. Both stories were written for a Continental French as well as an Algerian French audience but they are widely known and taught throughout the world as examples of great Western literature.

In both cases the nameless Arab is a key passive protagonist of the story while the European is a loner who finds communication difficult and is in some ways alien ('étranger') to his own social system. The title 'L'Hôte', meaning 'the guest' and 'the host', is unambiguously dual as suggested by the general title *Exile and the Kingdom* and by specific references in the story to the word 'hôte' (pp. 1611, 1615).[1] The Arab is the guest in Daru's schoolhouse but Daru is a guest in Algeria and the Arab in that sense is the host. Daru makes it clear that both the Arab and himself are in some ways in a symmetrical position: 'Dans ce désert, personne, ni lui ni son hôte n'étaient rien. Et pourtant, hors de ce désert, ni l'un ni l'autre, Daru le savait, n'auraient pu vivre vraiment' (p. 1615). (*'No one in this desert, neither he nor his guest mattered. And yet, outside this desert neither of them, Daru knew, could have really lived'* (p. 98). Daru, then, is in the situation of French Algerians born of European parents but whose 'kingdom', their native land, is Algeria whatever their ethnic background may be. The Arab, of course, is paradoxically and confusingly both a freedom fighter struggling for the liberation of Algeria and, according to French law (but not local law), a common criminal.

Because Arabs rarely appear in Camus's fiction,[2] the opportunities for comparison are few and, therefore, an examination of Camus's plots at a fifteen-year interval ought to be revealing. The fact that in one case an Arab is murdered and in the other an Arab is a double murderer (the second time by proxy) makes those rare appearances all the more significant. In addition, the fact that the title of 'L'Hôte' summarises in a nutshell the basic problem of displacement faced by the indigenous population and by colonists like Daru and Camus, makes it obvious that the fundamental subject of the story *is* on some levels at least colonialism. In that context, the charge of racism brought against Camus is worth considering.

Camus is a classic writer often regarded as a representative of humanism and Western civilisation. Because of this status, his work deserves the close scrutiny undergone by other writers who dominate the literary canon. For example, Montesquieu acquiesced to the infamous legal system against slaves (the 'Code Noir')[3] and Victor Hugo approved of France as a colonising nation because of its 'mission civilisatrice'. Similarly, the extent to which we may not or may assert that Camus as writer understood and cared about fundamental social values is the topic of this essay.

Apparently, the first mention of the plot of *L'Etranger* as racially problematic dates back to a piece written by A.J. Liebling for the *New Yorker* magazine in 1956:

Meursault is not just a man who has killed another man and cannot understand why there should be such a fuss about it; he is a North African of European origin who has killed that semi-abstraction known as 'an Arab,' and this increases his incomprehension of the trouble he finds himself in. The name of the Arab never appears ... [Meursault] even had the excuse of anticipatory self-defense, for the dead Arab, although reclining at the time Meursault shot him, was holding a knife in his hand. So when the court sentences Meursault to the guillotine, he is right in believing that the sad outcome must be attributed to extraneous factors ... There are Strangers everywhere, but in no other locale, with the exception of Mississippi, would society's reaction to Meursault's offense have seemed to society's victim [Meursault] so exaggerated and so clearly paradoxical. (p. 144)[4]

Among Camus scholars, Philip Thody is the only one to have presented openly this paradoxical premise presupposed by the plot of *The Stranger*. Thody presents his summary in the form of putative advice to a budding novelist. As such, his approach is not internal to the world of *L'Etranger* and complements usefully Liebling's view by presenting us with the kinds of thoughts Camus himself might have had:

> All right, you need a novel where a rather odd but basically attractive young man is unjustly sentenced to death. Have him shoot an Arab. This won't distract the reader's attention either from the other ideas you want to express or from the mysterious hard-done-by hero. It will also have the additional advantage of making the court which sentences him to death seem even more thoroughly an embodiment of an absurd Kafkaesque social order. After all, it isn't every day that a European is executed for killing a native, or a white man hanged for shooting a negro. There must therefore be some good – or bad – reason for this unusual event to take place. Concentrate on that and forget about the Arabs. They don't really matter anyway. (p. 65)[5]

In other words, the novel is written from the point of view of a French Algerian and is definitely *not* addressed to an Arab audience. But could Camus have told the story of *The Stranger* in a different way, thus avoiding the interracial issue which is not, one assumes, the main point of the novel? Camus certainly could have found other kinds of social outcasts: Raymond could have battered a European woman and Meursault could have killed a European social outcast. The tacitly targeted audience (French and other Western, mostly middle-class readers) being class conscious like all social animals would have found this quite acceptable. Certainly, Camus could easily have avoided the issue of ethnic or colonial conflict but – *if one accepts the basic premise and plot* – some down-trodden group had to become a scapegoat. Within the Algerian setting, Arabs were the scapegoats of choice.

Although the novel is not addressed to an Arab or Third World audience, the violence against the Arab is presented in a scrupulously fair way by Meursault as narrator. He lays little or no blame on the Arab: the self-defence argument could have been used at the trial but *we* would have known that it was not warranted from the facts as Meursault himself presents them. Aside from a slight defensiveness in the 'naturellement, j'ai serré mon revolver' (p. 1165) added by Meursault when he sees the Arab put his hand in his pocket – every point exculpates the Arab and puts the responsibility on Meursault's side. The Arab seems to be laughing (conceivably *at* Meursault), but as narrator Meursault stresses that this may be due to shadows on the Arab's face. When the Arab pulls out his knife because Meursault has moved forward yet one more step, Meursault does not present this as an act of aggression in and of itself, it is rather the sun's rays splashing over the steel blade that hurt him: the sun is the guilty party. The sweat becomes a blinding curtain of 'tears and salt'; the sun makes his temples beat so hard that he feels that they are being hit like cymbals: 'les cymbales du soleil'. Oddly, those cymbals appear to be symbols as are the stars in the last paragraph of the novel ('cette nuit chargée de *signes* et d'étoiles', p. 1209). In short blame for the event falls squarely on the sun so that it is poetically only fair that 'cymbales' and 'cinq balles' should be homonyms.[6]

But the sun can only be blamed for the initial shot. The narrator's text is abundantly clear about this: after a page of minute physical and emotional descriptions, there is a marked return to thinking and thoughtful action:

> J'ai secoué la sueur et le soleil. J'ai compris que j'avais détruit l'équilibre du jour, le silence exceptionnel d'une plage où j'avais été heureux. Alors, j'ai tiré encore quatre fois sur un corps inerte où les balles s'enfonçaient sans qu'il y parût. Et c'était comme quatre coups brefs que je frappais sur la porte du malheur. (p. 1166)

> *I shook off the sweat and sun. I knew that I had shattered the harmony of the day, the exceptional silence of a beach where I'd been happy. Then I fired four more times at the motionless body where the bullets lodged without leaving a trace. And it was like knocking four quick times on the door of unhappiness.* (p. 59)

Those lines at the very end of Part 1 are significantly different from the immediately preceding ones where Meursault's feelings are presented impressionistically. They are more like the ones *during* the confrontation where one finds verbs like 'j'ai pensé' or logical connectors like 'malgré tout' and 'à cause de'. In other words, there is not only a pause between the first shot and the others, but also a change of attitude: the first sentence explicitly says that Meursault has 'secoué la sueur et le soleil', i.e. got rid of the sun's hold. The second sentence explicitly says that he 'understands' – an act of intellect. Rhetorical devices appear: metaphors typical of poetical speech like 'équilibre du jour' and 'porte du malheur'; an imperfect of the subjunctive ('parût') typical of a heightened tone; and, as in the end of both *The Stranger* and 'L'Hôte', a pluperfect rather than an imperfect – 'où j'avais été heureux', a phrase that suggest awareness of the finality of his act.

For Meursault – as it ought to be – killing someone (even an Arab) obviously means the end of life as he knew it and the irony of the situation is that this is occurring *just when this loner was becoming socialised* – enjoying friends, women, and nature at the beach. As a consequence ('Alors', with a comma emphasising the word), now that the dream of happiness can never be – out of despair or anger one might think – Meursault shoots four more times. But the paradox is that this banal and expected anger against one's self or even (by projecting) the anger directed against the dead body is absent. The exact language of the last two sentences is strangely precise: after the 'alors' we have the contextually non-necessary logical connector 'encore' and the adjective 'brefs', neither of which evoke a feeling of violence unleashed. This is confirmed by the distancing effect of the indefinite article '*un* corps inerte' used instead of the definite article or better the demonstrative '*ce* corps'. Early psychoanalytic articles on Camus see this as a description of depersonalisation. Certainly everything is occurring too easily – 'sans qu'il y parût' – but the lack of anger or hatred is important, in another fundamental way: it enables us to accept the death of the Arab without attributing racial motivations to Meursault. (In fact hatred only appears, and quite unexpectedly, in the last words of the novel: 'cris de haine' (p. 1210).) The depersonalisation or odd distancing which accompanies the four final shots needs explaining but one of its most notable consequences is that it does not make an interpretation of Meursault's act as racist particularly convincing.

If anything, Meursault is unbelievably oblivious of race. Or if not Meursault, then Camus. At the opening of the second chapter of Part 2 (p. 1175), Meursault fearlessly and, as usual, thoughtlessly, tells his Arab cellmates that he has killed an Arab. The Arabs are silent but shortly thereafter help Meursault lay out his straw mattress. One has to wonder about verisimilitude. Why this odd kindness of the Arabs for a white Arab-killer? The point, perhaps, is that Camus protesteth too much: he too strenuously denies any hostility between his hero and the Arabs, thus suggesting that Camus was far from unaware of the racial overtones of his novel.

In effect, there are two worlds: the world as described by Meursault and, second, Camus's and his readers' actual world. Meursault's world, with its violence against Salamano's dog and against women, is not pretty and is presented in a rather realistic manner. Meursault is a part of that world and, although we may (or may not) think that Camus condones much of it in the name of the Mediterranean civilisation he loved, this fictional world is missing its most basic ingredient found in the world Camus actually lived in: the racism and colonial injustices Camus discusses, to an extent, in his early journalistic writings. In short, although in *The Stranger* one does occasionally find a typically colonial perspective on the Arabs (see Thody), there is nothing in Meursault that can be *directly* assigned a racist label. Even Meursault's tolerant attitude to Raymond's battering of his lover seems more directly linked to social attitudes towards women than to ethnicity. In effect, ethnicity is the reality Camus chooses for his story but without exploiting it: quite unrealistically no one utters racist or even racial remarks. On the other hand, the troubling presence of Arabs in the story – their silence, and other characteristics that make them seem like Camusian outsiders – suggests that they are there as an important subtext Camus wanted but did not or could not deal with directly.

Ethnicity and racism, then, are only marginally present in the story: for readers identifying with the characters and ignorant of the Algerian social world, this absence helps us focus on other human issues. The fact that the victim is an Arab certainly made the crimes of Raymond and Meursault less shocking to some Europeans; as such the choice is one a *European* novelist would have been likely to make. Camus, in his first and still best-known novel, apparently passively accepted the social system of his time and chose to tell a story in a way that took that society's racism for granted, in effect exploiting it for fictional purposes. Still in view of Camus's strong stands against injustice one wants to believe that the above interpretation is a misreading. Perhaps an examination of the more mature Camus of *Exile and the Kingdom* can offer a different perspective.

Both *The Stranger* and 'L'Hôte' are about *belonging*, but 'L'Hôte', as the double meaning of the title emphasises, is about belonging to a land one was born in but which was stolen from its previous inhabitants. 'L'Hôte' is about losing one's home. Whereas Meursault seemed like a loner who could have lived anywhere in the Mediterranean, Daru in 'L'Hôte' emphasises that Algeria is his home. The short story illustrates the colonialists' sad plight, *their* suffering and generosity. Witness Daru, a monk-like French Algerian schoolteacher living alone near the desert and feeding the bodies and souls of the starving Arabs around him. Not only is he the apparent embodiment of the good colonialist's 'mission to civilize', but Balducci, his friend the *gendarme*, is equally kind. By contrast the nameless Arab is a murderer.

As in *The Stranger*, we have no idea what the Arab's thoughts are since the story is told from the white man's point of view. The narrator tells the story from Daru's perspective, entering his thoughts but not those of Balducci or of the Arab. But Balducci is an open, friendly, talkative man who says what he thinks very directly whereas both Daru and the Arab, being perfect illustrations of one of the two basic themes of *Exile and the Kingdom* – the difficulty of human communication – are not overly loquacious. Had Camus chosen the standard omniscient narrator (say, à la Balzac) who could tell us why the Arab had committed his murder and what he thought, the story could not have been so easily interpreted, by critics, in racist terms.[7] However, unlike the descriptions in *The Stranger*, in 'L'Hôte', one does find several disturbingly stereotypical descriptions of the Arab as primitive, in particular his thick lips and his resemblance to animals: 'Daru ne vit d'abord que ses énormes lèvres, pleines, lisses, presque négroïdes' (p. 1611); '*Daru noticed only his huge lips, fat, smooth, almost Negroid*' (p. 90); 'il [Daru] voyait seulement le regard à la fois sombre et brillant, et la bouche animale' (p. 1617). '*He could see nothing but the dark yet shining eyes and the animal mouth*' (p. 100). But on the other hand, the Arab is never shown as having shifty eyes. All passages show him as looking at Daru very directly (p. 1611) particularly when he wants to speak to Daru about joining the rebels ('Viens avec nous', p. 1617). Paradoxically, even the notion that there is a rebellion and that he is a rebel is made less obvious by Camus's several changes to the manuscript of the story, as Maurice Roelens has shown.[8] In short, unexpectedly, it seems that the Arab, as seen through Daru's eyes, is more closely identified with the standard physical racist stereotypes found in colonial literature than were the Arabs in *The Stranger*.

The situation in 'L'Hôte' is odd on several counts. Daru's apparent reason for freeing the Arab is *not* explained by the narrator even though he can and does otherwise read Daru's thoughts. At any rate it is not because Daru believes that the Arab failed to commit a crime under his own people's rules that he lets him go; and it is not because he knows that the Arab is a freedom fighter (neither Balducci nor he seem to be clear about that point). It seems to be for one of two reasons: because he wants to avoid being a part of any social institution; or because Daru is metaphysically averse to the role of policeman – at least until war is officially declared, as he tells Balducci (p. 1612).

In addition, the issue is muddied by the choice of an Arab who is both a rebel *and* a murderer. The fact that the Arab is not a straight political prisoner turns the political war of liberation and the rebels' cause into a partisan affair. In that sense the Arabs' *brother*hood mentioned twice ('Tu viens avec *nous*' (p. 1617) and 'notre *frère*' (p. 1621)) appears more like an in-group kind of solidarity than like the universal brotherhood of freedom fighters or Daru's dreamt-of universal brotherhood of soldiers or prisoners at night, once they have doffed the clothes of civilisation (p. 1618). Both kinds of universalism tend, by definition, to reduce people and peoples to their most fundamental common denominator – their humanity (thoughts and feelings) – but in so doing people as social beings are ignored. The universalistic stance thus sees socially defined differences not as richness but as divisiveness and, consequently, the basic social fabric of life is devalued. People belong to nations, to ethnic and language groups, to a dominant or dominated group, and to the many other mediating social entities (groups, institutions) that help define a culture and, therefore, the nature of people's beliefs, values, and emotions. Here, such social forms of solidarity are devalued in favor of individualism and (unhappy) solitude.

Although the story is told by a narrator who takes Daru's point of view, one must not assume that Camus sides squarely with Daru and ignores mediating institutions such as the *gendarmerie* or the school system. In fact Daru is tacitly but strongly criticised, as we will show. Still, Daru's universalist position is presented as positive whereas the Arab's is not and would only be so if he were presented solely as a freedom fighter. The situation seems to have been conceived in this manner by Camus for a particular purpose: the plot is framed in an asymmetrical fashion precisely in order to have the Arab's status change for the better by the end of the story. At that point he becomes a new embodiment of the Noble Savage in his ability to adapt to another, assumedly better culture. The Arab will accept death in the name of the same kind of ideal Daru exemplifies:

the brotherhood of two men from different backgrounds living different situations but coming to comparably high moral decisions.[9]

In order to show that this is the case, we must attempt to make sense of the notoriously puzzling ending of 'L'Hôte'. One must assume that the men who write on the blackboard are the Arab's comrades-in-arms and that he contacted them during the night when he went out (in order to urinate, thinks Daru). The possibility of the presence of people around the schoolhouse is confirmed by the fact that Daru thinks he hears noises as he leaves (p. 1620) and that, when he returns, he finds the writing on the wall. Ironically, Daru wanted the prisoner to escape, either during the night or when he gives him money, food, and turns him bodily in the direction of freedom – thus unambiguously indicating what he would prefer the prisoner to do. The latter reacts with 'panic' (p. 1621) and wants to explain something to Daru who refuses to listen. This state of panic has occasionally been interpreted in a racist manner: a primitive Arab faced with the choice between liberty and doing what he is supposed to do, chooses the easy way out – taking the road to jail and death – as the stereotypical Arab fatalist ('insha Allah') might do.[10]

Before adopting such a facile reading, it seems preferable to link all of the unexplained parts of the tale together considering that, whatever one's final interpretation may be, we need to explain the writing on the blackboard and therefore the presence of other Arabs who knew that Daru was holding the Arab prisoner. The interpretation requiring the fewest inferences is the one that assumes that the Arab must have told his brothers during the night that Daru would take him to prison. This is reasonable since Daru refused to answer the Arab's insistent question about the 'Tu viens avec nous?' which means either 'Will you be accompanying Balducci and me to the prison?' or 'Will you join us rebels in our fight for freedom?' Daru having said nothing to the point, the Arab cannot but expect that Daru will act like Balducci. Such a reading also gives the Arab – and Camus – a noble, self-abnegating, and intelligent reason for going to prison: he knows that Daru is going to be killed and since Daru has refused to listen to him, he, the Arab, chooses to die too in order that some kind of poetic justice may come to pass. A true tragedy: both coloniser and colonised are good people but they both must die because of the social system they were born into – and because they do not make the necessary effort at communication.[11]

Our interpretation of 'L'Hôte' unexpectedly turns the Arab into a hero – a twist typical of the endings of *Exile and the Kingdom* but a twist which is not obvious to most readers. Among Camus critics, only Showalter seems to have considered it.[12] But there are good reasons for critics' not considering this interpretation. If there were other Arabs around the schoolhouse and if the Arab was able to talk with them during the night, why on earth did they not all flee together? Or why did they not attack Balducci earlier or Daru when he left the schoolhouse with the Arab? Camus has provided us with a story whose verisimilitude is in certain important respects lacking. But the choice is simple: either we accuse Camus of a certain lack of realism, which in a story with a moral focus – and in a collection with ' symbolic overtones – does not seem overly damning. Or we accuse him of providing an ending which is tragic for Daru but also blatantly told from a coloniser's perspective and blind to everything else.

In any event, Camus certainly does not present the coloniser as an innocent bystander. Willy-nilly, Daru is a participant in the French educational system: he teaches French geography, not Algerian geography. The point is mentioned at two crucial moments: the first and last pages of the story, and only there. It is definitely therefore a significant choice. In effect Camus has chosen a more graphic and practical equivalent of the notorious 'Nos ancêtres les Gaulois' which even African children were allegedly forced to learn in colonial times.[13] A map is an ideal objective correlative because the last words, condemning Daru to death, are written across the map of France on the blackboard, thus creating a strong symbolic statement of what the rebellion is about: France versus the Arabs. Further, Camus does not have Daru merely teach French geography: Daru had been teaching about the 'quatre fleuves de France' – teaching in the desert about an idyllic country with rivers. And it is across the meandering rivers that the Arabs appropriately write their message to Daru.[14] Camus cannot but be making a point about primary schoolteachers in Algeria who are part of a system that teaches not about Algeria but about France.

By contrast, towards the end of the story, the Arab becomes a man with the highest individual moral values, a perfect clone of Daru, the French Algerian loner who has isolated himself from the socio-political world. The Arab illustrates the 'eye for an eye principle' turned upside down: 'If Daru must die, then I shall die too so that a higher kind of justice may be served.' Camus's Arab is hardly realistic; rather he is the embodiment of the universalist ethic. Camus does not envision an Arab who would have the high ideal of refusing to waste his own life and death for reasons of personal morality; he does not envision an Arab who would want to dedicate his life and his death to the greater good of Algeria's freedom. To be sure personal morality is noble and tempting but what good would it do to die for a marginal, uncommitted French teacher named Daru who sadly could not choose between freedom and independence for Algeria and the colonial system he was born into?

Camus was obsessed with rebellion and even terrorism in the name of freedom. After *L'Etranger* he wrote *Les Justes* (1949), a play which discusses the 1905 attempt on Great-Duke Serge's life. Understandably Camus presented those issues more directly when the topic was far from home, as Russia was. As a result, in 'L'Hôte' we are left with a story that is so difficult to interpret that critics have easily attributed stereotypical motivations to the Arab. If readers adopt a reading that gives morality and nobility to the Arab and thus presents Camus in a favourable light – one must then assume that Camus wanted to present a situation that reflected his own sense of powerlessness and divided loyalties in the face of the nascent war of liberation. Yet neither his tacit criticism of Daru's teaching nor his positive presentation of the Arab's final sacrifice are highlighted enough to become a crucial part of the inter-pretations proffered by most readers. And, even if they were, the Arab's individualistic rather than social or political moral stance would still define him in terms that ignore his identity as an Algerian fighting a war of liberation.

In that sense, it is a failure of Camus's humanism and of ours that we have steadfastly focused on Daru, Meursault, and other emotional 'strangers' having difficulties of communication within their own society. They deserve to be heard but so do the under-class, those who are made to be invisible exiles in their own kingdom. Arabs in Algeria were the prototypical 'strangers' whose voices humanists like Camus ought to have heard – and whom they ought to have more loudly spoken for. Viewed with the comfortable superiority afforded by the passage of time, *L'Etranger* now seems like the swan song of a colonial society: the song struck a chord in many of us but the singers, Meursault-the-narrator and Camus, now sound oddly off. There they were telling a small story while the great songs of freedom needed to be sung.

Notes

1. All citations from Camus' works are from *Théâtre, récits, nouvelles* (Paris: Gallimard, Bibliothèque de la Pléïade, 1963). Translations are from *Exile and the Kingdom*, Justin O'Brien (trans.) (New York: Alfred A. Knopf, 1958) and *The Stranger*, Matthew Ward (trans.) (1988).

2. Alain Costes notes this and suggests (pp. 66 ff.) that Camus views Arabs as aggressors because Camus's mother was once attacked by an Arab, thus justifying on a biographical level Camus-Meursault's retaliation. ('Le Double Meurtre de Meursault' in Gay-Crosier, Raymond and Jacqueline Lévi-Valensi (eds) *Albert Camus: oeuvre ouverte, oeuvre fermée* (Paris: Gallimard, Cahiers Albert Camus: 5, 1985).

3. Louis Sala-Molins, *Le Code noir* (Paris, Presses Universitaires de France, 1987).

4. A. J. Liebling, *New Yorker*, 3, November 1956, p. 144. I owe this reference to Professor René Galand (Wellesley College).

5. Philip Thody, 'Camus' *L'Etranger* revisited' (*Critical Quarterly*, vol. 21, 1979, pp. 61–9).

6. Although a 'classical' writer, Camus is oddly fond of puns: the titles of most of the stories in *L'Exil et le royaume* are either direct puns as in 'L'Hôte' and 'La Pierre qui pousse' (it weighs down but also grows, being a stalactite or stalagmite) or at least plays on words as in the symbolic adultery of 'La Femme adultère' and the uncertainty of Jonas's spelling of 'solitaire ou solidaire' at the end of the story by that name. Whether the homonymy of 'cymbales' and 'cinq balles' is due to chance or not, it has a relatively small role to play in the story but does not seem untypical of what may happen during the creative process, particularly at key locations in Camus' works – titles, beginnings, and especially endings.

7. See, for example, Peter Cryle's excellent close reading of the story – but one unfortunately based on the notion of 'l'Afrique primitive' *Albert Camus*: 6 (Paris, Minard, Lettres Modernes, 1973, p. 137).

8. Roelens, 'Un texte, "son histoire" et l'histoire: 'L'Hôte' d'Albert Camus (*Revue des sciences humaines*, 42, no. 165 (1977) pp. 5–22.

9. Allegedly high moral decisions, since in Daru's case one is entitled to wonder about the reasons for his freeing the Arab. Nonetheless, one is, I believe, supposed to attribute to both Daru and the Arab an ethic of brotherhood and solidarity (cf. 'solitaire ou solidaire', the concluding words of 'Jonas', the story after 'L'Hôte'), which is a basic theme of *Exile and the Kingdom* and one that is closely linked to the second basic theme in *Exile*, communication and its failures.

10. See Peter Cryle (note 7).

11. 'L'Hôte' cannot be fully understood if it is taken out of the context of the difficulty of communication which is the central theme of every single story in *Exile and the Kingdom*. Difficulty of communication *and* the urge to communicate are essential commitments of Camus and his heroes from Meursault-the-narrator to Janine in 'La Femme adultère', to Jonas the artist, to Daru as schoolteacher. The conclusion of *Exile and the Kingdom* is 'Assieds-toi avec nous' said to dam engineer

d'Arrast by Brazilian natives. It is a fitting yet oddly ironic conclusion to a story where both the indigenous population and the white man are presented as stereotypes, but stereotypes succeeding in their effort at communication.

12. English Showalter Jr, '*The Guest*: The Reluctant Host, Fate's Hostage' in his *Exiles and Strangers* (Columbus: Ohio State University Press, 1981).

13. Blacks did not too often get the opportunity to go to school and, moreover, it took some time for the French to decide that their ancestors were the Gauls. On this, see Marc Ferro, *Comment on raconte l'histoire aux enfants à travers le monde entier* (Paris, Payot, 1981/1986) p. 37 ff.

14. The choice of the rivers (water) is also particularly significant. Recall that d'Arrast, in 'La Pierre qui pousse,' is building a dam and that Meursault commits his murder because he was seeking the refreshing presence of the spring on a hot summer day.

16

The Depiction of Arabs in *L'Etranger*
Jan Rigaud

Si nous avons un devoir en ce pays, il est de permettre à l'une des populations les plus fières et les plus humaines en ce monde, de rester fidèle à elle-même et à son destin.[1]

If we have a duty in this country, it is to permit one of the proudest and most human peoples in this world to remain faithful to itself and to its destiny.

Camus's most striking trademark as an 'Algerian' writer, as he once called himself, is the disproportion between his instinctive passion for Algeria, the land which exudes physical sensation, and his reflexive attitudes toward its inhabitants, Arabs, Kabyles and Berbers, which made up the Muslim communities. While the land's 'indifférence' captures the novelist's unreserved attention, the Muslim can only claim a modest place in the writer's fiction.

Camus's Algeria was a melting pot; the happy conjunction of two peoples, one Muslim, the other European but both Algerian, and if Camus, the man of letters, wrote about his country, Camus, the man, spoke for Algeria and for its two principal communities. The Maghrebine and the French of Algeria or *pieds-noirs*. He knew them and had ample access to both communities. More significantly, Albert Camus was one of the few French intellectuals to be actively engaged in Algerian affairs and to take a personal interest in the injustices of which Muslims were the victims.

At the time of its publication, *L'Etranger* drew very little protest from the young Algerian Arabs who read this work. French critics, on the other hand, unfamiliar with life in French Algeria moved rapidly to exploit the murder of an Arab committed by a *pied-noir*. Haunted by this crime, they assumed that the novel concealed a political message carefully planned by Camus. Had the writer through his protagonist become the *porte-parole* of the 'petit blanc' minority? Had he conscientiously ignored the Muslims? For years, Camus has been discredited for not having considered in his fictional work, the Arab 'reality'.

A political reading of *L'Etranger*, while inevitable and valuable, is incomplete because it focuses merely on one reality – the political reality – thus underestimating other realities, cultural, for example, which mattered much more to Albert Camus, the man and the artist, than politics.

Yet, Camus was no stranger to politics himself. For a while, he was an active member of the Algerian Communist Party, not by ideology but because he thought that the party was genuinely interested in Arab social and welfare reforms. Inevitably, Camus's sympathy for the Muslims led to conflicts with the Parti Communiste Algérien as he quickly realised that the party had altered its line and no longer supported Arab interests. Disillusioned and betrayed by the new anti-Muslim nationalism, Albert Camus withdrew. As Jacqueline Lévi-Valensi writes:

> Camus, who did not want to betray 'the true meaning of life' either in his action or in his writings, could not and would never be able to accommodate himself with cynicism to ideological strategy. Not only did he not accept 'the veering' of Communist party politics, but he did not accept having been misled, and having served a lying propaganda.[2]

A year later (1936), while working with the Théâtre du Travail, Camus met with Arabs and *pieds-noirs* during his extensive travels through the country. It was during this period that the young Camus witnessed first-hand the ills of colonialism – the misery of some and the unbearable poverty of others. Finally, in 1939, Camus was sent to the impoverished territory of Kabylia by the newly created leftist newspaper, *Alger Républicain*, to investigate the plight of the Kabyles' conditions. Not only was he fully exposed once again to the misery rampant at that time among the Kabylian population, but he also explored other dilapidated communities around the two cities of Oran and Tibet. His articles published in *Alger Républicain*, then in 1958 in *Chroniques Algériennes*, were provocative and unsettling to the French administration of Algiers. His anti-colonialism made him persona non grata with the government. Evaluating these articles, Camus's biographer, Herbert Lottman writes that 'his survey was clearly the product of legwork, of talking to rank-and-file victims of the colonial system.'[3]

Yet, when *L'Etranger*, his first published novel, appeared in 1942, Camus the novelist, had seemingly ignored the Muslim community which had previously earned the sympathy and commiseration of Camus the journalist. He who wrote not long after: 'Ce peuple n'est pas inférieur, sinon par la condition de vie où il se trouve, et nous avons des leçons à prendre chez lui dans la mesure où il peut en prendre chez nous',[4] *'This people is not inferior, except by the conditions in which they live, and we have lessons to learn from them just as they do from us'* had created in the midst of his fiction a Muslim community which remained the back drop of his novel. It was an idle population, deprived of its identity. For the sake of his literary career, Camus had sacrificed the Arabs' presence and self-esteem; Arabs had been relegated to the periphery of Camus's novel or served as 'accessoires et éléments décoratifs'. Hence, as a whole, the Muslim community suffered a kind of mysterious negativity which remained omnipresent throughout the entire work. That the Arab community existed in Algiers, *L'Etranger* does not deny, but its presence is only felt through nondescript and marginal references. Such lapses cannot be ignored.

The conception of *L'Etranger* was temporally so closely related to Camus's overriding concern with his country's social conditions, that one is unsettled and confused by his ambiguous treatment of his Arab characters. Camus's personal commitment to social and political justice, along with his sense of righteousness and hope for Algerian assimilation, find no voice in the author's first novel. Indeed, *L'Etranger*'s faceless Arabs appear embedded in a colonial society. Hardly defined, looking suspicious, wearing dirty working clothes, holding knives, they drift jobless, nameless or vacillate between idleness and promiscuity. As Jean Sarrochi explains: 'One must notice the break between the political man and the man of letters: there is a Camus who is sympathetic to the humiliated Arab, writing warm articles about him and a Camus who, from his writings, eliminates him or lowers him to shady roles.'[5] If this is true, why couldn't Camus express in his novel what he had so strongly exhibited in his articles about the Kabylians? Was his real intent to portray Arabs as reprobates, social failures, parasites of a Western society? Did his *pied-noir* status prevent him from transgressing the boundaries of social prejudices? Finally, could a plethora of Muslim details have been the marks of a militant Arabophile writer?

In the first part of the novel, the Muslim community is re-presented by only three Arab individuals: the nurse who cared for Meursault's mother, Raymond's mistress, and her brother. When Meursault enters the morgue, the first and only person at his mother's coffin is a Moorish nurse. Her face, partially hidden by the bandage tied around her head to conceal the ravages of cancer, suggests early signs of alienation from society. By standing un-obtrusively in the corner of the room, the nurse has distanced herself from the European inmates and avoided all contact with Meursault who, nonetheless, feels her presence. The illness she suffers, the job she endures and her triple conditions, as a woman, as a 'colonisée', and as an Arab, have pushed her to the bottom of society. Immersed in her job, she seems to flee the community. Her indifference to her surroundings, even more than her mutism, bespeaks hostility and suspicion. In this institution, the Arab nurse appears a likely outcast and her self-effacement betrays her de-meaning condition.

At night, however, the nurse fulfills her duty by returning to the room for Madame Meursault's wake. Yet, as the other inmates gather around the bier, she now moves further into the back of the room where she remains an unobserved presence. Meursault can only guess at what she is doing: 'la garde était aussi au fond, le dos tourné. Je ne voyais pas ce qu'elle faisait. Mais au mouvement de ses bras, je pouvais croire qu'elle tricotait' (p. 1131).[6] *'The nurse was on that side of the room too, but with her back to me. I couldn't see what she was doing. But the way her arms were moving made me think she was knitting' (p. 9)*. But the nurse's withdrawal reflex cannot be too foreign to Meursault, nor does it suggest to him any hatred. In-advertently, 'the absence of even a flawed contact reveals the conflict between Arabs and the *pied-noir* communities',[7] as Camus's bio-grapher Patrick McCarthy writes. Yet, the tentativeness ventured by 'le regard' of the narrator, conveys a sense of *rapprochement* which parallels the awkward mute rapport Meursault once had with his mother. In this depiction, the faceless Moorish nurse assumes a new identity conjuring up the vision of Madame Meursault mère. Whereas this association may have been overlooked at that time, it nonetheless demonstrates the consciousness of the narrator, whose distrust of France and guilt as a coloniser compels him to turn to the first native of Algeria. Some twenty years later, the protagonist of *Le Premier Homme*, Camus's unpublished manuscript, will be delivered by a Moorish nurse.[8]

Hence, the nurse's reserved attitude should not be viewed solely as a political emblem of a 'colonisée', but it should be recognised as a social and cultural reflex as well. The symbolic illness that afflicts the nurse may indeed reflect the inflexibility of a class structure like that of the *pieds-noirs* – or be the product of both the Islamic customs which have constantly denied women their rights, and the Arab culture which has reduced them to the degrading state where they still are today. Such evils explain the nurse's second-rate status in her own country. Consequently, the pathetic characterisation of the first Arab in *L'Etranger* emanates, in my opinion, from its socio-cultural reality and not from the fiction of 'a poor white type of liberal, a colonialist under the skin',[9] who knew nothing about Arabs' quest for national identity. In this unfortunate condition, the Muslim nurse is much more the victim of her own culture than that of an indifferent artist.

Raymond Sintès is a neighbour of Meursault. When we meet him, he wears a bandage on his hand because he just had a fight. He now invites Meursault for dinner because he seeks advice about a woman, his mistress. Suspecting her of cheating on him, Raymond asks Meursault to write a letter to ensnare his mistress and then to take revenge: 'Après quand elle reviendrait, il coucherait avec elle et "juste au moment de finir" il lui cracherait à la figure et il la mettrait dehors' (p. 1148). *'Then, when she came running back, he'd go to bed with her and right at the last minute he'd spit in her face and throw her out' (p. 32).*

One day, as Marie and Meursault are preparing for dinner, they hear a woman screaming. Raymond is beating his mistress. Alerted by the noise, the neighbours come out and an upset Marie asks Meursault to look for a police man. Meursault refuses because, as he says, 'je n'aimais pas les agents' (p. 1151), but the interference of a police man brought by a tenant reveals that social flaws were more harshly viewed than racial interaction. In his neighbourhood, Raymond is disliked, not because his mistress is a Moor, but because he is a pimp. More significantly, what emerges is the fact that the Arab victim is protected here and defended by both the *pied-noir* and the authority. Regardless of the victim's racial background, justice for Camus must prevail for all and should know no boundary. While a maudlin woman, who could have been charged with prostitution, is let go, a baffled Raymond is ordered to appear at the police headquarters.

Camus's neutral writing and objective narrative in this passage lead the reader to perceive both incidents – Raymond's fight with the Arab and the Mauresque's violent humiliation – as the results of personal and domestic conflicts rather than the corollary of a colonial system. In this story, for example, Raymond never alluded to the Maghrebine origin of the man with whom he had trouble, nor did he cause Meursault to suspect that his mistress is a Moor. Although the turbulent relationship revolves around a polarity between *pied-noir* and Arab, there is no evidence that Camus's narrative aimed at focusing on the ambiguities of ethnic diversities. Indeed, as Germaine Brée points out:

> What happens within the span of each life, however trivial, counts and counts absolutely. Hence Camus's outcry against all that mutilates human beings, and that outcry establishes the link between his fictional work and his socio-political actions. It is from that view of man that Camus postulated an ethic of commitment rooted in human emotions and solidarity. (Brée, p. 200)

However, sporadic uprisings, inherent mutual mistrust, and especially, 'the French-Algerian's reckless passion for life',[10] prompt us to acknowledge and not to dismiss the violence which eventually reappears the Sunday when Marie, Meursault, and Raymond leave for the beach: 'Ils [les Arabes] nous regardaient en silence, mais à leur maniére ni plus ni moins que si nous étions des pierres ou des arbres morts' (p. 1161). Once again, hostility has returned as evidence by the 'endemic regard' of the Arabs, who while seeming indifferent are viewed as threatening and provocative. Marie's impulsive reaction is, of course, to get away from them. But unlike Marie, whose concern is quite understandable, Meursault's neutral observation ('je lui ai dit que c'étaient des Arabes qui en voulaient à Raymond' p. 1161) compels the reader to reevaluate the flow of events, so that the presence of the Arab group on this Sunday morning should not suggest a recurrent provocation of the *pied-noir* trio, but a personal confrontation with Raymond who has so viciously humiliated an Arab Algerian woman.

Ironically, because of his association with Raymond, Meursault is inevitably linked with the same kind of violence that Raymond has committed towards the Arabs. Given the political climate of French Algeria in the early 1940s it is not surprising that the murder of an innocent Arab by a European which concludes the first part of the novel would be depicted as a politically inspired act of provocation. Although one can subscribe to Germaine Brée's

view that 'the innocuous life Meursault was leading reveals mal-
evolent potentialities '(Brée, p. 143), this is far from suggesting that
he was a ruthless coloniser and a militant advocate of French Algeria.
Furthermore, to infer that Meursault killed the Arab because he
was an intruder – or a rival – is to give Camus's literary expression
a political motive which the author would have repudiated, for 'as
an intellectual he would provide no verbal incitations to violence'
(Brée, p. 217). Also, it would suggest racial prejudices and a tacit
support of colonialism which cannot be attributed to the writer.
Even in the ample studies of intuitive analysis, such a proposal has
no foundation: 'Far from ignoring the colonial reality, Camus
would seem to be the product of it, but generally more deeply on
the "side of the Arabs than the French".'[11]

Meursault's indifferent relationships within his own community
(e.g. with Marie), his lack of personal ambition and his tepid
sentiments for people close to him are hardly the trademarks of a
violent militant coloniser. In the second part of the novel, Camus's
depiction of Arab prisoners will quickly put into focus all political
motives while probing more convincingly the sympathies of this
'unassuming hero'.

After killing the brother of Raymond's mistress, Meursault is sent
to jail. At first, when the prisoners, mostly Arabs, see him, they laugh
as if the presence of this European Algerian were a joke. Then, upon
hearing the truth, 'ce qui les a un peu refroidis',[12] Madame Faure
remarks ironically, they remain silent and the following long inter-
lude dissipates the resentment and minimises any hostile exchange
or harmful intention that could have burgeoned between the new
arrival and the other inmates. Instead, the Arabs explain to Meursault
how to make himself comfortable with the mat, 'en roulant une des
extrêmités, on pouvait en faire un traversin' (p. 1177). Among the
Arabs, Meursault finds real commiseration and justice. Such detail
must be pointed out for it exemplifies once again an awareness of
an Arab sensitivity toward the French-Algerian murderer. Furthermore, if earlier in the story – at his mother's wake, for example – a
guilty Meursault 'avait eu l'impression ridicule qu'ils [the inmates]
étaient là pour me juger,' (p. 1132), no such inference, however more
appropriate here, is made.

One can now foresee a strange communion between the two
social groups; a bond between Arabs and *pieds-noirs* is intimated.
The whole future of Algeria seems to have found its *raison d'être* in
this little cell, and for a moment at least, a sense of solidarity, a

relationship between the two communities has been effected; brothers – not rivals – for a night have emerged from the flaws and failures of Algerian colonialism. More importantly, by remaining silent, the Arabs have proven to Meursault that they have understood him, for, after all, both ethnic groups have been the victims of colonialism. At this instant, silence has once again been the catalyst for peace and understanding, the pivotal opening for communion and *rapprochment*. But, as a new day breaks, the dream recedes and yields to political realities: Meursault is moved away from his companions; the vision that he could be a viable part of Algeria has failed. Camus's personal interference is explicit. There is no illusion, no hope. With a harsh and poignant reality his dream of a Mediterranean Algeria has faded away.

The very last allusion to the Arab community in the second part of the work takes place again in prison as Marie visits Meursault. With rare exceptions, all the prisoners are Arab and when Marie meets Meursault she is surrounded by Maghreb women. Her visit underlines the dimension of two different mentalities. On one hand, Marie and the other *pied-noir* visitors cry at the top of their voices, engage in loud exchanges and gesticulate profusely; on the other hand, the Arabs, squatting on the floor, manage to communicate while keeping their voices down.

la plupart des prisonniers arabes ainsi que leurs familles s'étaient accroupies en vis-à-vis. Ceux-là ne criaient pas. Malgré le tumulte, ils parvenaient à s'entendre en parlant très bas … le murmure des Arabes continuaient au-dessous de nous. (pp. 1177–8)

*Most of the Arab prisoners and their families had squatted down facing each other. They weren't shouting. Despite the commotion, they were managing to make themselves heard by talking in very low voices …
The murmuring of the Arabs continued below us.* (pp. 74–5)

By stressing the ordinary habits in the *pied-noir* community and focusing on the visible and tangible behaviour with which he is most familiar, the writer has inevitably hidden the visibility of the Muslim community. Moreover, his omission of a definitive Maghrebine identity would lead critics to deem Camus an obdurate, unrepentant *pied-noir* and not the defender of Kabylian causes he once was. His earlier claim to be an Algerian writer would remain doubtful and as equivocal as Meursault's explanation for firing four bullets into an inert body. On the other hand, Camus's oblique reference to the Arabs functions as an authentic illustration of the Muslims' life under a colonial system, and his laconic manner brings out an 'arabisme' that has been objected to, or merely overlooked by readers. Indeed, it was certainly not Camus's intent to obliterate a community whose prejudices and injustices he had witnessed. Ironically, by holding back the visibility of the Arabs in his work, Camus has made their presence the premonitory sign aiming at a greater awareness of the Maghrebine social and political situation. As Herbert Lottman says: 'Camus and his comrades in the theatre group were taking giant steps into the future (and incidentally increasing distance from the majority of the French Algerian settlers.)'[13]

For those unfamiliar with his stand on Arab issues, Camus may seem to lack the evidence to make such a plea more cogent, especially since the Arabs are jailed, killed, or pushed into the background of his novel. Yet, his sentiments are nonetheless implicitly shown by the Arab's silence and self-effacement. Despite this ambivalence, Camus's sympathy is hardly equivocal: *pied-noir* characters may be the backbone of his narrative but they cannot be the real heroes. For behind each Arab character's anonymity, the disfigurement of the Moorish nurse, the verbal and physical abuse of Raymond's mistress and the absurd murder of her brother, lies a community which will no longer be silenced. Camus did recognise the inevitable sign of Algeria's future struggle for independence, as his journalistic work testifies, but in a continuous political climate his so-called inclination to be 'du côté des pieds-noirs' has prevented the writer from giving his Arab characters a deeper dimension. Therefore, one could concur with Patrick McCarthy's observation when he writes: 'Once one discards the hoary old myth that he [Camus] ignores Arabs, then the allusions to them might take on a coherent meaning.'[14] In this context, Camus's Arabs may well be the unlikely heroes of the novel, and their silence could conceal 'more things to admire than to despise'.

'Everything considered', writes the Algerian writer Kateb Yacine, 'he [Camus] was more French than Algerian. One cannot reproach him, but one must discard the myth of Camus "the Algerian".'[15] A half-century later, one can further dispel the myth of Camus 'le petit blanc'. Like Rodin's sculptures whose profiles can emerge only from the shadow which surrounds them, Camus's idiosyncratic, self-effacing approach to the Arabs in the midst of turbulent *pieds-*

noirs, has enhanced the startling reality and uniqueness of a community which otherwise would have been betrayed under a brighter light.

Notes

1. Albert Camus, *Essais* (Paris: Gallimard, Bibliothèque de la Pléïade, 1965), p. 938. Text from 'Misère de la Kabylie', 1936. Translation by Adele King.
2. Jacqueline Lévi-Valensi, *Camus et la politique*, Actes du Colloque de Nanterre, 5–7 juin 1985 (Paris: L'Harmattan, 1986), p. 149.
3. John Cruickshank, *Albert Camus and the Literature of Revolt* (New York: Oxford University Press, 1960), p. 16; Herbert H. Lottman, *Albert Camus* (New York: Doubleday, 1979), p. 199.
4. *Essais*, p. 942. 'Crise en Algérie', 1945. Translation by Adele King.
5. Jean Sarrochi, *Albert Camus et la recherche du Père* (Lille: Service de reproduction des thèses, 1979), p. 288.
6. Albert Camus *Théâtre, récits, nouvelles* (Paris: Gallimard, Bibliothèque de la Pléïade, 1962), p. 113; Translations by Matthew Ward, *The Stranger* (New York: Alfred A. Knopf, 1988). Page references within parentheses are to these editions.
7. Patrick McCarthy, 'The First Arab', *Celfan Review*, vol. IV, no. 3 (1985), p. 24.
8. Sarrochi, pt 5, ch. 3, 'La Mère', pp. 347–353.
9. Germaine Brée, *Camus and Sartre* (New York: Dell ,1972), pp. 152–3.
10. Patrick McCarthy, *Camus* (New York: Random House, 1982), p. 160.
11. Francesco Di Pella, 'Remarques sur l'Algérianité de Camus', *Albert Camus: à l'occasion du vingt-cinquième anniversaire de la mort de l'ëerivain*, Paul-F. Smets (ed.) (Brussels: Editions de l'Université de Bruxelles, 1985), p. 27.
12. Christiane Faure, Interview [sur Camus] accordée à Jan F. Rigaud in *Celfan Review*, vol. VI, no. 1 (1986), p. 19.
13. Lottman, p. 148.
14. McCarthy, *Celfan* vol. IV, no. 3, p. 23.
15. Cited in José Lenzini, *L'Algérie de Camus* (Aix-en-Provence: Edisud, 1987), p. 120.

Part Four
Comparative Studies

17

Camus, Faulkner, Dead Mothers: A Dialogue
Deborah Clarke and Christiane P. Makward

C : What do we want to achieve in undertaking a dialogue on Faulkner and Camus?

D : There are several things we can investigate in bringing feminist perspectives to authors who can be viewed as patriarchal, but invite new readings.

C : Usually critics do not look at the in-between in analysing gender but you are writing on the maternal metaphor in Faulkner and I wanted to do a new reading of *L'Etranger*. We know that Faulkner was fond of some things French and probably had read Proust, and again that Camus read Faulkner – eventually doing a stage version of *Requiem for a Nun*.

D : The French existentialists were among the first to praise Faulkner; Camus felt he was 'the greatest writer in the world' (Blotner, p. 1577). Also, both authors made rather provocative statements about mothers. Faulkner compared art and the mother with his famous declaration in a 1956 interview: 'If a writer has to rob his mother he will not hesitate; "The Ode on a Grecian Urn" is worth any number of old ladies.' Setting aside the obvious misogyny I note a close association between mothers and art. One must rob – and ultimately kill off – the mother in order to create as the title of my book (*Robbing the Mother*) indicates.

C : And Camus, quizzed about the Algerian War, made his famous statement about choosing his mother over justice. Obviously 'mother' is a value and we thought it was worthwhile pursuing the discourse of 'mother' or the maternal metaphor in those writers. First we must remember how tricky it is to develop an argument on the basis of single words in translation. In the

French text the first word is not 'Mother' or 'Maman' but 'Today'. The translators, not foreseeing gynocentric readings, reordered the words.

D: They induce a stronger feminist reading by putting the primacy on 'mother' rather than 'today'.

C: And Gilbert used 'Mother' rather than 'Mom' which suggests an intimacy subsequently found lacking in Meursault, so that's a problem. His translation was notoriously unscrupulous in places, particularly the shooting scene: he clearly departs from Camus's degree 0 style, to use Barthes' metaphor of transparent, communicative style. I find Ward's translation a distinct improvement though I question retaining 'Maman' in English, and leaving it in the initial position ... it smacks of the Victorian English novel ... So we are trying to achieve a new reading of Faulkner and Camus, and certainly of *L'Etranger* with reference to Faulkner and those mothers who have just died giving birth to a text, or a new consciousness in the characters.

D: This recalls Faulkner's comment on killing off the mother in order to create. Here the text is produced by that very process.

C: It is the image of the mother in the coffin that fascinates me. In Camus's text you can follow how 'Mom' retains personhood through the wake (she is referred to as 'Madame votre mère', 'Maman' and 'Mme Meursault'), but she loses it for objecthood when the casket passes the door into the sunlight. She dissolves into the scenery, even before she is buried. Indeed Meursault sniffs marine salt from over the hills and reflects, 'I could feel how much I'd enjoy going for a walk if it hadn't been for Maman' (Ward, 1988, p. 12). On the next page, the text resumes: '*Through* the rows of cypress trees leading to the hills near the sky, the reddish and green ground, the few sharply delineated houses, I could understand Mom' (*TRN*, p. 1135, my translation since Ward reads: '*Seeing* the cypress ... *I was able* to understand Maman *better*'). Those hills are in the direction of the sea, of course.

D: This raises the question of the ritual behaviour associated with the mother in the coffin. *As I Lay Dying* is a funeral journey, taking the dead mother to be buried in town. The neighbours, scandalised at what they see as impropriety and disrespect for the dead, comment, 'you've got to respect the dead themselves, and a woman that's been dead in a box four days, the best way to respect her is to get her into the ground as quick as you can.'

(p. 110) So we see a similar controversy over what constitutes respect for the dead mother but presented comically.

C : Meursault of course goes through the appropriate gestures except he does not cry, the (in) famous detail if we reduce the argument to the absurd.

D : And you get this curious inversion: the mother is a procreative force but through her death rather than her ability to give birth.

C : Apparently, there is not much to probe in comparing Faulkner and Camus at the level of style: we cannot imagine two more antithetical modes, and yet we want to pursue the topic a little. Leafing through Faulkner's novel, we can see how fragmented and 'pre-postmodernistic' it is. Can we see from the titles how they exemplify the authors' ideas of style?

D : Yes, 'the stranger' is one word identifying one character which seems to me to illustrate Camus's very pure and simple prose.

C : It is a minimal message although in translation, both *The Stranger* and *The Outsider* could be kept in mind to think of the text.

D : *As I Lay Dying* comes out of *The Odyssey*. When they meet in the underworld, Agamemnon tells Odysseus how Clytemnestra stood over him as he lay dying, and refused to shut his eyes and perform the standard rituals for the dead. So even beyond its shocking quality, the title focuses our attention on burial rites and respect for the dead. It's a far more encompassing title than 'l'étranger' and I think it exemplifies Faulkner's exuberant and wordy style . . .

C : In sharp contrast with Camus. That's why Gilbert's translation overlooks the essentials of *The Stranger*'s voice: the shooting scene is over-translated – Halloween style – with the 'blade of light . . . gouging into [Meursault's] eyeballs', also making the erotic symbolism explicit: 'I felt the smooth underbelly of the butt' becomes 'the smooth underbelly of the butt jogged my palm.' Such inflation – even in this surreal Doomsday scene – contradicts Meursault's manner, which is the understatement, far from the expressionistic imagery Camus will use for a crazed character such as Caligula, or 'The Renegade'. So we were going to look at the question of metaphorical discourse in Faulkner because it seems absent in Camus though other dimensions of metaphor can be considered. What kind of metaphorical function is illustrated in Faulkner's *As I Lay Dying*?

D: First, I'd like to refer to Domna Stanton's essay 'Difference on Trial'. She argues that metaphor suggests being, offers a way to understand the unknown. Metonymy, on the other hand, 'evokes the more numerous elements that are missing and thus, in contrast to metaphor, suggests lack of being' (1986, p. 175). This is a distinction that we'll want to apply, as Stanton does, to the issue of the maternal metaphor. But for now, let me say that Faulkner's characters speak in a highly poetic language using simile more than metaphor, producing the dual effect of being and non-being. Faulkner uses many linguistic tricks, most notably surrealistic imagery as in Vardaman's famous line, 'My mother is a fish' (p. 79).

C: Indeed that is striking image, akin to Breton's title: *Soluble Fish*. And the speaker of that image is not deranged, or playing, or quoting a nursery rhyme . . .

D: No, he is a nine year old trying to understand death. He catches a fish nearly as big as himself, cuts it up and reappears 'bloody as a hog to his knees' (p. 37). Shortly after that his mother dies but he can't accept the fact of her death. He can only understand it by transposing her into the fish and thinking of the fish's death, something he can comprehend. When he says 'My mother is a fish', he is trying to understand death without saying 'My mother is dead'.

C: This brings up the interesting distinction I have tried to make discussing the metaphor 'writing the body' in an article, long before I read Sterling's. The substitution Vardaman makes of 'fish' for 'death' suggests that Faulkner's genius has captured some fundamental truth which is that there are various types of body consciousnesses. Sterling distinguishes – as Merleau-Ponty had – between consciousness of the body, body-consciousness and consciousness as we normally understand it: the state of mind that is reflexive and uses and controls language to some extent. Meursault says he smiles looking at himself in the bottom of his tin-dish but his image does not smile. Of course the clinical term for this is a schizoïd psyche, a 'divided self'. But here, we have an artist's hunch about the gap between the reflexive self, and the body-consciousness as separate from the consciousness of the body . . . It is that same body-consciousness that is years behind the reflexive self in Proust's famous masquerade dinner scene, at the close of his novel. Much as we cannot conceptualise objectively our aging body, Faulkner's character will not conceptualise accurately the mother's dead body. Sterling quotes Camus on the necessity, in order to understand the body's central truth, to approach a corpse with 'the eyes of the body'. In Vardaman's case, it seems that the child, having seen and handled a dead fish, has a physical awareness of the experience of death but cannot/will not transfer it/meta-phorise it: he fends off the experience of his dead mother's body ...

D: For Vardaman indeed the trope is metonymy: he denies death physically as well as verbally when he drills holes through the lid of the coffin to give her air (since she is not dead), and of course, with typical Faulknerian black humour, he punches the awl right into her face which they then have to veil.

C: What Faulkner suggests is that at that age there is no symbolising the concept of death: there is just a physical, metonymical association with the experience of a dead fish. We can't say this applies to Meursault because losing his mother is not a learning experience for him. His most important death lesson occurred years earlier when he had to interrupt his studies. Behind that is a biographical trace: Camus was sentenced to death at least in his imagination at age seventeen, when diagnosed with tuberculosis ... So he had been initiated in the flesh to the threat of death and he projects that on the character of Meursault.

D: You are suggesting that the death of his mother wasn't learning experience because there was nothing more to learn about death for him.

C: That's right, in fact he explicitly says so at the very end. 'Nobody, nobody had the right to cry over her' (Ward p. 122). No one should have cried because there was nothing tragic about her death or her life in the retirement home. Crying over people's deaths makes no sense, obviously we grieve over ourselves. But of course his story, the outsider's, is indeed the story of an initiation into death at a different level. Could we say that Faulkner's novel is a dramatisation of learning death for a set of characters or a particular character?

D: More for some characters than for others. It is for Vardaman, and for Jewel, Addie's favourite son. The rest are more concerned with their own motives and problems, and interestingly enough, her only daughter Dewey Dell, feels she has no 'time to let' her mother die because she is so intent on getting an abortion (p. 114).

C : A nice example of the metaphorical style of Faulkner; it is also the deeper meaning of Meursault's 'matricide', and the second level of his initiation. The real fable of *The Stranger* is learning 'the happy death' as his mother had done before him. I was happy with my first reading when we started this dialogue: it was a metaphorical reading achieved when you superimpose a triad of signifiers. Camus represents Meursault circulating between three maternal signifiers, traditionally intermeshed in the French literary imagination. Any number of poets have played with 'mer', 'mère', and Marie, or 'marine' from Desnos and St-John Perse to Duras and Irigaray ... By the way, Meursault does not 'pick up a girl' called Marie, as some critic put it: they were acquainted, and this time he bumps into her in the sea ... she is marine Marie/Venus of the sea indeed. In his ultimate ecstasy, the maternal metaphor is there as well as the memory of the mother: peace enters Meursault like a 'marée' (tide). It makes a lot of sense to read Meursault as a character who is 'different' because indifferent to everyday concerns, not that he is really indifferent but he will not fake feeling, he does not cry and that is why he is beheaded in the end. But he certainly must also be read as outside paternal law.

D : If we think about those three signifiers and perform a metaphorical reading, would you say that this brings us to a greater understanding of the maternal or the feminine?

C : Certainly I come to a greater acceptance of Meursault ... I become able to encompass him (metaphor intended) as a strange and in fact impossible character, but only *logically* impossible. That's how I first read Meursault: as a rigged character, probably under the influence of Sartre's piece on *L'Etranger*. I used to read it as one of three emblematic protagonists Camus had selected to illustrate the absurd. At that stage I was not very involved in the non-psychology of Meursault. And then I rediscovered it years later: I was alerted as a feminist critic to the discourse of the body prevalent in this text. What I could add to Sterling's is my gynocentric reading: Meursault's (in)difference as un-differentiation from the maternal. So my latest view was to understand Meursault's bizarre psyche as a mind-body without a psyche in the usual social, symbolic sense; absurd – which means discordant – in that he lives a very physical life and doesn't think about anything beyond the immediate. Then he also makes sense as an icon of contemporary man, that is an emotionally desensitised or a differently sensitive, pleasure-oriented humanoid. This is what *L'Etranger* can be construed as.

D: The issue of writing the body can be applied to Faulkner but in very different terms. His characters, particularly his men characters, use words like Hamlet; they would rather speak than do. But you can't get away from the literal body in this novel because it is centred on a corpse, the corpse of the mother. This is a journey of the body for both mother, whose body is being carried to the grave, and daughter, desperately seeking an abortion. The novel writes the maternal body not the generic – and thus male – body.

C: The characters in Faulkner are at the stage where they discover the treachery of language and it's very clear that Meursault is beyond that point in maturing or philosophising, in making sense of reality and language.

D: That's true for Addie who gets to Meursault's state by the end of her monologue (particularly striking since it takes place many days after she dies). Her son Darl also focuses on the problematic nature of language. He intuits things, Dewey Dell's pregnancy for example. She says, 'He said he knew without the words ... and I knew he knew because if he had said that he knew with the words I would not believed' (p. 26). This non-verbal communication, which Darl holds with lots of people, reveals not so much the treachery as the uselessness of language.

C: But you see this again can be construed or rationalised by referring to the body-consciousness, of this other sense, this intuition we call 'picking up vibes'.

D: But this seems to be 'feminine intuition', and one of my arguments about Darl, who goes insane by the end of the novel, is that he is too feminine. His permeable ego boundaries, his intuition, and his use of non-verbal language make him a 'feminised' character who cannot survive.

C: And Meursault is unfit too: nothing makes any difference to him. So, my new reading is to take Meursault's indifference to social conventions and order as being non-differentiated from the maternal, the archaic in the Kristevan or Lacanian sense. This would explain his apparent indifference or constitutional difference: if you can focus on the fundamentals of existence much as an oriental yogi, then indeed you are able to keep symbols at a distance and not react to the trivial or even the tragic. In addition, Meursault was no longer familiar with his mother by the time she died.

D: So he was not that close but yet he was still not really separate from her.

C: It sounds paradoxical only if we collapse the mother and the maternal which I don't mean to do. Rather I would associate bodily gratification, being in touch with your body, with femininity, at least as a reflection of the feminine condition. It is considered a trait more developed in women, to be more aware of the material, to be less a creature of project, of system and of power. As you know Meursault declines the opportunity to go back to Paris and build a career: that has no meaning or value for him. He even declines to occupy both rooms of the apartment after his mother leaves: he literally 'cocoons' in his own bedroom (with a view).

D: We could superimpose much of this on Darl. Part of his difference also is in his lack of separation from the maternal. He is most like his mother even though they don't like each other. Darl himself more than any of the other men has a focus on the body. He talks about the taste of water which has set in a cedar bucket, and about how much he likes lying in bed at night and feeling the cool wind over his body.

C: And his are the kind of fluid ego boundaries, or a weaker ego altogether, which Camus has illustrated in 'The adulterous woman', a short story. Meursault is very much an embodiment of that purely physical person, male in this case, but it is hard not to see the feminine in him behind the Mediterranean machismo, and the colonial heritage.

D: Certainly, Nancy Chodorow and Luce Irigaray have identified fluidity and permeable ego boundaries as feminine.

C: We could even credit Simone de Beauvoir with theorising women's cultural (not essential) heritage as 'immanence', a propensity not to define oneself separately, not to conceive power-oriented lifestyles, and not to pursue them.

D: We've gotten ourselves into a position where we are talking about two male characters in two texts by two male authors whom we are identifying as essentially feminine. What do we do with that?

C: We remember that great minds can only be bisexual and great writers in particular, because language is the realm of infinite nuance and suggestion. I followed that in detail in Claude Simon quite a while ago, but I'm absolutely convinced of it. It is the only way out of the segregation of the sexes, it's a way of accounting for sexual differences without relating sex to art, only gender ... always a matter of representation, and of the ability to tune in to differences.

D: Actually, there's an excellent book on bisexuality in Faulkner by Minrose Gwin, called *The Feminine in Faulkner* (1990).

C: It is a fruitful approach, and so is construing Meursault's psychology as someone not separate from the body, the pre-oedipal, the archaic 'mother'. Then there is the other area we want to explore: the question of language because in feminist theory a prevailing idea has been to view the gender of language as masculine, though it has come under fire more recently.

D: Well it is a very problematic notion since we are speaking as women in a discourse designated as masculine.

C: Yes, but they told us it was impossible: Granoff reading Freud (*La Pensée et le Féminin*) shows that when women speak or think, it is the masculine in them that speaks: they are no longer female the minute they are not silent.

D: Then there is no way out of the trap. You are either silenced or you are speaking as a man.

C: If you define the feminine as that which cannot be symbolised then of course inevitably I'll never be a woman as I speak, and yet here we are, embodying the paradox. Is there a point of comparison between Meursault's relation to language and Faulkner's characters?

D: There is some comparison to Dewey Dell who is unable to 'speak' her pregnancy. In addition, Addie begins her soliloquy talking about how words are no good; they are simply shapes to fill a lack. She repeats the names of her husband and sons over and over again until the words solidify and take on a shape and then they die away. Ultimately she comes to the realisation that language is not going to help her, that she has been tricked by words like love and motherhood. And this could be the reason that she dies, remembering the lessons of her father: 'the reason for living is getting ready to stay dead' (p. 167).

C: Perhaps she dies to avenge herself: remember the oath she forced on her husband, to take her back to Jefferson? She said 'my revenge would be that he would never know I was taking revenge' (p. 164). This incredibly protracted, hallucinating burial is her wish.

D: She's comparable to Meursault when she says of her neighbour, Cora, 'she believed I was blind to sin, wanting me to kneel and pray too, because people to whom sin is just a matter of words, to them salvation is just words too' (p. 168). That's precisely what Meursault refuses to become involved with: communicating with the chaplain.

C : The priest annoys him tremendously, triggering an explosion which constitutes a very significant step in his progress toward harmony with the universe and peace. Camus also wants us to believe Sisyphus is happy pushing his rock back up the hill through eternity. We are led to believe that Meursault dies happy because cleansed of any hope, 'désespéré' as Gide put it, asserting hedonism. Meursault, accepting the inevitable, asserts his radical alienation from a blood-thirsty human horde.

D : This detachment parallels Addie's condition but not Faulkner's. Addie may feel that you must empty yourself of hope and of feeling, but in the rest of the characters and in the novel itself, there's a vitality and continuity which I don't see in Camus.

C : But this is early Camus: he didn't uphold this commitment to focus on death and he calls 'an imbecile the one who is afraid of jouissance' (*Noces*, p. 59) Meursault is an impossible character, but he makes a lot more sense once we pay attention to the intervention of the mother and the father figures. After Meursault is deprived of his body, cut off from the maternal that is, the physical life, the sea, and Marie, he is forced to go through the final stage of learning death or 'conscious' death.

D : What about that newspaper story of the mother who kills her son?

C : That is when the spectre of the bad mother comes in, the one who does not know her own flesh. So far 'mother' or the archaic has been positive, pleasurable. It was the only realm to live by: not indifferent but reliably present, and accessible. I don't think nature is labelled 'indifferent' in the first part of the story (the sun of course is hostile at the opening and at midpoint, since these are the scenes of death). It is only at the very end . . .

D : When he's looking up at the stars and experiences that 'tender indifference' of the world . . .

C : But this world is not nature, not the sea, not the beach, not concrete nature: it is an abstract 'world'. Remember that from his cell all he can see is the sky, a night full of signs and stars. And so the reference is to the world in the masculine (in French) and to the 'fraternal'.

D : Rather than 'mother nature' which is, of course, not indifferent to us.

C : What has just irrupted – and disrupted his time – is two father figures, a memory of his father and the prison chaplain who suggests that they come closer calling each other 'father' and 'son'. His protective gesture revulses Meursault: calling this man 'father' would draw him inside the patriarchal value system which he rejects. His biological father isn't mentioned until the metaphorical mother is lost, while the real mother theme recurs at the very end.

D : Faulkner, in contrast, twists that circle. The novel opens with Addie still alive and closes with: 'Meet Mrs Bundren'. She's been replaced.

C : A critic has said that young Camus was almost obsessed with dying, and that he feared death 'except his mother's'. This statement seems to be projected onto Meursault who does not react to his mother's death, either because he has lost her a long time ago or because he finds her in his other 'mothers': he has incorporated the idea of death. We might say he has regressed (progressed, in Camus's didactic perspective) to a pre-oedipal (pre-phallological?) stage which would account for his favouring 'Mom' over the formal 'Mother'.

D : Now in Faulkner you get two contrasting responses from two different sons. Jewel, Addie's favourite and illegitimate son, goes through a classic oedipal struggle and is forced to sell the horse which has served as his mother substitute. Darl, on the other hand, is much more like Meursault when he says 'I cannot love my mother because I have no mother', a suggestion that can be read on many levels. One can say that his mother – who never cared for him while he was alive – was simply a body who provided various maternal services. Once that maternal body ceases to function, he has no mother. Darl does not believe in the maternal metaphor. Indeed, he resents this long journey with a stinking corpse, eventually he sets fire to a barn housing the coffin. This behaviour gets him committed to the state asylum, and it stems from a refusal to see the corpse of the mother as a metaphor. Rather, he sees it as metonymy, a lack of being. This parallels Meursault's behaviour which damns him at his trial.

C : What constitutes Meursault's difference, is that he does not 'buy' words and therefore uses as few as possible. I am interested in Kristeva's theory of the 'woman effect' as that which is either unexpressed or repressed, since part of my reading of Meursault is that, not paying his dues to the symbolic and social order he is the silent one, and as such, rejected and destroyed. The memory of the father is a very crucial episode in Meursault's march towards the guillotine, and his terminal sense of self. Could he be released, he would obviously go back to the same lifestyle, because his lifestyle is authentic. He would not become power or success oriented. But he does achieve the ability to declare himself at one with the universe, which means essentially become 'God' in having a divine understanding of reality.

D: But hasn't he achieved this stage once before when he had to give up his studies? Isn't that what has resulted in his current life?

C: He had broken away from the banal lifestyle having had to face the issue of death, but I don't think he had experienced a profound and definitive harmony with the universe, as he puts it, which is happiness. I don't think he has experienced this before. It took losing the body, being forced to go within himself and face the destruction of his body to reach that higher stage of consciousness which is Camus's ideal.

D: And which is becoming a man, which is leaving behind the maternal. So for him is happiness predicated upon a male discourse?

C: It's not the only way to become a man; there is the lyrical essay 'Nuptials' where, having spent the whole day at the beach, Camus felt he had done his job 'as a man' (*Noces*, p. 60) But in the situation Meursault is in, which is inescapably facing death, he has to go through another degree of initiation.

D: But this still leaves the maternal behind. And where does this leave us as feminist critics?

C: Well, it suspends my proposed reading of Meursault as being on the side of the maternal, and feminine, and destroyed as such, but is also leaves me unhappy with that kind of teleological reading because I think it is an initiation into death-consciousness and acceptance, which of course is very 'male', death-oriented.

D: The most you can say in terms of the feminine is that it is not death-oriented, but having said that, we are still focused on the issue of the patriarchal structure.

C: I think it's quite clear that very often, and for reasons that may not be easily articulated, men are much more concerned with, obsessed with, controlling death, coming to terms with death.

D: That makes Addie very male-oriented. She has appropriated a male identification since she is obsessed with death and since she, like Meursault, remembers the father. That's one of the reasons she wants to be buried in town, to show that acknowledgement of her father rather than of herself as mother. She is perfectly willing to sacrifice and forego, even for her favourite children, her maternal role in order to assert an identification with the father, and the idea of death.

C : There is no objective reason for Addie to have such a sinister attitude. I wonder if Faulkner's suggestion is really a vindication of the rights of women or a denunciation of the condition of the woman.

D : It could certainly be a denunciation of the position of women. And you can also say, whether or not you believe it is a good thing, that Addie as a woman is able to cross conventional gender boundaries, which does mark a step towards psychobisexuality. Both Addie and Darl move in that direction. Darl is committed to an asylum at the end and so is 'killed off', but not before we recognise that part of his artistic creativity – and his insanity – comes out of his 'feminine' nature. And you still have Dewey Dell, who has been unable to abort her fetus. You can read that as reinforcing women's conventional roles, but you also see in Dewey Dell the glimmerings of some recognition of what this all means, of the problems of language and maternity. It's not simply a blind continuation.

C : Would you not agree that the true outsider in this batch of characters is the dead/dying mother?

D : Yes I would. To a lesser extent you could sometimes see Darl in that role, but Darl experiences greater intimacy with some of his siblings than Addie seems to have with anyone. Actually, Dewey Dell could also qualify, for she is isolated is her pregnancy, realising that 'the process of coming unalone is terrible' (p. 59).

C : In evaluating my attempted feminist reading of *L'Etranger*, I'm aware that it is not the most encompassing reading. I think I would sustain my original interpretation which is that he is a rigged character, created to illustrate Camus' ethics: the dignity of man is to be as lucid and aware as possible of his finitude, of being a body for death. On the other hand, it is the early Camus, and the rest his work certainly qualifies that highly teleological – some have argued pre-theological – reading of *L'Etranger*. In short, I don't think that gynocentric reading of *L'Etranger* is the most convincing one although it helps throw light on Camus's bisexuality.

D: And that may ultimately be what we want to get to: we probably can't, nor maybe should we, try to protect these authors too vehemently against charges of phallocentrism. But we can certainly find value in a feminist reading even if it doesn't change – as you suggested with *L'Etranger* – the overall interpretation of the novel. It nonetheless opens up new questions and points out some interesting concerns.

C: Certainly I wouldn't elaborate a gynocentric reading of *La Nausée* because it's so obvious what goes on in that text. There is such a rejection, a revulsion before the feminine, not only of the female body but matter, any and all flesh. What Meursault/Camus does is valuing the body as the only and ultimate reality other than death, while Roquentin is pure intellectual mush, the reverse of Meursault, who tries to live a pure body until he can become pure consciousness of death at the end because he's lost the body, so he's forced into this new intelligence of the universe.

D: So one of the things that we can discover through these feminist critiques is that a focus on writing the body, and the awareness of gender as a point of interrogation, or a point of examination can help clarify many of the issues in both Camus and Faulkner. This brings us back to the issue of gendered language.

C: Yes, I would say if we want to conclude on that, the question of the gender of discourse, in this case, rather than language in general. I'm not convinced, after twenty years of feminist criticism, that language is male. It's only male because it's male controlled, mastered, and that's a situational quality or situational advantage and privilege; it's not essential, although it is in the Lacanian system but we're out beyond that. So if we should try to evaluate the feminine quality of these discourses, I would certainly give the advantage to Faulkner but again we know it's not all that fair to compare *L'Etranger* which is this simplified, highly trimmed French-style demonstration of something to this extraordinarily complex, elusive, mindboggling novel.

D: Genre enters in as well as gender.

Works Cited

Blotner, Joseph, *Faulkner: A Biography*, 2 vols (New York: Random House, 1974).

Camus, Albert, *L'Etranger* (Paris: Gallimard, 1942, Bibliothèque de la Pléïade, 1962).

Camus, Albert, 'Noces à Tipasa' (1939), in *Essais* (Paris: Gallimard, Bibliothèque de la Pléïade, 1965).

Camus, Albert, *The Stranger*, Stuart Gilbert (trans.) (New York: Alfred A. Knopf, 1946; Vintage Books Edition, 1954).

Camus, Albert, *The Stranger*, Matthew Ward (trans.) (New York: Alfred A. Knopf, 1988; Vintage International, 1989).

Clarke, Deborah, 'Gender, Race, and Language in *Light in August*', *American Literature*, vol. 61, no. 3 (October 1989) pp. 398–413.

Faulkner, William, *As I Lay Dying* (New York: Random House, 1930; Vintage Books, 1964).

Makward, Christiane P., 'Corps-écrit, corps vécu: de Chantal Chawaf et quelques autres', in S. Lamy and I. Pagès (eds) *Féminité Subversion, Ecriture* (Montréal: Editions du Remue-Ménage, 1983).

Stanton, Domna C., 'Difference on trial: A Critique of the Maternal Metaphor in Cixous, Irigaray, and Kristeva, in Nancy K. Miller (ed.) *The Poetics of Gender* (New York: Columbia University Press, 1986).

Sterling, Elwyn F., 'A Camus: The Psychology of the Body and *The Stranger*', *University of Southern Florida Language Quarterly*, no. XXV, nos 3–4 (1987) pp. 11–20.

18

L'Etranger and the New Novel
John Fletcher

If taken literally, Alain Robbe Grillet's remarks about Camus's 'tragic humanism' in *Pour un Nouveau Roman* might lead the reader to suppose that he – and other *nouveaux romanciers* along with him – reject Camus outright. Robbe-Grillet says:

> Aussi le livre n'est-il pas écrit dans un langage aussi *lavé* que les premières pages peuvent le laisser croire. Seuls, en effet, les objets déjà chargés d'un contenu humain flagrant sont neutralisés, avec soin, et *pour des raisons morales* (tel le cercueil de la vieille mère, dont on nous décrit les vis, leur forme et leur degré d'enfoncement). A côté de cela nous découvrons, de plus en plus nombreuses à mesure que s'approche l'instant du meurtre, les métaphores classiques les plus révélatrices, nommant l'homme ou sous-tendues par son omni-présence: la campagne est 'gorgée de soleil', le soir est 'comme une trêve mélancolique', la route défoncée laisse voir la 'chair brillante' du goudron, la terre est 'couleur de sang', le soleil est une 'pluie aveuglante', son reflet sur un coquillage est 'une épée de lumière', la journée a 'jeté l'ancre dans un océan de métal bouillant', le cap 'somnolent', la mer qui 'halète' et les 'cymbales' du soleil ...
>
> La scène capitale du roman nous présente l'image parfaite d'une solidarité douloureuse: le soleil implacable est toujours 'le même', son reflet sur la lame du couteau que tient l'Arabe 'atteint' le héros en plein front et 'fouille' ses yeux, la main de celui-ci se crispe sur le revolver, il veut 'secouer' le soleil, il tire de nouveau, à quatre reprises. 'Et c'était – dit-il – comme quatre coups brefs que je frappais sur la porte du malheur.'

L'absurde est donc bien une forme d'humanisme tragique. Ce n'est pas un constat de séparation entre l'homme et les choses.

C'est une querelle d'amour, qui mène au crime passionnel. Le monde est accusé de complicité d'assassinat.

Nor is the book written in as purified *a language as the first few pages might lead one to suppose. In fact it is only those objects which are already loaded with flagrant human content which are carefully neutralised, and for moral reasons (such as the old mother's coffin, where we are given a description of its screws, their shape, and depth of penetration). Side by side with this we discover the most revealing of classical metaphors, which become more numerous as the moment of the murder approaches, and which either mention man or assume his omnipotence: the country is 'gorged with sunlight', the evening is 'like a melancholy truce', the pot-holes in the road reveal the 'shining flesh' of the tar, the earth is 'the colour of blood', the sunlight is a 'blinding rain', its reflection on a shell is 'a sword of light', the day has 'cast anchor in an ocean of boiling metal' – to say nothing of the 'breathing' of the lazy waves, the 'drowsy' headland, the 'panting' sea and the 'cymbals' of the sun ...*

The key scene of the novel gives us a perfect picture of a painful solidarity: the implacable sunlight is always 'the same', its reflection on the blade of the knife the Arab is holding 'wounds' the hero in the middle of the forehead and 'searches' his eyes, his hand tightens on the revolver, he tries to 'shake off' the sun, he fires again, four times. 'And', he says 'it was as if I had given four short knocks on the door of misfortune.'

The absurd, then, is indeed a form of tragic humanism. It is not a recognition of the separation between man and things. It is a lovers' quarrel, which leads to the crime of passion. The world is accused of being an accomplice to murder.[1]

But Camus was pretty much of their generation: born over a decade after Nathalie Sarraute, the same year (1913) as Claude Simon, a year before Marguerite Duras, and a decade (more or less) before Robbe-Grillet, Robert Pinget and Michel Butor; so any rejection of Camus by the *nouveaux romanciers* would be the rejection of a contemporary or near-contemporary, not of a precursor. When *L'Etranger* appeared in 1942, Claude Simon had written his first novel (*Le Tricheur*, 1945), and Nathalie Sarraute had already published her first book (*Tropismes*, 1939), so any disagreement between Camus and the *nouveaux romanciers* would be more in the nature of a squabble between siblings than the traditional rejection of the preceding generation.

In any case, what could be more characteristic of the *nouveau roman* than Camus's handling of Meursault's rhetoric in *L'Etranger*? The cunning with which Meursault manipulates the reader and alienates his/her sympathies away from the murdered Arab is the invention of a writer who was fully aware that reality is created by language – a premise of the *nouveau roman* – rather than being straightforwardly conveyed by it, as Balzac (or the Balzac whom Robbe-Grillet sets up as Aunt Sally in *Pour un nouveau roman*) assumed. A close reading of *L'Etranger* shows how Meursault, by a cunning use of tenses and of other rhetorical devices, *creates* the version of events which virtually every reader accepts and retains: that the Arab's death was at worst a regrettable incidence of manslaughter and at best a legitimate action, on Meursault's part, in self-defence, rather than, as the prosecution allege at Meursault's trial, murder in the first degree.

That close reading has to begin at the first word, *aujourd'hui* ('Today Maman died'). Although this word is at once qualified by the words 'or yesterday maybe', the text creates a feeling of *present* time which continues throughout the first two paragraphs. For convenience, I shall refer to this feeling as the 'dramatic present', even where it is not necessarily aroused by a preponderant use of the present tense proper but by other parts of speech (such as temporal adverbs like 'today').

The third paragraph opens with a *passé composé* ('J'ai pris l'autobus à deux heures', ('*I took the two o'clock bus*'), p. 1125).[2] This constitutes one of the most important time-shifts in the whole novel, but because the *passé composé* is ambiguous in French – it can apply to a very recent occurrence, and usually does, but (particularly in colloquial usage) it can also refer to the remote past – the reader is not at once aware that the narrator Meursault is gliding from an ostensible stance 'on top of events' in the first two paragraphs to a position considerably more removed in time. How far removed, the reader has no way of telling: the *passé composé* would be used by a speaker quite naturally to relate even remote occurrences, and it is this informal mode which characterises Meursault's style. Indeed, in abandoning the traditional *passé simple* (preterite) tense in favour of the more colloquial *passé composé* (perfect) tense, Camus broke new ground in French narrative prose. The reason which is usually given for this is that he wanted to give Meursault's account a conversational immediacy which would make his hero more *sympathique* (likeable) to the reader, and undoubtedly it helps in that regard. But a more important reason was the temporal ambiguity of the *passé composé*. Indeed, the first two paragraphs of the novel are fraught with ambiguity, even deceit, on the question of when the story was composed: the use of the future tense in particular ('Je prendrai l'autobus à deux heures ... je rentrerai demain soir,' ('*I'll catch the two o'clock bus ... I'll return tomorrow evening*', p. 1125) artificially but very effectively appears to situate the narration between the mother's death and her funeral.

With the third paragraph of the novel, however, we are withdrawn imperceptibly into a structure of less immediate, more distanced narrative. The use of the preterite tense would have made this break crudely evident. The *passé composé* allows a smooth and virtually unnoticed shift. It is some while, in fact, before the reader becomes aware that Meursault is not, temporally speaking, on top of the events he is describing; by using a shrewd blend of the dramatic present and the ambiguous past, Meursault is able to create an illusion both of immediacy and of objective veracity.

In fact, it is not until the fifth chapter of Part 1 that we are given some 'back perspective' on Meursault's existence *prior to* the main events of the novel, when he tells us how he had been ambitious as a student and informs Marie that he had once lived in Paris. By this point he is preparing the reader for the revelation that he is far more aware of the implications of his actions – hitherto presented as spontaneous and unconsidered, with one event simply following upon another – than, for rhetorical reasons, he has been willing to do up till now. The revelation comes on p. 1157: 'J'ai répondu', he begins, and then adds as if in parentheses, 'je ne sais pas encore pourquoi' ('*I answered, I still don't know why*'). Those last few words – je ne sais pas encore pourquoi – lift the narrative clear out of ambiguous time and situate it firmly in the *un*ambiguous remote past, since they refer to the 'real' present, and betray the fact that the account is being written with the benefit of considerable hindsight.

How much hindsight, the reader must still wait to discover, but in due course, by a process of elimination, he/she establishes that the book, which at the outset appears to be a diary, is in fact *entirely* composed, from beginning to end, in the days (or hours) which follow the rejection of the prisoner's appeal and the consequential certitude it brings that the time he has left is finite. How then does

Meursault spend the precious hours (or days) before his execution? On something which, unlike his naive student aspirations, he has at last found to possess 'real importance': nothing less than conducting his defence all over again, not the assize court affair which resulted in his conviction for first degree murder, but the trial he pleads before us, the jury composed of his posthumous readers. For it is *our* favourable verdict that he is after, and our sympathy which is of supreme importance to him. He is thus a more self-aware and sophisticated narrator – and indeed a more consistent character – than is usually supposed. He is, in fact, a writer, constructing a text and therefore – Robbe-Grillet has taught us – a *reality* which *his* text calls into being.

It is consummately done. Indeed, Meursault gives at first such a powerful impression of near-imbecility that most readers are taken in by him and fall into precisely the trap he lays for them, which is to accept his special pleading as factual and the prosecutor's rhetoric as gross distortion, an act of flagrant and wilful misunderstanding. But is it? The republic's legal representative is doing his job as well as most French lawyers could; anyone who has sat through a French murder trial will find little out of the ordinary about the business which the accused claims to experience – and thereby induces us to experience – as frighteningly unreal. The difficult rhetorical exercise triumphantly succeeds, so that few readers pause to examine how Meursault has persuaded one jury, at least, of his complete innocence of the crime for which he is under sentence of death.

Thus the text of *L'Etranger* so structures reality that Meursault is exonerated, and his murder trial ends favourably after all, with his acquittal by the jury of his readers. Theirs is of course a *literary* tribunal, and the triumph of pleading achieved before it is a specifically *literary* triumph. It is therefore a striking example of *nouveau roman* techniques deployed ten years before the *nouveau roman*.

And there are other parallels. In Nathalie Sarraute's *Le Planétarium*, (1959) different views of the novelist Germaine Lemaire are expressed, and conflicting versions of the same incident are confronted, leaving the reader to determine which to accept. Although this is a more open structure – at least in appearance – than Meursault's 'speech' in his defence, it could hardly have been written in the way it is without the example of the ways in which fictional rhetoric can be deployed that Camus provided in *L'Etranger*.

The same is true of *Le Voyeur* by Robbe-Grillet (1955). It would be easy to reconstruct, from the various indications given in the text, how the precocious teenager Jacqueline was sadistically and methodically tortured, raped and killed by Mathias the watch salesman, watched all the while by Julien, the voyeur of the title, and his terrifyingly accusatory eyes. But this is precisely the black hole into which the text lures the reader, who is intrigued by a gap in Mathias's painstakingly detailed sales schedule, a period of about an hour, long enough to permit Mathias to seek Jacqueline out, torture, rape and murder her, and throw her body off the cliff into the sea. The text circles around this blank spot, as if the void itself presided over the composition – which in a sense it does, since this absence is the true generator of the text.

There are at least three possibilities in *Le Voyeur*, as there are at least two in *L'Etranger*. In *L'Etranger*, Meursault shot the Arab either because he was a rather limited person dazed by the heat and the glare, or because he was a callous sadist: the reader is invited, as we have seen, to choose between these two versions of the central episode of the novel. In *Le Voyeur*, Mathias may be a sex-murderer; but if he is, why is he not investigated by the police instead of being left free to embark for the mainland on the next ferry? Or else the girl's falling off the cliff may have been an accident, as the islanders believe, and Mathias had nothing to do with it; but in that case, why does he miss the first ferry and prolong his stay on the island, obsessively (re?)visiting the cliff top where the accident (crime?) took place. The third possibility, and probably the most plausible, is that Mathias is not a rapist and murderer but a sadist-fantasist – a sort of pornographic Walter Mitty – whose diseased imagination transforms Jacqueline's accident into a lurid sex-crime committed by himself; this would explain why he misses his boat and returns obsessively to the scene of the accident, making it into a crime in his mind. But then why does Julien watch him as he searches the cliff top for incriminating evidence – is it incriminating in the sense that it points to his guilt, or in the sense that it enables him to 'construct' a crime?

Claude Simon's novel *La Route des Flandres* (1960) raises a similar question: did Captain de Reixach ride deliberately into the sniper's ambush and thereby disguise his suicide as death in action? The narrator (a former trooper who served under Reixach) is not sure: 'Mais l'ai-je vraiment vu ou cru le voir ou tout simplement imaginé après coup ou encore rêvé?' (*'But did I really see it or think I saw it or* merely imagine it afterwards or even only dream it all?'), he asks on the last page of the novel.[3] The reader is once again invited to decide whether what the trooper thought he saw did, in fact, take place, and if it did, what meaning to attach to it: death in action or suicide? And once again, the example of L'Etranger would have been instructive in showing Simon how the same event – in this case the death of an officer on a Flanders road – may be seen in more than one light, with profoundly different implications. If Meursault's shooting of the Arab was justifiable homicide, then he should have escaped the guillotine; if Captain de Reixach did not ride deliberately into a death-trap, then all of the romantic embroidery of the event by Georges and the other prisoners in the stalag becomes pure fiction, truly – as Reixach's widow says, when Georges looks her up after the war – the dirty-minded fantasies of sex-starved POWs.

Finally, in Michel Butor's La Modification (1957), the narrator first tells himself that he is going to leave his French wife for his Italian lover, then changes his mind and decides not to desert his wife, all this during the hours taken by the express he is travelling in to cover the distance between the Gare de Lyon in Paris and the Stazione Termini in Rome. The 'modification' of his plan is prompted by his rehearsal, during the long journey, of the two scenarios, setting up house with his lover, or staying with his wife; and the difficulties and contradictions inherent in the former course of action lead him to abandon it. Once again, a version of events (in this case, a version of possible future events) is tested for plausibility in the very public arena of the text's readership, where (as we have seen) Meursault chose to plead in his own defence.

These nouveau roman examples are all instances where the unreliability of data is emphasised, and which show that the lesson of Part 2 of L'Etranger was learnt by the new novelists. For Part 2 is very different in tone from Part 1. For one thing, Meursault intervenes much more in the narrative than he did in the first part. He claims, for instance, that the proceedings before the examining magistrate all seemed like a game to him, and he justifies the passivity which he displayed in the first part by telling his lawyer – and thereby the reader too – that in recent years he had lost the habit of introspection. He also makes no attempt any longer to conceal the fact that he is composing an account (he goes in for redactional asides of the 'if I might put it so' variety). In the carefully managed pathos of the court scenes, Meursault's seemingly most trivial actions of the first part, such as taking Marie to a Fernandel movie or failing to refuse the offer of coffee at his mother's wake, are systematically 'read' by the prosecution in a manner calculated to cast him in the worst possible light. But Meursault is of course blurring the distinction between crime and social lapse, as Camus did too in his famous remark – whose paradoxical nature he freely admitted – that in our society a man may be condemned to death for not shedding tears at his mother's funeral (p. 1920). The Algiers court is shocked by his callousness not so much because of his insensitivity but rather as the key to his motivations. Camus skilfully induces us to misapprehend this perfectly reasonable forensic test, and so overlook the fact not only that Meursault has committed murder, but also that he feels no remorse for having taken a human life. Normal people are extremely upset even if they kill someone entirely by accident; the Algiers tribunal was not being unreasonable in expecting Meursault to show some regret for having shot dead a man whose only weapon was a knife, and to have compounded the offence by firing four more shots into the man's dead body. But we, the readers, have been treated to the magnificent flight of rhetoric which concludes Part 1, particularly to Meursault's cunning use of passive forms – of the trigger 'giving', not being pulled, of the revolver going off, not being fired – and he now has us in the palm of his hand, and he can afford to abandon the pretence of being obtusely unaware of what he was doing.

He can, in fact, come clean about the fact that he is a writer, that is an artist, shaping his text along consciously literary lines, and anticipating innovations made – as we saw above – by Camus's contemporaries, the *nouveaux romanciers*. The time-scheme of the second chapter of Part 2 is rather complex, for instance. Ranging back and forth over the months in gaol, Meursault generalises about the experience and does not record events in strict chronological sequence as he had done in Part 1. He conveys this new impression of generality by an increased reliance on the imperfect tense, which as mentioned above was not the standard tense of Part 1. In other words, a more 'writerly' approach to fictional narrative is establishing itself after the pseudo-naive style of Part 1. When, for instance, Meursault says that the period before his arrest now seemed a long time ago to him, he is indulging in poetic licence; it cannot really seem all that long ago or he would not recall it as vividly as the full account in Part 1 reveals that he does. For him, it can hardly be remote; but the rhetoric he deploys induces the reader to feel its remoteness and the consequent horror of the captivity which causes Meursault's life as a free man to appear so distant. In fact, despite his affected indifference to the past, Meursault betrays a detailed, if selective, recollection. And that selectivity is the hallmark of an artist who knows his *métier* and the rhetoric it commands. In Part 2, that includes imperfect subjunctives, conditionals and pluperfects. There is, in fact, a continual process of temporal expansion and contraction at work, between the event and the close 'dramatic present', and the event and its more distant 'narrative past'. This systole-diastole effect is reinforced by temporal indications like 'I recall . . .', by dramatic breaks in the narrative, by redactional asides, by authorial commentary, by the skilled deployment of imagery, and above all by the controlled use of pathos. All this adds up to a formidable massing of literary artillery trained on our sensibilities and sympathy, so that long before we read of the death of the Arab we are unhesitatingly on the side of the brilliant advocate who convinces us indubitably of his essential innocence by portraying himself as a harmless, uncomplicated individual who only asked for a quiet life, but found himself instead caught up by a vindictive destiny in a tragic mesh beyond his understanding or control.

We can, moreover, reconstruct three clear phases in Meursault's existence on the basis of indications concealed in the text, itself a very *nouveau roman* thing for readers to do: the years of the student who read books, had ambitions, and lived in Paris; the time of the mature man who is content with humble clerical work because he has come to believe that nothing of that had any real importance; and the period of the condemned prisoner who sees even this renunciation in an unfamiliar light. To discern this evolution in the character is simultaneously to dispose of the common complaint of ineptitude levelled at Camus. The accusation of inconsistency goes like this: we are presented in Part 1 with an inarticulate moron who is unconvincingly transformed, only a few months and a hundred pages later, into an eloquent intellectual whose fluent rhetoric silences even a man of words like the prison chaplain. The truth is, of course, that in Part 1 Meursault conceals his intellect and understanding so that his fate may appear in retrospect all the more unjust and unfair. His advocacy is therefore an artifice, a construct, a *literary* creation; and his *literary* triumph will make it possible for him, in the magnificent closing words of the novel, to glory in the expression of hatred that, once he steps onto the scaffold, he expects to hear from the ignorant mob, so different from the Stendhalian 'happy few' of his readers.

We are now in a position to return to Robbe-Grillet's comments on *L'Etranger* which I quoted at the outset, and see that they are more disingenuous than appears on first reading. Robbe-Grillet reproaches Camus with indulging in sentimental anthropomorphism which leads him to spoil, in the later pages of *L'Etranger*, the overwhelming effect of an admirably neutral opening. What *I* would have done, Robbe-Grillet implies, is to continue in the same objective and object-oriented vein – it is significant that he notices the detailed description (p. 1127) of the screws on the mother's coffin and especially of the depth of their penetration into the wood – and so avoided all that 'complicity', all that 'connivance' between mankind and the world. But he quite misses the point, that the 'connivance' is purely *apparent*, a pose (I have been arguing) which Meursault adopts for rhetorical reasons, to show how unjustly he has been treatred. He does indeed suggest, as Robbe-Grillet notes, that it is really *things* that are finally responsible for pushing him into crime, but he does so not out of philosophical naivety or post-Christian delusion as Robbe-Grillet claims, but out of a concerted reader-persuasion strategy. Robbe-Grillet is too intelligent a critic to have overlooked such a crucial distinction; he ignores it deliberately, for rhetorical reasons as well. These are connected with his *own* project, which is to press a thorough-going atheism, the conviction that there is no God of the sort which, he insinuates, Camus so grievously lacked, or rather so grieved to lack.

Other readers, too, can be tempted to see Camus as God-starved, or even – like Hamm in Beckett's play *Endgame* – as railing at God for His failure to exist. But a fair-minded reading of the Camus canon by anyone with no ideological axe to grind must conclude that Camus was no crypto-Christian. His atheism was as solid as Robbe-Grillet's; it merely draws different conclusions about mankind's proper response to the death of God. Where Robbe-Grillet asserts robustly that no God means 'no fret' – the universe neither loves nor hates us, it is just *there*, and to talk even of its indifference is to indulge in a treacherous anthropomorphism – Camus acknowledges that it is hard for human beings to come to terms with the fact of the universe's unconcern. As Flaubert says of Madame Bovary and her kind, people *will* persist in beating on the cracked cauldron of language in a vain attempt to move the stars to pity.

But that is not the subject of *L'Etranger*, the least didactic of Camus's novels. Like all great works of art, it does not carry a simple message, and Robbe-Grillet's misreading is wilful, though perfectly understandable in the context of the polemic in which he is engaged in *Pour un nouveau roman*. Notwithstanding this, Robbe-Grillet does not conceal his admiration for Camus, whose 'economy' and 'subtlety' in his 'great novel' he singles out for special mention in the essay. And he is thereby doing no more than justice. Without *L'Etranger*, just as without *Madame Bovary* and *Du Côté de chez Swann*, there could have been no *nouveau roman*. As the same Robbe-Grillet acknowledges in the same essay, it was on the names of their precursors that the *nouveaux romanciers* found it easiest to agree. And whatever Robbe-Grillet may, for polemical reasons, have said at the time, the Camus who wrote *L'Etranger* was an indispensable precursor. But unlike Flaubert and Proust, who were dead ancestors and so could be venerated without embarrassment, Camus was an older brother, still alive, and sibling rivalry made it impossible to acknowledge his contribution. But to re-read the magnificent sequence of sentences beginning 'Aujourd'hui, maman est morte,' and to know, as we now do know, that mother did not die that day, but had long been buried in Marengo cemetery when those words were uttered, is to experience again the *frisson* that only great art gives us, a *frisson* we may be sure Robbe-Grillet felt when he too read them for the first time.

Indeed, every reader will remember his or her first encounter with Meursault. For me, it was on a Cambridge college lawn in the summer of 1957. I should have been doing a Latin prose, but the weather was too good to make work indoors feasible, so I took a cushion and a copy of the 'Livre de poche' edition of *L'Etranger* outside and read it straight through. I felt very sorry for Meursault by the time I finished it. Older and wiser now, I no longer feel sorry for him; in any case, such sentiments towards a fictional character would be naive in a professional literary critic. But I remain, if anything, more admiring than I was in 1957 of the novel's consummate artistry, which left me so wholeheartedly persuaded, on that sunlit day, of a murderer's innocence. If I was impressed, how much greater must the impact have been on Robbe-Grillet and the others as they searched in the novels of the past – to use a Georges Perec term – for a new literature's *mode d'emploi*?

Notes

1.   Alain Robbe-Grillet, *Pour un nouveau roman* (Paris: Editions de Minuit, 1963), pp. 57–8, translated by Barbara Wright as *Snapshots* and *Towards a New Novel* (London: Calder & Boyars, 1965), pp. 85–6. All other translations are my own.

2.   *Théâtre, récits, nouvelles* (Paris: Gallimard, Bibliothèque de la Pléiade, 1963). Future references are to this edition.

3.   Claude Simon, *La route de flandres* (Paris: Editions de Minuit, 1960), p. 314.

19

Camus, Orwell and Greene: the Impossible Fascination of the Colonised
Patrick McCarthy

In Part 2, Chapter 2 of *L'Etranger* there is an intriguing passage:

> Le jour de mon arrestation on m'a d'abord enfermé dans une chambre où il y avait déjà plusieurs détenus, la plupart des Arabes. Ils ont ri en me voyant. Puis ils m'ont demandé ce que j'avais fait. J'ai dit que j'avais tué un Arabe et ils sont restés silencieux. Mais un moment après, le soir est tombé. Ils m'ont expliqué comment il fallait arranger la natte où je devais coucher.

> *The day of my arrest I was first shut up in a room where there were several other prisoners, most of them Arabs. They laughed when they saw me. Then they asked me what I had done. I told them I had killed an Arab and they were silent. But a moment later it was evening. They showed me how to arrange the mat I was to sleep on.*[1]

As so often in *L'Etranger*, the seemingly precise temporal indications belie the place these sentences occupy in the time of the novel. Meursault was arrested at the beginning of Part 2, Chapter 1 which depicts his interrogation by a lawyer and a judge; their view of him may thus be contrasted with the Arabs' view. At the outset of Part 2, Chapter 2 Meursault tells us that a few days went by in prison before he became aware of the grim situation in which he found himself. So this passage is suspended in a limbo and, like so many other fragments of *l'Etranger*, it does not fit in with what follows. Nor does it seem an important passage for it is not given a paragraph of its own.

Not all the other prisoners are Arabs but, since the non-Arab contingent is not defined, the Arabs may be said to have hegemonised

221

the group. The laughter, far from seeming malicious, is a sign of recognition. The interest of the question is that it does not ask – as the lawyers and judges ask over and again – why Meursault did what he did. Explanations belong to the world of authority, whereas prisoners limit themselves to facts. In this they are demonstrating a solidarity with Meursault who is unable to answer the question why.

The solidarity is interrupted when Meursault tells them he has killed an Arab. But the change from day to evening ends the interruption because – as will be expounded in *L'Exil et le royaume* – the day is associated with public roles and the evening with personal contacts. Now the prisoners initiate Meursault into their group by showing him how he and they are to sleep. A bond is established between a French-Algerian, or *pied-noir*, and Arabs.

The seriousness of Meursault's action demonstrates how strong the bond is. Although he has killed an Arab, he may be embraced by Arabs because he is, like them, a prisoner. He is no longer a coloniser who is linked with the French state; rather he is its victim and hence a colonised. In the prison the colonial relationship breaks down and *pied-noir* and Arab are one. There is an ironic footnote to the passage: bed-bugs run over Meursault all night long. Such is the price of becoming an Arab.

The passage leads nowhere for there is scarcely a further mention of Arabs and Meursault is tried for not mourning at this mother's funeral. The conflict of Part 2 is between French authority and a Meursault who may be perceived both as an 'existentialist' individual and as a member of the *pied-noir* working-class.

If the passage is intriguing it is because it is an odd postscript to the theme of the Arab in Part 1. Here he is depicted, however obliquely, as Meursault's rival. The first Arab character is the nurse who watches over his mother's coffin and is a surrogate mother; like the real mother she may be assumed to inspire in him a mixture of love and resentment. The second character, Raymond's mistress, moves the discussion into the political universe by offering an example of colonial violence. The third, her brother, is Raymond's rival for control over Arab women. His battle with Raymond's friend, Meursault, is set amidst the sea and the sun which have been depicted not as generic nature but as a specifically Algerian nature.[2]

None of this could be stated clearly in an Algeria which was considered not a colony but an integral part of France and where the official ideology was assimilation. Such hints do, however, allow the reader to perceive Part 1 of *L'Etranger* as colonial novel. As a member of the *pied-noir* working-class Meursault is caught between the French authorities and the indigenous population. Unable to identify with the former, he is menaced by the latter.

The value of the odd postscript is that it allows the reader to perceive the fascination which is the other face of the rivalry. Although one has to stretch Memmi's definition of the coloniser who refuses to make it include Meursault, he does reject the official values of the French state: ambition, morality and a logic which is the façade of power. To all of these he opposes his indifference. Inevitably he is drawn to the Arab who is more different, more silent and still further removed from career and morality.

The ordinary coloniser feels for the colonised a hostility – Ellis in *Burmese Days* is a good example – which is inspired by the need to exploit or even to suppress the indigenous population in the name of a superior European society. Meursault, however, wishes to be an Algerian and to unite with the Arabs. Not that this frees him from the temptation of violence because, when his quest proves impossible, he strikes against the Arabs. But his is a different attempt to cope with the alienation of the colonial relationship.

In this essay we shall ask two questions. Firstly, whether the discourse of fascination, which flickers so obliquely and so briefly in *L'Etranger*, may be found in other colonial novels such as *Burmese Days* and *The Heart of the Matter*. Secondly, how Camus develops the discourse when he returns to it in his last fictional portrayal of Algeria, *L'Exil et le royaume*.

One might not expect to find this fascination in Orwell. There is in *Burmese Days* a hatred of Burma – of the heat and the loneliness. There is also a sympathy for the average Anglo-Indian who is exposed to them and who is exploited by the English upper-classes, the owners of the timber companies and the aristocrats like Verrall. Orwell is harsh on Burmese and Indian characters whom he perceives as corrupted by colonialism, whether the fawningly pro-English Dr Veraswami or Ma Hla May who just wants to be a white man's mistress. *Burmese Days* is a deliberately simple novel and lacks the ambiguity on which the discourse of fascination thrives. The Empire is nothing more than a money-making operation and the solution for the British characters is to go home.

Yet Orwell's critique of colonialism leads him to dwell on the figure of the colonised who succeeds. U Po Kyin sees through the rhetoric of the white man's burden and, by his bribe-taking, he participates in the thievery of the Empire. His merits are lucidity, cynicism and irony. In turn they allow him to live part of his life outside the Empire: he prefers Burmese cigars and 'never smoked English tobacco, which he declared had no taste'.[3]

As a collaborator U Po Kyin is the objective ally of the British authorities and his enemy is Flory, the coloniser who refuses. At the end of the book he blocks Flory's marriage, which allows the Deputy Commissioner to marry Elizabeth. However, just as his view of Empire resembles Flory's, so he also indicates the possibility that there may be another Burma, an uncorrupted Burma.

This hope haunts Flory who, having rejected the English community, sets out on his quest. The episode that depicts it is set between his dismissal of Ma Hla May and his meeting with Elizabeth (pp. 53–8). He goes into the jungle which near his house is mere scrub and is haunted by a 'poisonous, ivy-like smell'. Then, as he leaves behind the town, the jungle grows lusher and cleaner. Flory bathes ritualistically in a pond beneath a peepul tree that is alive with green pigeons. This is the world of Burmese nature, untainted by colonialism but also devoid of Burmese.

However, Flory meets a Burmese cart-driver who takes him to a village. Although it consists of 'twenty ruinous wooden huts roofed with thatch', there are white egrets overhead and a woman is playing happily with a dog. The village economy consists of subsistence agriculture and making cart-wheels, neither of which involves the British. Flory is treated as a guest rather than as a superior and his initiation takes the form of drinking green – the colour green recurs here – Burmese tea. Flory even tries to enter the non-scientific culture: when he asks whether the well water is drinkable, the headman replies ' those who drink it, drink it ... and those who do not drink it, do not drink it'. Flory concludes that this is wisdom.

So Flory has discovered a peepul tree that does not exist for the greater glory of timber companies and Burmese who seem to exist outside of colonialism. The contrast with Ma Hla May is obvious, but Orwell does not send Flory in search of a pure Burmese woman. Instead Flory, when he meets the Englishwoman Elizabeth, sets out to win her over to his other Burma. His compromise is that he will live as a colonial in a non-colonial country. He will be a timber merchant and the husband of an English woman and yet he and she will live within Burmese culture.

The irony is that Elizabeth was born to be a *memsahib* and ends as one when she marries the Deputy Commissioner. Flory's attempts to interest her in Burmese dance, in the bazaar or in the language merely irritate her. He impresses her when he takes her shooting, where he slaughters the green pigeons, or when he plays out the role of the male coloniser by protecting her against the animals and the people of Burma.

Flory's journey to the peepul tree and the village is retrospectively revealed as an illusion. The discourse of fascination breaks down against the reality of colonialism and Flory's last contact with a Burmese is once more with Ma Hla May.

In *The Heart of the Matter*, a book which Orwell disliked, Greene is more willing to gamble. Here again the majority of the English community wallows in miserable hatred. 'I hate the place, I hate the people. I hate the bloody niggers', says one.[4] Wilson, the spy, is attracted by an African girl whom he sees nude to the waist, but the next moment he is disconcerted by the unreliability of his African informers. He concludes the cycle by going to a brothel, which is a recognition of his inability to confront the real Africa, whatever it might be.

Scobie, by contrast, is maligned by the other whites because he 'sleeps with black girls' (p. 17). The reproach is ironic but justified, because Scobie, a policeman, is another coloniser who refuses. To him, the stone building of the police station and the lawcourts stands 'like the grandiloquent boast of weak men' (p. 15). Unlike Wilson, he appreciates the unreliable African witnesses because he perceives in their lies a protest against an imported Western brand of justice.

There is a link between this view and Scobie's Catholicism which leads him – the fairest of men – to spurn the lay values of fairness and logic in the name of love, pity and the relationship with a remote but merciful God. In *The Heart of the Matter* humans are not closed, finite beings; they are unpredictable and prone both to evil and to good. This vision spreads through the novel an ambiguity which is very different from the ambiguity of *L'Etranger*. In Camus there is much – at least in Part 1 of the novel – that is simply not known; in Greene the unknown is a potential that marks the possible presence of God. At every point in the book and especially at the end the reader is confronted with various interpretations of the characters' behaviour. His task is not to choose among them but to perceive in their multiplicity the mark of the infinite.

No attempt can be be made here to examine Greene's Catholicism in detail. But in the context of the West African colony it acts as a seditious force because it undermines the pretence of law and duty. Scobie likes the colony because 'human nature hasn't had time to disguise itself; (p. 35). The poverty and misery of the colony present man as God sees him.

Passed over for promotion and distrusted by the English community, Scobie studies the Mende language and learns to appreciate the beauty of black woman. Years before he 'had begun to desire these people's trust and affection' (p. 20). Not content with mitigating the effects of colonial justice, he seeks personal relationships with them. The discourse of fascination unfolds in Scobie's relationship with his boy Ali. It goes through three phases and is punctuated by his dealings with Yusef.

Ali has been with Scobie for fifteen years, one year longer than Scobie has been married. In a sentence reminiscent of the passage from *L'Etranger*, Greene writes that Ali had been in prison but that this did not alter his relationship with the policeman Scobie because there was 'no disgrace about prison' (p.23). When Scobie cuts his hand, his wife shrinks from the blood but Ali bandages it, his hands 'as gentle as a girl's' (p. 40). On the journey to Bamba Ali tends Scobie, bringing him tea and watching over him when he has fever.

The homosexual element in the relationship is established first jokingly and then seriously. When Scobie's wife accuses him of loving no-one but himself, he jests that he also loves Ali. On the road to Bamba he notes that 'this was all he needed of love or friendship' (p. 84). Although Scobie's dealings with Ali are open to a criticism which is discussed below, he considers the relationship a close one.

It is challenged by Scobie's growing friendship with Yusef who is a more complex U Po Kyin. As a Syrian, Yusef is the necessary middleman in the colony, accepted neither by the Africans nor by the British. Like U Po Kyin, he has a lucid view of the Empire, desiring to profit from it. He expresses his aims in political language when asked to explain why he is plotting against another Syrian: 'It is no good the Syrians being in two parties. If they were in one party you would be able to come to me and say, "Yusef, the government wants the Syrians to do this or that" and I should be able to answer "It shall be so" ' (p. 151). Scobie's initial dislike of Yusef is not merely the distaste of an honest policeman for a scoundrel but also the doubting coloniser's distrust of colonialism's objective ally.

Unlike U Po Kyin, Yusef is an ambiguous figure. Even as he blackmails Scobie, he protests that he cares for him and that he is drawn to Scobie's essential goodness. There is no reason to disbelieve him, the religious values of good and evil being interwoven in *The Heart of the Matter* and united in their opposition to lay values. Moreover Scobie himself has become ambiguous: a corrupt policeman who betrays his office to protect his wife and an unfaithful husband who commits adultery to protect his mistress. A bond is created between the Syrian middle-man and the English renegade.

When Scobie was ill at Bamba, Yusef arrived and tried to tend him, thus challenging Ali. As Scobie draws closer to Yusef, he moves away from Ali and then, trapped in the web of deceit, he starts to distrust Ali. He becomes an orthodox coloniser who lives out the West African dictum that you can 'never trust a black' (p. 237). Logically he turns to Yusef, the collaborator of colonialism, who sets in motion the events that lead to Ali's death.

But here begins the third phase of Scobie's relationship with Ali where the discourse of fascination reaches its climax. Scobie's onslaughts on Ali coincide with the blows he strikes at God by receiving communion in a state of mortal sin. At his death Ali is fused with Christ on the cross. Scobie has summoned him with a rosary and, when he looks at Ali's corpse, he sees it as a broken piece of the rosary: 'a couple of black beads and the image of God coiled at the end of it' (p. 247).

But if Ali is a Christ-figure, then he cannot entirely die and his sacrifice must create good. Scobie had struck at him because he was losing the goodness which had lain in their relationship; now it will be restored to him. Scobie's suicide is less an act of despair than a refusal to continue hurting Christ by receiving his body in sacrilege. Ali will be Scobie's guide into death.

Gazing at the corpse Scobie declares: 'I loved him' (p. 248), which is his third and clearest statement. Once more he chooses between Ali and his wife, Louise. She is falsely happy because Scobie has at last been promoted and because she interprets his willingness to receive communion as a sign that his affair with Helen is over. 'You've got to put it behind you. You can't help Ali now' (p. 252), she tells him, eager to take her rightful place in colonial society. But Scobie ignores her and presses on with his suicide, his last words reserved for Ali and for God. If, as the ending suggests, there is spiritual value in Scobie's death, then it comes in part from Ali.

Rarely can the discourse of fascination have been taken further than in *The Heart of the Matter*. The colonised is Christ on the cross whose role is to damn colonialism and to save the coloniser who refuses. The criticism that one cannot refrain from making is that all this is a European invention. Like Orwell and Camus, Greene makes no pretence of reconstructing the world as the colonised sees it. The point of view is always the European's, which is honest because a European novelist should not masquerade as an African. It exposes Greene, however, to a question: why should Ali be killed so that Scobie may be saved?

The Heart of the Matter invites us to reread *L'Etranger* and to reconsider the murder of the Arab and its odd postscript. As Scobie strikes at Ali because of Ali's goodness, so Meursault kills the Arab because of his greater authenticity. The night in prison is a hint of the reconciliation that takes place between Scobie and Ali after Ali's death. Although Camus will never go as far as Greene, he will spin out the discourse of fascination in *L'Exil et le royaume*, enveloping it in religious and sexual language of his own. Finally he will depict its collapse as colonialism itself breaks down.

Published in 1957 *L'Exil et le royaume* corresponds to a different historical period from *l'Etranger*. By now the Front de Libération Nationale uprising had destroyed assimilation, had exposed the colonial conflicts in Algeria and was menacing French rule. This in turn allowed Camus to write less obliquely.

The dream of union between coloniser and colonised is briefly realised in *Les Muets* where the approximately fifteen striking workers include one Arab, Saïd. He is not the equal of the *pieds-noirs* because much of his work consists in bringing them the tools they need. Then, the first day after the failed strike, the main character, Yvars, notes that Saïd has no lunch. Saïd's posture is distinctive: he is lying down, 'le regard perdu vers les verrières bleuies par un ciel maintenant moins lumineux' (p. 1605). Camus frequently associates the colour blue with Arabs and here it links Saïd with the natural world. Yvars shares his sandwich – a version of communion bread – with Saïd, who also drinks the coffee which has been given to another *pied-noir* worker by a grocer sympathetic to the strike. So the colonial conflict is suspended during a moment of working-class solidarity. The moment does not last because at the end of the day the *pied-noirs* go off to wash while Saïd remains to sweep the workshop. As in *L'Etranger*, the *pied-noir* must be humiliated – by the failure of the strike – before he can find kinship with the Arab.

The quest for such a union and the notion that the colonised possesses a naturalness which the coloniser, who is aware of his alienation, lacks and desires, are the themes of '*La Femme adultère*'.

Significantly, the coloniser is not a 'he' but a 'she' while the protagonist of 'L'Hôte' who confronts the futility of fascination is male. The traditional division of female–male roles allows Camus to depict Janine's experience in erotic-mystical language. However the ingredients of the colonial theme are all present.

Unlike *L'Etranger*, *'La Femme adultère'* depicts two Algerias. Algiers is cut off from the sea because Janine's husband has deserted the beaches. It is a bastardised city – Janine lives in a half-European and half-Arab neighbourhood – and it is dominated by money making. Although she has heard Arabic all her life, Janine does not speak it. However, the bus journey brings her into Southern Algeria where there are no cities but mountains and oases. Beyond lies the open desert and the nomads 'qui ne possédaient rien mais ne servaient personne' (p. 1570). This is the magic realm that stands outside colonialism. Even in the Southern mountains there are few French-Algerians and the Arabs are prouder than in Algiers. The first Arab shopkeeper refuses to buy Marcel's cloth.

Janine's awakening takes the form of an estrangement from her husband as she realises that she has allowed her life to be dominated by his need of her. Her revolt as a woman does not go far because she continues to live under the *regard* of men: in the oasis 'il semblait à Janine qu'elle n'avait jamais vu autant d'hommes' (p. 1568). But the men are Arabs. Janine is moved by the countryside, the wind and the cold, but there are sexual elements in the culminating experience of the story. She abandons her husband's bed and goes among the Arabs whose robes brush against her. The night sky takes possession of her and throws her moaning on the ground.

Does Janine want an Arab to make love to her? Certainly, but such an explanation is absurdly reductive. Camus suggests this interpretation by his choice of title but the reader has learned from the very same Camus the value of wariness. Janine's response to the nature of Southern Algeria is not a pretext; rather nature shapes and is shaped by the Arab. Shepherds emerge from the duststorm to surround the bus, children spin around in the wind. If the Arabs are repeatedly described as 'thin' (pp. 1561, 1567), it is because their asceticism fits the harsh mountains.

Nor should the mystical language in *La Femme adultère* be dismissed. Just as Greene's Catholicism leads him to perceive Ali as a Christ figure, so Camus's sense of the possible oneness between man and nature makes him admire in the Arab the incarnation of such harmony.

As a coloniser who refuses, Janine seeks out Arabness. It is a dangerous quest because the Arabs' *regard* is indifferent, which destroys her
identity as a traditional woman. Similarly the nomads' proud poverty
mocks Marcel's shopkeeper mentality. But the nomads promise a
liberation from the alienation of Algiers and in the desert night Janine
experiences, however briefly, totality – 'il lui semblait retrouver ses
racines, la sève montait à nonveau dans son corps' (p. 1574).

'*La femme adultère*' is set not long after the Second World War,
whereas '*L'Hôte*' takes place shortly before the outbreak of the Front
de Libération Nationale uprising in 1954. As an elementary school
teacher Daru represents the benevolent face of assimilation: on the
blackboard he has drawn the rivers of France. During the drought
he distributes to his pupils grain which is being shipped from
France. But the prospect of Arab rebellion transforms Daru into a
policeman and compels him to realise the complementary nature of
the two professions.

He also realises – as Scobie could have taught him – that Western
ideas of justice and morality have no meaning in Algeria. Why did
the Arab kill his cousin? Balducci, the policeman, does not know –
native affairs are illogical. Does the Arab feel remorse? He does not
understand the question. The impenetrability of the murder takes
us back to *L'Etranger* and causes us to brood – yet again! – on the
Arab elements in Meursault. But in '*L'Hôte*' there is a political interpretation of the Arab's arrest: to his village it is an arbitrary exercise
of colonial power. Once more Daru is dragged into politics.

'*L'Hôte*' has presented itself as a discourse about official colonialism
but now the secret discourse of fascination unfolds. Daru is not a
Frenchman but a *pied-noir* and Balducci, who would not have trusted
a Frenchman, trusts him: 'Tu es d'ici. Tu es un homme' (p. 1616).
However the *pied-noir*'s identity links him to the Arab: 'hors de ce
désert, ni l'un ni l'autre ... n'auraient pu vivre vraiment' (p. 1617).
In this story the city of Algiers has vanished and there remain the
cold hills and the land of the nomads. Unlike Janine, Dary belongs
to the mountains and is the Arab's brother. When Balducci's
request that he turn in the Arab forces him to realise that he can no
longer be *pied-noir* and Arab, he tries to opt for the Arab.

Daru makes bread, which may once again be seen as communion
bread, and eats with Arab. They sleep in the same room and there
are hints of homosexuality in that Daru is naked. Since this is the
fraternity of 'soldats ou prisonniers' (p. 1620), Daru, the supposed
jailor, has become an honorary prisoner.

The break-down of fraternity is explicitly political. True to his belief in morality, Daru leaves the Arab free to decide whether he will go alone to prison or whether he will head toward the nomads. Clearly Daru wants the Arab to go South, thus freeing himself and, by implication, Daru. But the Arab goes off to prison as the colonial authorities have instructed him. Despite his efforts Daru has played out his role as a policeman.

The ending of 'L'Hôte' sees the entry of a new historical protagonist. The writing on the blackboard challenges the rivers of France and foreshadows a different state – independent Algeria. But it refers to Daru by the familiar 'tu' form only to contrast the 'tu' with 'notre'. This is the rejection not of French assimilation but of the *pied-noir*'s dream of becoming an Arab. Cruelly for the *pied-noir* the two projects collapse together.

The writing on the blackboard reminds us that until now Camus has, correctly, reconstructed Algeria from the *pied-noir*'s viewpoint. Retrospectively the discourse of fascination is made to appear solipsistic: the coloniser has been inventing the colonised. Does this mean that of our three writers Orwell was the most perceptive in flatly rejecting the theme? No, because the value of colonial writing lies in its awareness of the contradictions of colonialism and in its desperate if unsuccessful bid to resolve them. Camus lived out those contradictions, testing the limits of assimilation in *L'Etranger*. The discourse of fascination, which flows beneath the surface of the novel and comes into the open in *L'Exil*, is important precisely because it is impossible.

Notes

1. Albert Camus, *Théâtre, récits, nouvelles* (Paris, Gallimard, Bibliothèque de la Pléiade, 1962), p. 1177. References to *L'Exil et le royaume* are also to this volume. The translation is my own.
2. For a fuller treatment of this interpretation see Patrick McCarthy, *Camus: 'The Stranger'* (Cambridge: Cambridge University Press, 1988) pp. 41–62.
3. George Orwell, *Burmese Days* (Harmonaswon: Penguin Books) p. 13. All references are to this edition.
4. Graham Greene, *The Heart of the Matter* (Harmonaswon: Penguin Books) p. 13. All references are to this edition.

20

Strangers and Brothers in the Works of Albert Camus and Jules Roy
Catherine Savage Brosman

Like contrary forces in a historical field, the metaphors and themes of stranger and brother, alienation and fraternity, mark and act as organising principles in the works of both Albert Camus and his Algerian compatriot and friend, Jules Roy, whom Philippe Bernet called his 'héritier spirituel'.[1] The parallelism, suggested by the titles *L'Etranger* and Roy's *Etranger pour mes frères* (1982), goes well beyond the use of the term. To the lyrical passages in *Noces* and *L'Eté* concerning the fraternity between the speaker and the natural world correspond similar passages by Roy, notably in *Les Chevaux du soleil* (1968–75), a series of novels concerning Algeria. Camus's far-sighted criticisms in *Misère de la Kabylie* (1939) of the unconscionable inequities in the Algerian economic system and social fabric are echoed in Roy's *La Guerre d'Algérie* (1960) and *Autour du drame* (1961). Finally, the sense of exile and alienation visible in Camus's 1942 masterpiece and elsewhere is paralleled, in its own register, in a number of Roy's books. However, between the positions of the two writers, who were close friends from 1945 until Camus's death in 1960 and who held many views in common, there was also, at the time of the Algerian war, a distance that did not mar their friendship but sheds a critical light on the texts of the Nobel Prize winner, including *L'Etranger*.

To tens of thousands of students in English-speaking countries who read Camus's masterpiece in a college edition, with a preface by the author, Meursault is 'le seul Christ que nous méritions'.[2] The novelist's a posteriori judgement of his hero as a Christ figure doubtless represents an over-simplification of his significance, even a distortion: after all, Meursault is morally passive, if not neutral, most of the time, denies all religious transcendency, and is certainly

232

not *only* a victim. Camus's evaluation does, however, have the merit of calling attention to elements of the novel, apparently morally indifferent, that may be interpreted as value oriented. It also draws attention to, and perhaps indicts, the *nous* – the collective social body, embracing author and readers alike and representing the other. In this context, the thematics of strangers and brothers is particularly pertinent.

The term *étranger*, which, strikingly, does not occur anywhere in the *text* of Camus's narratives,[3] has been given multiple meanings, which bear reviewing. Meursault is commonly thought to be an outsider with respect to social mores; he does not play the right role, say the right things in connection with filial relationships, marriage, and a career, for instance, adopting instead either an attitude of indifference, or seeing his function differently.[4] He seems especially alienated from the suppositions and mechanisms of the criminal justice system, which one may take as representing the core of a society built on proscriptions, and from religion, equally central to the European civilisation that is represented, at least on the surface, by the French presence in Algeria. His indifference can be blamed as pathological maladjustment – the conservative attitude, expressed within the novel by the examining magistrate and the court system in general – or can be praised, as by many critics, as the only authentic recourse possible in society as Camus saw it. A variation on this interpretation is that Meursault is not only relatively, but absolutely 'strange' (not, of course, the same as being a 'stranger') – a pathological case because he lacks 'meaning endowing facility' and the 'principle of unity and continuity that characterises man'.[5]

By other readers, Meursault is viewed as a metaphysical outsider, representing man as depicted in *Le Mythe de Sisyphe*, cast into an uncaring universe that does not respond to his demands for meaning and value and puts at the end of his projects the absurd finality of death. 'Dans un univers privé d'illusions et de lumières, l'homme se sent un étranger' (II, p. 101).[6] It is perhaps significant that the word *étranger* appears in this sense in Camus's most metaphysical essay, published the same year as the novel. Still other readers see Meursault as a stranger to himself, vaguely schizophrenic and lacking in self-awareness; one can cite, in support of this reading, the episode in which, as a prisoner, he looks at his reflection in his metal dish without being able to identify with it, significantly on the same day he acquires an awareness of time that he had heretofore suppressed (I, p. 1181).[7] He can also been seen as a stranger to France, a reading particularly pertinent to the purpose at hand. Although of French citizenship and language, he is Algerian to the core, feeling at home only there and espousing its sea and sky as his sufficient world. More will be said on this later.

Finally, by virtue of his racial antecedents, he may be viewed as a political intruder, a member of a colonial caste and an oppressive race exercising unjustified dominion over a people whose territories have been seized and occupied. He has not chosen his situation as a European in a colonial society; but he accepts it without question and, implicitly, benefits from it (for instance, in his wages, higher than those of a native). Such would be the reading of anyone who accepts Frantz Fanon's view that no European presence in Africa is legitimate.[8] It was proposed shortly after Camus's death and has been suggested since, but, as Louise K Horowitz has observed, has generally remained in the background.[9] To borrow John Erickson's words concerning Camus himself, Meursault belongs to 'a country within a country and ... a culture superimposed from without' (p. 73). Culturally speaking also, he would, from this perspective, be an outsider to the degree that his discourse reflects, indirectly, the native culture that is not his, which he takes cognizance of from the exterior. One can argue also that, paradoxically, Meursault is a stranger to the landscape, whereas the Arabs, even under the burning sun, seem to belong to it. Every reader is aware of the hostility of the sun the morning of the funeral procession and the day of the murder; Camus calls the landscape 'inhumain'. 'L'éclat du soleil était insoutenable' (I, p. 1134). At the beach, while the sun is 'écrasant', Raymond and Meursault find the Arabs near a little spring; 'Ils avaient l'air tout à fait calmes et presque contents'; as the Europeans approach, the others slip (the verb is *couler*, like the flowing water) behind a rock (I, pp. 1163–4).

However, one can turn this argument around and suggest that the murdered Arab himself is the stranger, *marginalisé*, as Raymond Gay-Crosier has put it,[10] out of place in his society and on the beach, where he is killed. He is, in a word, the quintessential other, by whom one acquires a sense of the self.[11] The Berber and Arab natives are nearly invisible in the novel, even though they composed at the time of its writing some nine-tenths of the population; those with whom Meursault gets involved are silent, like animals, watching the Europeans in the awareness that they represent a political and a physical threat and, in response, seeking to objectify them with their gaze: 'Ils nous regardaient en silence ... ni plus ni moins que si nous étions des pierres ou des arbres morts' (I, p. 1159). His attitude toward the natives reflects this marginalisation; on the beach *they* are seen as intruders, representing a threat.

In a number of these readings, Meursault is viewed as heroic, whether as a modest Sisyphus toiling in an absurd world and refusing the consolations of belief, or as the sole honest man in a society that demands respect for conventions and institutions and devalues, even fears, the exercise of individual choice. One should note, however, that he does not refuse all conventions. There are at least two areas in which his behaviour is the most conventional possible: his attitude toward women and natives and his relationships with his male friends. He is not distressed by Raymond's pimping, nor by the latter's treatment of his native mistress, whom he routinely knocks around before the ritual 'reconciliation' through possession of her body. He accepts as a matter of course the easy pacts that men in his society make with fellow European males against those not in their group, and thus is willing to assist Raymond in punishing his indigenous mistress. From this perspective, he is an *insider*, representing the North African *machisme* that characterised Camus throughout his lifetime and that Roy subsequently criticised.[12] He is thus a stranger to some of the humanistic values that have long been associated with his creator.

Nevertheless, his role as victim, since an oppressive society seems to be using his capital sentence to compensate for its own inequities, would seem to justify the author's likening of him to a Christ figure. To what degree this victimisation can compensate for his undeniable attitude of superiority toward the silent race of Arabs around him is open to debate. It is he, not Raymond the pimp, who becomes most seriously involved in the beach fight; he is convicted of killing a *man* and acknowledges it himself (I, pp. 1169, 1191), although he told his fellow prisoners that he had killed an *Arab*, and is sentenced to death, as if that man had been a fellow European. While it seems unlikely on both internal and external grounds, one could argue that this sentence is the author's reply to the racism shown by Meursault and to his fellow European Algerians, whom he had criticised in *Misère de la Kabylie*. A contrary interpretation has been proposed by O'Brien: the novel, 'by suggesting that the court is impartial between Arab and Frenchman, ... implicitly denies the colonial reality and sustains the colonial fiction' (p. 23). Whatever the case, the hero remains unaware of the social implications of his sentence, and instead, even in the second part, his role as 'stranger' seems to be confined to the alienation between him and the society into which he is not, by its standards, integrated, and which condemns him, by its own rules, for the wrong reasons. The problems of the colonial European and their implication for a comprehensive understanding of modern alienation – social and metaphysical – remain unexamined.

Another possible offsetting factor to the hero's racism is his function in a barely visible thematics of brotherhood. I do not have in mind his friendship with Emmanuel, which foreshadows his involvement with Raymond, nor the male bonding between him and the latter, which draws him into the quarrel with the Arabs. But, after his arrest, his fellow prisoners, all Arabs, to whom he has admitted killing one of their fellows, show him how to roll his mat for the night, as if their common detention erased any racial differences between them (I, p. 1175). The day of Marie's visit, he seems to feel less close to Marie than to his fellow-prisoners, mostly natives, especially the one who says nothing but only looks at his mother (I, pp. 1176–7); and, during his trial, he is sensitive to the kindly feelings of journalists and others in the courtroom, especially those who testify in his favour – the watchman at the asylum and Céleste, whom he feels like embracing. Implicitly, at least, this fraternity extends to the wider world in his recollections of the city he can no longer even see and the life that cannot be his. Purged of his 'mal' by his anger against the chaplain, 'je m'ouvrais à la tendre indifférence du monde. De l'éprouver si pareil à moi, si fraternel enfin, j'ai senti que j'avais été heureux' (I, p. 1209). Unfortunately, the weight given to his fraternity in the novel is less than that attributed to it by countless readers.

While echoing the work of Camus in numerous respects, Roy's Algerian writings, both essays and fiction, seem intended, if unconsciously, to remedy some of the defects in his friend's position by dissolving the differences between races and proclaiming 'strangers' to be brothers. Such was not his original intention, by any means. When the two met in the last spring of the war, Roy was an army major, just back from England, where he had flown thirty-seven missions with the Royal Air Force. By the 'fraternité d'élection que l'Afrique du Nord avait préparée', he recognised in Camus, six years younger than he, not only a kindred soul, but a great stylist, an original mind, a literary and moral master.[13] He was the recognised leader of the small group of North African writers, mostly of European descent, who gathered in Paris in the mid-1940s around the publisher Edmond Charlot, who had brought out works by several of them in Algiers before moving his firm to Paris. Camus was also the one who had criticised eloquently, if not the colonial system as such, at least the most extreme exploitation of Algerian natives by the *métropole*. 'Il reste à l'origine du libéralisme qui prit naissance dans quelques esprits algériens.'[14] Roy's own writing then was focused on the war and the experience of flying, but he was homesick for Algeria and concerned for its future. The uprisings in Sétif in May 1945, which he witnessed, and consequent repression shocked him and, as he said, made him ashamed of his uniform; Camus's comments on the event added to his malaise.[15] 'Camus ... m'avait fait découvrir en 1945 que les Arabes avaient une âme.[16]

In the next decade or so his awareness of the scope of injustice in his homeland and the political dilemmas it posed increased, partly under his friend's influence. He credited Camus with having led him, ultimately, to embrace the cause of Algerian independence, which Camus himself continued opposing until his death, favouring instead some form of federation.[17] As long as he was on active duty, Roy was not in a position to comment in print on the Algerian situation. Moreover, he considered Camus to be the spokesman for those who shared his views on the need for reforms in the territory.[18]

In 1953, after having travelled to Indochina to survey the war there and discovering what he considered to be abominations, Roy returned home and resigned from active duty. By 1955, he published in *L'Express* an article entitled 'Mes camarades, je ne vous envie pas', in which he dared to say that his fellow officers were performing a police action in Algeria, not fighting a war, and that he could not approve of it.[19] This article not only shocked and angered many military men; even Camus remarked, 'Tu y vas un peu fort'.[20] Perhaps injured by the remark, and certainly unwilling to seem to be attacking the army, of which he had been a part for a quarter-century and which had suffered at Dien Bien Phu just the previous year one of the worst defeats in all of French history, Roy resolved to keep his thoughts to himself and let Camus be the spokesman: 'En quoi avais-je besoin de prendre position? Camus était là pour dire ce que nous avions à dire, le plus simple était d'y souscrire' (*EF*, p. 109). Roy did not comment on the latter's articles in *L'Express* and *Le Monde* and his unsuccessful plan for a civil truce in 1956 and subsequent silence, nor on the Battle of Algiers.

After Camus's fatal accident, which to Roy was a personal tragedy, circumstances suddenly seemed very different. An invitation to visit North Africa that spring was like a summons from beyond the grave. His tour produced his controversial *La Guerre d'Algérie*, which enraged some quarters of opinion, while appealing to others. Returning to the criticism voiced in the 1955 article, it went much further than Camus himself had ever chosen to go, stating plainly that, despite Roy's deep attachment to his native territory and its culture, despite the fact that his brother was still living in Algiers, he was in favour of cessation of the repression and a negotiated peace, with gradual autonomy for the former colony. Yet this was written in the spirit of justice for which Roy gave credit to Camus, while acknowledging that the latter, if alive, might not have agreed with him and 'peut-être même nous serions-nous séparés'.[21] 'Mon gouru n'a pas vu ce que j'ai vu, et peut-être n'a-t-il pas voulu le voir' (*EF*, p. 127). 'La Justice passe avant la Mère', a commentator wrote concerning Roy's *reportage*, in an allusion to Camus's controversial Stockholm statement to the effect that, before justice, he had to prefer his mother.[22]

Perhaps unconsciously echoing Camus, Roy uses a thematics of alienation and fraternity (even maternity, since Algeria itself is seen as his *mère*) to inform his Algerian writings. It is embodied – in the truest sense – in the figure of the bastard. The term has a double reference. One is literal illegitimacy, the illegitimacy that marked Roy's own life both before and after his tardy discovery of it; the other is figurative, indicating the marginalised and oppressed. Whether of the first or second type, the bastard is a stranger to those who should be his fellows.[23] Because his sense of inferiority is bound up with his deepest image of himself, moreover, there is a sense in which he can never feel at home in the world; social hostility stands for metaphysical hostility.

In *La Guerre d'Algérie*, the writer says that the natives have been treated like bastards by the 'legitimate' sons of France, although they are both born of the same mother – the Algerian soil. He now knows, he writes, who is his mother, who are his brothers – all who suffer from injustice – and he demands full fraternity and intergration for the natives. If the supporters of 'L'Algérie française' ever see in their gunsights a tall bastard with white hair fighting with the rebels, it will, he writes, be he.[24] In *Autour du drame*, the theme appears in the form of the *frères ennemis*, brothers who do not recognise each other as such. The author wonders whether the

Arabs to whom he offered help when they had broken down on the highway would have believed him if he had told him he too was one of theirs, a bastard (*AD*, p. 220).

Roy's series of Algerian novels, *Les Chevaux du soleil*, contains, from the beginning, suggestions of both alienation and fraternity; the French invaders in 1830 are clearly strangers, and their descendants' relationship with the natives is one of exploitation, and yet fraternity is not ruled out. Hector Koenig, the auto-biographical hero, feels, despite belonging to two superior castes – the race of Europeans that colonised and still dominate Algeria, and the army – that he is in exile, an outsider, forever marked by his inferiority as a bastard. Despite the racism that has been bred into him, he recognises obscurely that the natives around him, some of whom serve France under his orders in the military, are similarly illegitimate, strangers to the ruling caste, estranged from the land that should be theirs, and, worst of all, schizophrenic, estranged from themselves, since, in a world whose values are all European, and in a position of social and political inferiority, they cannot know full personal identity. Walking in the dark in a moment of crisis, he meets other 'strangers', with whom he feels an obscure fraternity. He understands the widely criticised marriage of his cousin with a native, reflecting: 'Pourquoi pas rompre avec toutes ces haines et ces saletés en épousant un étranger, un Arabe?'[25] The term *étranger* comes from the vocabulary of the French colonists, but he undermines its negativity by assuming it for himself and imagining marriage with the Other. Significantly, when he is about to shoot himself in despair with his own service pistol, it is his native orderly, Boualem, who interrupts him and gives him the will to keep living by stressing the fraternity that would be possible in Algeria if, as he says, all the French were like Hector.

Finally, in the autobiograpical *Etranger pour mes frères*, Roy associates, in a rhetorical and moral tension built on the principles of difference and resemblance, the tragic alienation that separated him from many of those towards whom he felt fraternity – including the Arabs with whom he played as a child but whom society shortly separated from him – with the sense of brotherhood. The title suggests a historical and political estrangement from his *native* brothers, whom he explicitly recognises as such, and, even more, estrangement from his *French* brothers, especially the *pieds-noirs*, who could not accept the positions he had taken on Algeria. Retracing the development of his thinking, from a conservative to a liberal stand, he again credits Camus with alerting him to what he calls the Arab 'soul'. 'Si j'ai été plus loin que lui, c'est parce qu'il m'a ouvert les yeux' (*EF*, p. 128). Bertrand Poirot-Delpech identified Roy as the most lucid and courageous of strangers, the self-aware colonist: unlike Camus, he 'a eu la force de se reconnaître "étranger" sur sa terre natale et de ne plus avoir pour patrie que la vérité dont aucun intellectuel de la métropole, pas plus que le FLN et l'OAS, ne s'est vraiment soucié'.[26]

In *L'Etranger*, Meursault reveals nothing of this awareness of either political alienation or identity between him and the natives in whose drama he becomes embroiled. The system of images that Camus uses for his experiences, and to some degree these experiences themselves, suggest, however, a greater resemblance between him and the Arabs than he realises himself. Perhaps one can apply to him the words of Jean-Pierre Millecam concerning the *pieds-noirs*: 'Ils ne savaient pas qu'ils aimaient les Arabes.'[27] Meursault's dislike for Paris, with its 'cours noires' – what Roy called 'une métropole froide et constipée' ('La Tragédie algérienne', p. 200) – marks him as a son of the bright Mediterranean skies; his taste for swimming, the port and the beach, the odours and sounds of his city, indicate that, despite his European antecedents, he belongs to Algiers. He is that Mediterranean man whom Camus analysed, who is indifferent to the mind and worships the body. It is significant that Roy called Camus 'un Algérien' in his obituary column in *Le Monde* (6 January). Both authors had the intuition of a Mediterranean race that could found a new culture on the African shores, where, as Camus put it, 'la grandeur de l'homme trouvera enfin son vrai visage' (II, p. 74).

One final way to read the title of the novel is thus to see Meursault and the Arabs together as strangers to the European Other: a culture that would impose upon them, from another continent, conventions and expectations that they cannot meet – including a Christian belief that Camus rejects in the name of the lessons of the natural world – and which, in particular, would weaken, if not destroy, the bond between them and nature. 'Notre vraie patrie était pour nous tous le soleil', wrote Roy.[28] One cannot imagine Meursault living elsewhere than Algeria, outside of the setting, both natural and cultural, to which he is knitted by more than habits – by the only myth that has meaning for him, the myth of nature. In the fraternal Algeria of which both Camus and Roy dreamed, before it became clear that hostorical forces working against it were too strong, Meursault would have been at home; instead, the brilliant sun turned murderous, this time against not an Arab but the European exploiters, pursued by their fellow North Africans with the cries of hatred Meursault expected to hear from the crowd at his execution.

Notes

1. In his 'L'Etonnant Retour en Algérie du pied-noir Jules Roy', *L'Aurore*, 1 April 1975, p. 2.
2. See the edition by Germaine Brée and Carlos Lynes Jr (New York: Appleton-Century-Crofts, 1955), p. viii.
3. Manfred Sprissler (ed) *Albert Camus: Konkordanz zu den Romanen und Erzählungen*, vol. 1 (Hildesheim and New York: Georg Olms, 1988) p. 699.
4. This is Camus's own view: 'Dans notre société tout homme qui ne pleure pas à l'enterrement de sa mère risque d'être condamné à mort' (1955 edn, p. vii). It has been taken to heart, or arrived at independently, by countless critics.
5. Madeleine Tison-Braun, 'Silence and the Desert: The Flickering Vision', in Bettina L. Knapp (ed.) *Critical Essays on Albert Camus* (Boston: G.K. Hall, 1988), p. 49. This commentator goes on to say, however, that Meursault is not *really* lacking in interpretive ability, nor shallow; the proof is that, as she claims, he keeps a diary, where one would not 'record ... what any third person would notice at first sight' (p. 50).
6. *Essais* (Paris: Gallimard, Bibliothèque de la Pléiade, 1965). Future references are marked II.
7. *Théâtre, récits, nouvelles* (Paris: Gallimard, Bibliothèque de la Pléiade, 1963). References are marked I.
8. See his *Les Damnés de la terre* (Paris: Maspero, 1968).
9. I am indebted to Horowitz's lucid article surveying the relatively limited critical literature that has focused on racial matters in Camus, including *L'Etranger*: 'Of Women and Arabs; Sexual and Racial Polarization in Camus', *Modern Language Studies*, vol. 17, 3 (Summer 1987), pp. 54–61. Pierre Nora and Henri Kréa commented in *France-Observateur* in 1961 on Camus's racialist views; Conor Cruise O'Brien took up the question again in his *Albert Camus of Europe and Africa* (New York: Viking, 1970), but critics often have retreated after acknowledging the undeniable racist elements. See also John D. Erickson, 'Albert Camus and North Africa: A Discourse on Exteriority', in Knapp, pp. 73–88.
10. In 'Algérianité et marginalité: Le cas d'Albert Camus', a paper delivered at the MLA convention, 1988.
11. 'Once the subject seeks to assert himself, the Other, who limits and denies him, is nonetheless a necessity to him; he attains himself only through that reality which he is not ...' Simone de Beauvoir, *The Second Sex* H.M. Parshley (trans) (New York: Bantam, 1961), p. 129. See also Edward Saïd, 'Representing the Colonized: Anthropology's Interlocutors', *Critical Inquiry* vol. 15 (Winter, 1989), pp. 205–25.

12. For glimpses of this *machisme*, see Simone de Beauvoir, *La Force des choses* (Paris: Gallimard, 1963), p. 208: 'Méditerranéen, cultivant un orgueil espagnol, il ne concédait à la femme l' égalité dans la différence et évidemment ... c'était lui le plus égal des deux.' For Roy's analysis of Camus's *machisme*, see his autobiographical novel, *La Saison des za* (Paris: Grasset, 1982), pp. 106, 117–23, 125.

13. Jules Roy, 'Camus, Prix Nobel,' *Nouvelles Littéraires* 1673 (24 October 1957), p. 1.

14. Jules Roy, 'La Tragédie Algérienne,' in *Camus*, R. -M. Albérès (ed.) (Paris: Hachette, 1964), p. 212.

15. See my *Art as Testimony: The Work of Jules Roy* (Gainesville: University of Florida Press, 1989), p. 15. Roy wrote concerning colonialism then: 'Quel pied-noir le connaissait? Aucun. Camus a été le premier à se rendre compte – le premier et le seul, pendant longtemps. Sans lui, il n'y aurait eu personne d'autre.' See Jacques Roque, 'Jules Roy ou la Rigueur', in Jules Roy, *Une Femme au nom d'etoile* (Paris: Talandier/ Cercle du Nouveau Livre, 1971), p. 18.

16. See introduction to *La Guerre d'Algérie*, 10/18 (Paris: Christian Bourgois/Dominique de Roux, 1971), p. 9.

17. See 'Camus: Prix Nobel', p. 1, and Roy's 'Un Africain', *Le Monde*, 6 January 1960, p. 2.

18. See Maurice Robin, 'Remarques sur l'attitude de Camus face à l'Algérie', in Jeanyves Guérin (ed.) *Camus et la politique* (Paris: L'Harmattan, 1986), pp. 185–90, for a friendly evaluation.

19. This article was reprinted as 'Dans une Juste Guerre', in *Autour du drame* (Paris: Julliard, 1961) (henceforth *AD*). In *La Saison des za*, he writes, 'Peut-être parce que sa mère était morte, Berg, qui n'était plus militaire, s'était déjà presque malgré lui laissé entraîner plus loin [than Camus]; à la place des Arabes, il aurait lutté pour l'indépendance, comme Camus dans sa jeunesse' (p. 83).

20. See Jules Roy, *Etranger pour mes frères* (Paris: Stock, 1982), p. 109. Subsequent references will be abbreviated in the text *EF*.

21. Francis C. Bueb, Jules Roy: Un Moraliste de notre histoire', *Magazine Littéraire*, vol. 31 (August 1969), p. 41. In 'La Tragédie algérienne', he admits that they were 'à l'opposé l'un de l'autre' (p. 200).

22. 'Je crois à la justice, mais je défendrai ma mère avant la justice' (II, p. 1882). For the quotation on Roy, see cover comment on *EF*. It should be noted that he was aware of his friend's controversial remark and deliberately pointed to his own mother as one who inspired his stand. See Brosman, pp. 82–4. Roy sometimes stated that if Camus had lived he would not have gone to Algeria and written his documentary (*EF*, p. 127), and elsewhere wondered whether 'ce témoignage aurait été écrit sans la mort de Camus'. See the 10/18 edition of *La Guerre d'Algérie*, p. 9.

23. As a former seminarian, Roy cannot have been unaware of the Biblical overtones of the word *stranger*. Most of the OT occurrences devalorise the stranger as an ethnic alien, one with whom there should be no dealings. In Psalm 146, however, the Lord is said to protect strangers, and in Matthew 25: 35, the word stands for the recipient of charity, indeed Christ himself: 'I was stranger, and ye took me in.'

24. *La Guerre d'Algérie* (Paris: Julliard, 1960), p. 181.
25. Jules Roy, *Les Ames interdites* (Paris: Grasset, 1971), p. 500.
26. *Le Monde*, 25 April 1975, p. 19.
27. In his reply to an *enquête*, 'Que signifie pour vous le mot 'pied-noir'?' *Figaro Littéraire*, 22 June 1987, p.v.
28. Preface to Gabriel Audisio, *L'Opéra fabuleux* (Paris: Julliard, 1970), p. 12.

21

Camus and Sartre
Olivier Todd

October 1938: Albert Camus, a twenty-five year old journalist on a North African progressive daily, *Alger Républicain* reviews Sartre's *La Nausée*. His article is balanced, insightful, double-edged. *La Nausée*, writes Camus, is 'an extravagant meditation' reaching 'a kind of perfection'. Yet in this book 'theory harms life'. And it isn't really a novel. It looks more like a monologue. What should we then call *L'Etranger*? A narrative. Sartre comes close to Kafka although the young critic feels 'a kind of embarrassment'. Nevertheless, from this Monsieur Sartre 'one expects everything ... We are impatiently waiting for the works and lessons to come'.

Plenty of friendships, many love affairs start like that, in a haze of admiration and reservations.

Tackling *Le Mur* the following year in the same paper, Camus sounds more enthusiastic. These short stories are 'prodigiously interesting'. Monsieur Sartre converts the reader 'to nothingness but also to lucidity'.

September 1942: in occupied Paris, Sartre, thirty-eight, indulges in a long essay around *L'Etranger*, an instant best-seller. Sartre had also read *Le Mythe de Sisyphe* in manuscript. His essay scintillates, toing and froing from Camus's novel – sorry, narrative – and his essay. Now Sartre finds it hard to pigeon-hole *L'Etranger*. A novel? Well, up to a point. Rather in 'the tradition of a Voltaire tale'. Sartre relishes Camus's 'dry and neat style' but distances himself from the thinker. The essayist, writes Sartre, deals 'with death, the irreducible pluralism of truths and beings, the unintelligibility of the real world, and chance ..., poles of the absurd. Truly these are not original themes.'

The title of Sartre's first digression on Camus is pretty patronising: 'Explication de *L'Etranger*'. Decode it: as an *agrégé de philosophie* and a *normalien*, let me tell you, young man, what *you* actually mean and, also, where you get off.

The two established authors met when *Les Mouches* was premiered in Paris in 1943. It was love at first sight. Sartre – he made no bones about it – did not, on the whole, like the company of men. Camus was handsome and elegant. With a 'gutter-snipe' touch, said Simone de Beauvoir. With all his charm, Sartre was neither handsome nor elegant. Camus, a meritocrat, had been brought up by his mother, an illiterate cleaning lady. Sartre was constantly denouncing the bourgeois scion in himself and others. Camus's investigative reporting in Algeria had been factual and militantly anti-colonialist. In France, Camus was an active member of the Resistance. Contributing to underground papers, Sartre remained more aloof. *He* took to politics late in life.

Both had, so to speak, benefited from *not* having a father. Both had justified literary ambitions. Both loved sports and jokes. Both enjoyed women.

Camus had acted and directed plays. Having dashed off *Huis-Clos* in two weeks, Sartre asked Camus to stage it and to take on Garcin's part. Rehearsals got off the ground in a small flat, with Wanda Kosakiewicz, an important planet of Sartre's feminine constellation. Albert flirted with Wanda, to Sartre's slightly voyeuristic amusement. 'The Russian soul', he explained in a letter to Simone de Beauvoir, 'is not familiar' to Camus. Eventually, Camus did not direct or act in *Huis-Clos*.

Then came the heady days of the Liberation. 21 August 1944: *Combat*, an excellent underground paper, comes out in the open. *Combat* flashed a sub-titling motto: 'From the Resistance to the Revolution.' Camus proclaimed that 'fighting invaders and traitors, the Home French Forces (the FFI) are re-establishing the republic in our country'. In those days, politics looked pretty simple, Sartre and Camus were on the same wavelength. Editing *Combat* with rigour and vigour, convinced that 'the journalist is the historian of the moment', Camus encouraged Sartre to write his first reportages, beginning with descriptions of Parisians attacking the last Germans stuck in Paris.

As a guest of the Office of War Information, Sartre flew to the USA. To *Combat* he cabled somewhat dry, technical articles, concentrating on the Tennessee Valley Authority, dealing with economics – never Sartre's or, for that matter, Camus's strong point. To the resurrected *Figaro*, a respectable, bourgeois daily if ever there was one, Sartre, to Camus's irritation, sent more impressionistic pieces.

In July 1945, Sartre delivered some definitive pronouncements in *Vogue*. 'The Resistance,' he asserted, 'taught that literature is no fancy activity independent of politics.' There were two generations of French writers. One, pre-warish with Blanchot, Bataille and

Anouilh; Leiris, Cassou and Camus stood for the new school. Sartre raved over Camus. Here was indeed the archetype of the committed writer (emphasis on both words). Camus represented the chance of 'a new classicism'. Sartre had perused another Camus manuscript, *La Peste*. 'The main characteristics of future French literature', Sartre predicted, 'can probably be detected in Camus' sombre and pure work.' Sartre claimed that 'the belief in austere, modest and useful action' distinguished Camus' generation from Malraux's. The mind boggles! Forever, Sartre remained strong on generalisations and short on facts. Yet could one be more flattering about Camus? Sartre was then at the centre of the literary and philosophical scene – outside academia. With their novels, their plays, their essays, Sartre and Camus were conquering Paris, France, all continents.

Camus did *not* join the editorial board of *Les Temps modernes*, Sartre's monthly review and the ultimate Vulgate of assorted Sartrists and Sartrologues.

Philosophically, through an unwritten gentlemen's agreement, the two writers kept apart. Sartre derived his prodigious inspiration from Husserl and Heidegger, Camus more from Russian nihilists. Sartre, *crescendo*, Camus, *moderato cantabile*, belonged to the grand French Rationalist (as opposed to Empiricist) tradition. With them, one is never quite sure where philosophy ends or literature begins. And vice-versa. Camus played around with 'the absurd', Sartre with 'contingency', 'the thing-in-itself' and countless concepts or creatures of his 'ontological phenomenology'. November 1945: Sartre confides: 'Camus is not an existentialist.' December, same year, Camus confirms: 'I am not an existentialist.' Camus saw himself first as an artist, Sartre perceived himself foremost as a philosopher. Well, Voltaire was sure *he* would mainly survive as a dramatist.

The reading public and some unread critics tended to lump Camus and Sartre together for anecdotal reasons. Didn't they refuse the Legion of Honour ribbon at the same time?

In March 1947, after a boozy evening, Camus rowed with the then Sartrian Maurice Merleau-Ponty over Communism. With rumours about concentration camps in the USSR, with quasi-insurrectional strikes in France, headed by CP unions, with the Communist coup d'état in Czechoslovakia or the West Berlin blockade on the political horizon, this delicate subject of Communism could hardly be avoided. In the early 1940s, the USSR was part of 'the democratic camp' against Nazis and fascists. Sartre sided with Merleau-Ponty and did not speak to Camus for four months.

The two authors buried the hatchet and got together again. They were sufficiently close to watch each other's plays being rehearsed. Sartre admired *Caligula*, a supreme example of 'simple, concise dialogue'. Modern playwrights, Sartre ruled, were interested 'in going back to tradition rather than in innovating'. So much for Ionesco or Beckett. Camus and Sartre went into adaptations, Sartre over Alexandre Dumas, Camus with Dostoievsky. Unlike Sartre, Camus kept away from film scripts. Sartre was a prolific and impatient genius. Steadier, Camus rarely left something unfinished.

Sartre had a double approach to Camus. In print or during lectures, he would praise him. Privately, he suggested that Camus was 'no genius'. Sartre was a master at successive sincerities.

Politics brought out their disagreements openly over Gary Davis, in June 1948. Camus endorsed the citizens-of-the-world-unite-and-burn-your-passports line. Camus, a bit of a moral yoga, supported peaceful men of good will. Sartre, a metaphysical commissar, thought Davis utopian, if not crackers. This American overlooked social and economic parameters. Camus could sing of innocence, Sartre of experience.

This minor Davis incident was the tip of the iceberg.

Camus and Sartre went along with the Rassemblement Démocratique Révolutionnaire (RDR), a small political movement, hardly qualifying as a party, almost entirely made up of intellectuals in search of a unicorn, the third force, between Right and Left for some, between Gaullism and Communism to others, between the 'capitalist' USA and the 'socialist' USSR for almost every RDR member. At a meeting in the Salle Pleyel in December 1948, a solemn Camus and a smirking Sartre sat side by side with other European luminaries. Camus spoke darkly about 'the world in which inquisitors are sitting in ministerial armchairs'. Where? In the White House, Matignon, the Kremlin? Sartre was not amused.

The iceberg was emerging.

The break-up came in a true Parisian and French fashion. Since Zola and going back to Voltaire, French men of letters conclave and separate on principles, poetical, philosophical and, more and more, political. Camus and Sartre parted through a magnificent polemic.

Camus published his most ambitious essay, *L'Homme revolté* in 1951, at a high point of the cold war. Revolt, Camus argued, did not merely come through being oppressed. It was also generated by the oppression of others. 'Metaphysical revolt is the movement through which a man rebels against his condition and the whole of creation.'

Starting with Sade's absolute negation, Ivan Karamazov's refusal of salvation and Nietzsche's absolute affirmation – all somewhat woolly notions – Camus examined the relationship between individual revolt and collective revolution. He dealt with Louis XVI's execution. Camus maintained that, through state terrorism, a revolution turned against revolutionaries who rebelled against the revolution. Art, Camus concluded, was a revolution which allowed us to reach happiness. The book was well received.

Now it looks like a disconnected series of essays. Lautréamont and the surrealists bump into Rousseau or Hegel. Form overtakes content. Anyway, Camus utterly rejected revolutions which produced police states.

That did not wash with the Sartrians. Sartre had exposed what would be called the Gulag, but he talked, wrote and behaved as if concentration camps were merely an epiphenomenon of socialism, the most unfortunate Stalinist accident. To Sartre 'an anti-communist was a bastard' (*un chien*). To Sartre, until a few months before his death, communist parties, with all their errors and crimes, remained the incarnation of the proletariat. Sartre gave up third-forcism and, in a manicheeistic frame of mind which to him was solid realism, sided with the USSR against the USA. Camus's siding against Communism (with a C or a c) annoyed Sartre who believed that Marxism, with a few existentialist alterations, embodied the Truth about the universe.

The *Temps modernes* tribe pondered over *L'Homme revolté*. How could one deal with such a book? To Sartre, Camus was still a friend. On the other hand, he hated what he'd read of *L'Homme revolté*. Sartre dallied for six months. He finally decided that Francis Jeanson would review Camus' essay. Simone de Beauvoir said that Sartre wanted a courteous piece. Yet he wished *L'Homme revolté* to be damned – a typical Sartrian reaction. As Jeanson was polishing his article, Sartre met Camus in the street and warned him: *Les Temps Modernes* would be 'negative' about the book, sorry about that.

Jeanson's twenty-five-page review was condescending, insulting, vitriolic from the very title: 'Albert Camus or the rebel soul.' Camus, Jeanson argued, was in a general sense guilty since right-wing critics had praised his book. Camus's thinking was 'inconsistent', as well as 'indefinitely plastic and malleable'. Jeanson spotted in Camus 'a vague humanism with the required touch of anarchism'. The writer's style, Jeanson admitted, was 'almost perfect'. The main point was that Camus 'refused to give historical and economic factors their due in the genesis of revolutions'. Worse still, Camus tried to demonstrate that 'Marx's doctrine logically leads to the Stalinist regime.'

Jeanson proceeded to bulldoze Camus's other books. *La Peste* was 'a transcendental chronicle'. Camus, a pseudo-philosopher and pseudo-historian, turned out to be 'out of history'. No doubt Camus was heading for literary retreat in an ivory tower. How sad.

Camus was invited to reply. He did. His epistle began with a formal: *Monsieur le Directeur.*

Camus by-passed Jeanson, addressing the editor, *le Directeur*, Sartre himself. (Camus always used ceremonious vocatives when writing to papers or reviews.) In this piece, he dissected Jeanson's 'intellectual method'. Camus calmly said that if he believed truth to be on the right, then he would be right-wing. In a now very famous remark, he exclaimed that he was rather 'tired of being lectured to by censors who had never pointed anything but their armchairs in the direction of history'. *L'Homme revolté*, he claimed, had 'an exclusive topic, revolt and terror in our times'. In a footnote he asserted that as far as he was concerned, Marx had 'mixed the most valuable critical method with the most controversial prophetic messianism'. This was characteristic of the 1950s in France. And, by the way, Camus inquired, was there anything wrong with writing well?

Since Camus had sent *him* a reply, Sartre felt he must join the fray and the fun. His piece was cruel, brutal, satirical and dialectically devious: another epistle in a modern mood – rejected lover's farewell letter. Sartre and Camus were, in fact, fighting again the French 1789 and the Russian 1917 revolutions. Implicitly, Sartre was a Jacobin and Bolshevik, Camus a Girondin and Menshevik. Once more very much the *agrégé de philosophie*. Sartre, using the method of authority, lectured Camus: 'And suppose your book simply showed your philosophical incompetence?' *L'Homme revolté*, Sartre added, was stuffed with 'second-hand knowledge'. At his most arrogant and insulting, Sartre suggested that Camus should read *L'Etre et le néant*. If he could manage it, of course. Camus, Sartre conceded, was the better 'writer' but Jeanson reasoned better. Camus and Sartre were back to square one: to Sartre's early essay on *L'Etranger* and *Le Mythe de Sisyphe*, years before. Sartre now discovered that *La Peste* was a 'mystification', since microbes in that novel symbolised the Nazis. Sartre saw in *La Peste* an example of 'collaboration between classes'. The adrenalin flowing and amphetamines helping, Sartre went on and on ...

One of Sartre's accusations encapsulates the core of the dispute: 'We are all', he wrote, 'concerned by the scandal of the (*Soviet concentration*) camps: the Iron Curtain is only the mirror, every half of the world reflects the other half. Whenever we turn on the screws *here*, they turn them on *there*.' In other words, the ultimate cause of concentration camps is the West's early opposition to communism. Not Stalinism, Leninism or Marxism. Capitalism forced Communism into repressive policies. For Sartre, there was somewhere, in limbo, a possible socialism with a human face. Those were very much the French 1950s.

Bickering over Communism, Camus and Sartre insisted on the police state, never on the total economic inefficiency of 'real socialist' régimes, especially for the underprivileged. It would take the French left-wing, non-communist intelligentsia another forty years or so, and the 1989 events in Eastern Europe, to acknowledge the social failings and economic failures of all Communist systems.

Sartre ended his piece kindly: 'Whatever you may say or do to reply, I refuse to fight you. I hope our silence will induce people to forget the polemic.'

Throughout the Algerian war, Sartre and Camus disagreed. Francis Jeanson was head of an underground movement, *le réseau d'aide au FLN*, helping Algerian nationalists in France, providing them with flats and handling funds collected among Algerian immigrants. Camus asked the French army and police, as well as the FLN (Front de Libération Nationale) forces in Algeria, to spare civilians. Privately, Camus helped individuals on both sides. Sartre explained revolutionary violence away, Camus hated all types of violence. Sartre stuck to the idea of revolution, Camus to evolution. The 1980s have vindicated Camus.

They went on writing. Camus withdrew slightly from politics, Sartre got more and more involved. Camus *seemed* more conformist: he accepted the Nobel Prize, which Sartre refused – and not because Camus got it before it was offered to Sartre.

I lunched with Sartre in Paris for the last time on 23 February 1980, shortly before he died. As often, I brought up Camus. Once more, I asked Sartre what was Camus's best book.

– Unquestionably *La Chute*, Sartre shot back.

– Why?

– Because he put himself and hid himself in it more than in any other work.

Clamence, the judge-penitent, reflects Camus's solitude, perhaps also his disillusioned sensuality and, up to a point, his growing conviction – which eventually was Sartre's – that ideas don't change the world. Clamence is a powerful caricature of cynicism, which had tempted Camus. Sardonically, Clamence exalts servitude. After the *Temps modernes* polemic, Camus noted in his diary that the Sartrians were fascinated by servitude. Jean-François Revel would call it the 'totalitarian temptation'. *La Chute* reflects the difficult experiences of an age which saw its moral and political values shattered. To Camus, Clamence was 'a small prophet. One of those who don't announce anything ... who can't do better than accuse others by accusing themselves'. Clamence can equally be seen as a caricature of Sartre. A careful comparative analysis of *Les Mots* and *La Chute*, two masterpieces, would no doubt bring that out. Hence, Sartre's interest in *La Chute*?

January 1960. After Camus's death, in *France-Observateur*, Sartre published a moving, warm tribute to Camus. He wrote that Camus, before his fatal car crash, was 'provisionally torn by contradictions we should respect ... We thought that he was changing the world, like any of us: that was enough for his presence to remain alive.' Not given to sentimentality or praise, forgetting his you-are-no-philosopher diatribe, Sartre went as far as to claim: 'We lived for or against his (Camus's) thinking'. Camus had been an 'austere and sensual humanist.' A 'Cartesian of the absurd' he held the world in 'his clenched fist'. Camus was one 'of the main forces in our cultural field'. Some readers, then, may have remembered a sentence of Sartre's outrageous piece in *Les Temps modernes*. He had written that Camus 'had been – could still become again – the admirable conjunction of a person, an action and literary achievements', (*l'admirable conjonction d'une personne, d'une action et d'une oeuvre*).

In this obituary, Sartre admitted that he had liked Camus very much ... '*pour tous ceux qui l'ont aimé*'. The French verb *aimer* translates to love and to like. Robert Gallimard, who dealt with both writers at Gallimard's and remained on good terms with the two, always says that the Sartre – Camus relationship was 'a failed love story'. Sartre was the joyful victim of many parricides from his fellow-writers and philosophers, what with Etiemble, Merleau-Ponty, Jean Cau, Claude Lefort ...

With Camus it was fratricide.

Index